VIOLENCE IN A TIME OF LIBERATION

VIOLENCE IN
A TIME OF LIBERATION

Murder and Ethnicity at a South African Gold Mine, 1994

DONALD L. DONHAM

with photographs by Santu Mofokeng

Duke University Press

Durham and London

2011

© 2011 Duke University Press

All rights reserved

Printed in the United States of
America on acid-free paper ∞
Designed by C. H. Westmoreland
Typeset in Arno
with News Gothic display by
Tseng Information Systems, Inc.
Library of Congress Cataloging-
in-Publication Data appear on the
last printed page of this book.

Duke University Press gratefully
acknowledges the support of
the Division of Social Sciences,
University of California, Davis,
which provided funds toward the
production of this book.

For friends — Charles, Rudy, Terry

CONTENTS

PREFACE

IT WAS WHOLLY BY ACCIDENT that I conducted field research in times and places caught in great upheaval—first in Ethiopia in the midst of a revolution that replaced an emperor with a socialist regime, then in South Africa as apartheid disintegrated and its black people became, at last, citizens in their own land. I am more grateful than I can say for the provocation of what overtook and sometimes overwhelmed me.

The uncertainties of historical rupture often open spaces that otherwise would be closed. This was certainly the case in both Ethiopia and South Africa.[1] In the latter, I gained access to the social life of a gold mine, with its white officials, black compound, and work underground. I would like to thank Charles van Onselen, then director of the Institute for Advanced Social Research at the University of the Witwatersrand, with which I was affiliated while doing research. It was at the institute that I first met Santu Mofokeng, whose photographs do so much to enhance this book. Had it not been for the assistance of Eddie Webster at the Sociology of Work Unit at Wits, this study might never have been accomplished. Sakhela Buhlungu provided additional help and advice. Finally, most of all, I want to thank the National Union of Mineworkers (NUM) and management at the mine I am calling Cinderella, especially "Charles du Toit," for permission to carry out this study. I shared the penultimate draft of this book with both—a consultation that should not be taken to indicate that either party endorses what I present. In any case, this process saved me from serious errors, and I am grateful to both the NUM and management at Cinderella for their willingness to engage with an independent researcher.

This research was supported by grants from the Social Science Research Council, the Wenner-Gren Foundation, and the Fulbright-Hays Program. I began writing while I was a fellow at the Woodrow Wilson International Center for Scholars, in Washington.

What follows is a story, a complex story that will take the reader into a gold mine just as the new South Africa was being born. At the outset, let me confess to a particular addiction to detail, and to a hope that the list of groups and timeline that appear after this preface prove useful to readers, particularly those with little knowledge of South Africa. Some social scientists may complain that I do not utilize "theory," that this book is "only a story." But such objections overestimate the purpose theory can serve in this case.[2] There has been altogether too much (premature) theorizing about ethnic violence when what is required, first, is a deeper inquiry into just what constitutes a case. The particular methodological difficulty that must be faced is that social actors' own narratives *after the fact* cannot necessarily be accepted as indicators of how and why violence developed.

If violence is one keyword in the analysis that follows, national liberation is another. The elections of 1994 in South Africa have been justly celebrated. That national liberation entailed a darker side has also long been appreciated. One of the purposes of this book is to capture this contradiction in the lives of black workers at a gold mine. The elections gave black South Africans democratic rights in return for the protection of a purified but conservative capitalism — an economic system that has produced greater social inequalities than apartheid, along with systemic unemployment for at least one-third of the black population.[3] My goal is to make the micro-history of one gold mine illuminate national liberation as it actually occurred and as it continues to shape the new South Africa.

Many colleagues have helped me with this study, and I would like to thank the following: Belinda Bozzoli, Fred Cooper, Dunbar Moodie, Kent McNamara, Sakkie Niehaus, and Carol Smith. The readers for Duke University Press were also helpful. The intellectualism and moral passion of academics in South Africa has been inspiring. Finally, I would like to thank editors Linda Forman and Patricia Mickelberry.

November 2010

GROUPS AT CINDERELLA IN 1994

Afrikaners	Whites descended mainly from Dutch settlers in South Africa. Their language is Afrikaans. (Most white workers at Cinderella were Afrikaners.)
amabutho	The "regiment," a secret Xhosa-speaking group in the compound, who used traditional fighting techniques (in alliance with the NUM).
ANC	African National Congress, Nelson Mandela's political party.
IFP	Inkatha Freedom Party, a mostly Zulu political party headed by Chief Mangosuthu Buthelezi.
Inkatha core	The approximately 50 out of the 350 Zulus in the compound who belonged to the IFP.
NUM	National Union of Mineworkers, a labor union in alliance with the ANC (the union recognized by management at the time of the violence).
Shangaans	Mostly foreign black workers from Mozambique, comprising almost 60 percent of the black workforce.
Sothos	Mostly foreign black workers from Lesotho, but also some from South Africa, comprising about 15 percent of the black workforce.
UPUSA	United People's Union of South Africa, a labor union informally allied with the IFP.
Xhosas	South African black workers from the Transkei and Ciskei, comprising about 15 percent of the black workforce. (Pondos are a subgroup of Xhosas.)
Zulus	South African black workers from KwaZulu, comprising only about 7 percent of the black workforce.

LOCAL TIMELINE IN RELATION
TO NATIONAL LIBERATION

1986	An attempt by the NUM to organize black workers at Cinderella fails.
February 1990	Nelson Mandela is released from prison, and the ANC is legalized.
1990	UPUSA begins organizing black workers at the mine.
December 1992	Du Toit initiates new management strategy by encouraging unionization by the NUM.
April 1993	Van Zyl shoots a Mozambican worker, and a strike is called by the amabutho.
July 1993	Strike over wages takes place, with some NUM involvement.
late 1993	Recognition agreement is reached between management and the NUM.
February 1994	Buthelezi and the IFP call for a boycott of the upcoming elections.
February 1994	Voter education takes place in the compound.
20 March 1994	A mine security logbook records a threat against Zulu workers.
28 March 1994	Bloody Monday takes place in Johannesburg, as Inkatha marchers are murdered in front of ANC headquarters.
1 April 1994	Good Friday: Attacks take place against Zulu workers in the compound.
3 April 1994	Easter Sunday: Inkatha core attempts to reenter the compound, but all Zulus are separated out by management.
April–May 1994	Zulu workers are sent home for a cooling-off period.
20 April 1994	Inkatha boycott of the elections is called off.
27–28 April 1994	National elections take place.

9 May 1994	Nelson Mandela is inaugurated.
15 June 1994	The first batch of Zulus return from home leave unexpectedly.
16 June 1994	Soweto Day: Two Zulus are murdered, and another five sustain life-threatening injuries.
18 July 1994	350 Zulu workers are fired.
August 1994	Three Xhosa-speaking Pondos are arrested for the murders.
September 1994	Charges are dropped against those arrested.
September 1994	UPUSA, representing the fired Zulu workers, brings a case against management in Industrial Court.
May 1996	Zulus win additional compensation but not reinstatement.
June 1999	Thabo Mbeki succeeds Nelson Mandela as president of South Africa.
August 1999	Cinderella goes bankrupt.
March 2000	Cinderella reemerges with black ownership.
December 2007	Jacob Zuma, a Zulu, becomes the president of the ANC.
May 2008	Pogroms against black foreigners take place at Cinderella squatter camp. Two foreign mine workers are killed.
September 2008	Thabo Mbeki resigns as president and is succeeded by Acting President Kgalema Motlanthe.
November 2008	Underground work at Cinderella is suspended.
January 2009	Over 1,400 Cinderella workers lose their jobs.
April 2009	Jacob Zuma is elected President of South Africa.

VIOLENCE IN A TIME OF LIBERATION

INTRODUCTION

ON THE EVENING OF 16 JUNE 1994, at a South African gold mine I will call Cinderella (figs. 1 and 2), black workers ganged up on the Zulus among them and slowly, determinedly hacked two to death.[1] It took some time to kill with knobkerries, those short, thick sticks with heads that can be used either as walking sticks or clubs; with pangas, the long, broad-bladed knives used by cane-cutters; and with the various steel-tipped weapons that workers had jerry-rigged from materials taken from underground. Even so, two Zulu workers lay dead and many more were seriously injured before mine security could intervene to end the attack.

The murderous split among black workers came just six weeks after the famous elections that freed South Africa from white rule.[2] Celebrated across the globe, the end of apartheid can be seen as the final chapter in the long process of decolonization, of national liberation on the African continent.[3] When Nelson Mandela was inaugurated as state president on 9 May 1994, he proclaimed, "Never, never, and never again shall it be that this beautiful land will again experience the oppression of one by another."[4] But at Cinderella, a gold mine just east of Johannesburg, just weeks after Mandela assumed power, something knottier than the clean outlines of liberation occurred: (oppressed) black workers killed other (oppressed) black workers.[5]

Had blacks at Cinderella risen up against their erstwhile white masters, that would have made some immediate sense. Gold mines, after all, had been critical sites in which much of racial oppression had first been constructed. Mining in South Africa had driven the only industrial revolution on the continent, producing prodigious wealth, and in both the black and white cultural imaginations — in music, novels, and local TV programs — mines had become iconic, condensed symbols of the nation.[6] Had black workers cleansed the mine of whites, who

1. A modern shaft at Cinderella

2. An older shaft dating back to the early part of the twentieth century

continued to occupy nearly all of the supervisory roles at Cinderella, Frantz Fanon's thesis that violence provides a necessary catharsis in national liberation would have been affirmed.[7]

But that is not what happened. Instead, by the end of the conflict, almost everyone at Cinderella, black and white, interpreted what had occurred in ethnic terms: Xhosas had attacked the Zulus. Framed this way, the conflict was assimilated to literally hundreds of others that had erupted around Johannesburg after 1990.[8]

Pitched battles broke out in Sebokeng in late July 1990, and spread quickly to Katorus. Over 1,500 people were killed in the last half of 1990 alone. On average, the police were collecting eight bodies a day. The scale was truly horrifying. Between June and October 1990, approximately 550 people died in a single township, virtually on or around a single street: the infamous Khumalo Street in Tokoza. On one occasion, in a single day, 143 people were killed. Violence remained high right up until the first democratic election in April 1994. Around 1,000 people died in 1991, double that the following year. Violence peaked in 1993, when more than 2,000 people were killed in fighting. A total of 754 died in 1994.[9]

By 1994, there was an established script to this violence. It opposed Zulus to others, principally Xhosas.[10] The killing (which took place in black townships and squatter camps around Johannesburg, generally not in gold mines) has been called the East Rand War.

This violence was a part of the momentous political changes under way in South Africa at that time. After Nelson Mandela was released from prison in 1990, it was clear to everyone that apartheid was coming to an end. The only question was on exactly what terms this would happen. The political party in power, the National Party, the original architect of apartheid, delayed the process as long as it could, attempting to play one black political party against the other. On one side was the long-established African National Congress, the ANC, Mandela's party, which had just been legalized. The ANC strenuously rejected black ethnic division and argued for a nonracial future. On the other side was the hastily organized Inkatha Freedom Party, the IFP, led by Chief Mangosuthu Buthelezi. The IFP celebrated Zulu ethnic identity, at times Zulu chauvinism, and demanded ethnic autonomy within any new dispensation.

According to rumors of the time—later confirmed—elements of the old apartheid security apparatus secretly provided arms and training to Inkatha provocateurs.[11] These Zulu men carried out some of the most horrendous acts of the East Rand War. Their white instigators were apparently motivated by the desire to present the National Party as the only political organization capable of restoring order to an increasingly chaotic situation.

Beyond events in South Africa itself, the Cold War had recently ended and the Soviet Union was disintegrating, international sea changes that, ironically, provided the coup de grâce to the colonial project on the African continent. South African whites could negotiate away apartheid without fearing communist redistribution of their wealth. Capitalism could be purified, and everyone start anew, now as formally equal individuals in a free market (even if the new state was committed to some forms of affirmative action, or what it termed black empowerment).

In the globalizing world in which apartheid ended, we have come to expect ethnic violence. We read about it everyday, from Bosnia to Darfur to Georgia. Ethnicity seems the natural basis on which social actors compete in times of upset and uncertainty, particularly among those Fanon evocatively called the wretched of the earth. And yet if we examine specific cases, looking beyond the initial newspaper reports, this clarity invariably begins to blur.[12] At some point the question arises: Was this, in fact, an ethnic conflict? What is ethnic violence, after all?

To preview, the denouement of the conflict at Cinderella in 1994 was delineated in ethnic terms. Those attacked and killed were Zulus (or mistaken as Zulus). Less clearly, those who carried out the murders seem to have been overwhelmingly Xhosa (or from closely related, Xhosa-speaking ethnic groups). But what I shall show over the course of this book is that sheer cultural difference — or hatred of an ethnic other — had little to do with the causes of the conflict. Heightened ethnic identity may, rather, have been one of the principal outcomes of the violence.

What motivated the murderers was the struggle for national liberation.[13] June 16th was, after all, not just any day. It was the first celebration of a new national holiday, initially called Soweto Day, later renamed Youth Day. By 1994, South Africans saw the 1976 Soweto Uprising as the beginning of the struggle that had so recently produced liberation. On that ritually marked day at Cinderella, when all those who had given their lives for the new nation were remembered — eighteen years from the day on which white policemen shot down black Soweto schoolchildren — Zulus were banished from the mine as traitors, as undeserving and inauthentic national subjects.

In the very first sentence of *Wretched of the Earth*, Fanon wrote: "National liberation, national reawakening, restoration of the nation to the people or Commonwealth, whatever the name used, whatever the latest expression, decolonization is always a violent event."[14] But this way of casting the historical process is misleading. The notion of the nation is not so much *reawakened* or *restored* (even if these are the terms in which nationalists always speak). The nation is, rather, created in the struggle itself, particularly at moments of new beginning, like 1994 in South Africa.

Those beginnings persist even as the patterns they establish are transformed in some ways. Nationalism has its dialectic. To define those who have struggled and sacrificed for liberation as the only authentic subjects of the nation sets up shifting possibilities for categorizing non-nationals, particularly in an economic context that does not provide much improvement for the bottom half of society. By May 2008, the boundaries of black South African nationalism would again be dramatically emphasized, this time by a series of pogroms directed against black foreigners, including one at the squatter camp founded by mineworkers at Cinderella. At that point, Zulus had been ushered back into the nation — if nothing else by the rise of Jacob Zuma, a Zulu, as president of the ANC. Zimbabweans, Mozambicans, and other foreigners remained the objects of attack, much as Zulus had been at Cinderella in 1994.

If black nationalism is key to the events I describe in this book, it was nevertheless entangled with ethnicity in those events. The objects of the attack at Cinderella were Zulus — and not just Zulus who belonged to the IFP, the political party that, by allying with white power, had, from a certain point of view, betrayed the national struggle. And the attackers were an ethnically homogenous, secret gang who called themselves simply the *amabutho*, the "regiment" — inheritors of a long history of ethnic gangs on the mines, but in this case mobilized by a nationalist, rather than an ethnic or a criminal, agenda.[15]

After the killings, there were two fundamentally different accounts of the violence at Cinderella, which have much wider relevance in the world today. In the first, black workers were always already ethnic subjects. Apartheid, like communism, was a social order founded on coercion. When that coercion faltered, according to this narrative, black ethnic groups came into conflict, as they began to compete in new ways for resources and power; it was only a matter of time until something like the events at Cinderella occurred. This is what might be called the ethnic story, an account that made sense to all whites at the mine and to many black workers as well. A variant was put on display, for example, by mine management when, in July 1994, after weeks of attempting to reconcile the black workforce after the murders, it fired all of its approximately 350 Zulu-speaking employees. The Zulus comprised only a small percentage of the 5,000 or so black workers at Cinderella and thus could be let go without jeopardizing the enterprise. Management emphasized that it regretted this action, but that it could not be held responsible for solving the "age-old animosities" of black South African ethnic groups.

The other story, told principally by black clergymen who attempted to mediate the conflict and by the head office of the National Union of Mineworkers (NUM), the union recognized at Cinderella, proceeds from assumptions that contradict those of the first. According to the second story, blacks were never ethnic, at least not in the ways that whites assumed. The huge apparatus of apartheid half-convinced some blacks that they had opposing interests, but in reality all blacks occupied the same position vis-à-vis apartheid. Therefore, those in power had to go to greater lengths to stir up trouble among blacks, and this was precisely what occurred at the end of apartheid: as a last desperate attempt to influence the transition, a "third force," organized by elements of the old white regime, instigated conflict among black factions. This plot, one that Fanon himself might have offered, I call the black nationalist story.

Neither of these explanations turns out to be convincing in the case of the Cinderella events. Both management and the NUM acted in surprising ways. After long years of resisting unionization, management, for example, invited the NUM to unionize its workforce in the early 1990s. With the end of apartheid clearly on the horizon, the company realized it could not run its enterprise without the help of legitimate black authority. There is no evidence that the company instigated rivalries or attempted to divide the workforce, and there is no indication of third-force involvement at Cinderella (as there is in some other conflicts).

The actions of the NUM also confound expectations. Despite the anti-ethnic platform at the NUM's head office, local organizers self-consciously used ethnic strategies at Cinderella to unionize the workforce. One of the two NUM organizers was himself Xhosa, and he targeted Xhosa workers as members. The union piggybacked on the secret Xhosa regiment already at the mine and used it at critical moments as an "enforcer" during strikes. When shaft stewards were elected after union recognition in late 1993, Xhosas, far beyond their proportion in the workforce, dominated local union leadership.

Not much in this case is as it first appears. In this respect, the murders at Cinderella resemble the structure of the mine itself, whose most critical areas were hidden two miles beneath the surface.[16] After

the end of the Cold War, ethnic violence has become all too familiar. Ordinary citizens, not to mention policymakers, daily confront the
question of how to interpret violent events — many of which are presented in newspapers, court records, and government reports as matters of ethnic (and sometimes religious) difference. It is my purpose
to illustrate a critical methodology for reading ethnic violence.[17]

Given the labor involved, not every conflict can be submitted to the
kind of scrutiny I have applied to Cinderella. Years of probing and
rethinking preceded the writing of this book, and still uncertainties
remain in my analysis. Nevertheless, I hope, by elucidating how this
conflict came to be "ethnic," to impart a certain sensitivity that will be
useful for reading other cases.

The first methodological challenge involves the peculiar complexity
with which identity terms are socially mobilized.[18] At base is the issue
of how an individual views him- or herself: "I am Zulu," "I am black,"
"I am Jewish." But no individual unilaterally determines these terms.
Others label him or her as well: "Yes, she is Zulu," "He's not really
black," "She's not an observant Jew." How any one person ultimately
views him- or herself is the result of a dialectical, always social, not
just individual, process. Moreover, organs of society, like the state,
also classify persons, and such classifications, given their institutional
power, carry a weight of their own.[19] The apartheid state (as well as
management at gold mines) magnified the weight of these schemes
about as far as was possible, categorizing not just races, but African
tribes as well, each purported to have its own traditions, laws, character, and even work abilities.

When violence is introduced, this picture becomes yet more complex. The dead man on the ground was Zulu, and, yes, let us say that
the man who murdered him was Xhosa. Although one might think
that such violence can be considered ethnic only if the Xhosa man
acted because of the dead man's Zuluness, the matter cannot be contained by ascertaining the murderer's true, inner intention. Inevitably,
those who witness the event and who construct accounts of it afterward impute motives (which can be different from the murderer's
original intention). A case of violence becomes ethnic finally because
of a semiotic process that deems it so, through narratives that become
collectively shared to some important degree.[20] It is therefore crucial
to appreciate just how the process of collective narrativization occurs.

Not every story of ethnic violence gains any traction of course. In
any particular case there is a complex dialectic between narratives cre-

ated to explain events and the actualities of what transpired. No theory can assist us in the understanding of this complexity.[21] Rather, each case must be examined in its own terms to furnish a micro-history of how ethnic narratives come to persuade in relation to particular events, particular contexts. This operation constitutes "theory" in another sense.[22]

Almost no analyst of violence—whether reporter, police officer, judge, anthropologist, or political scientist—personally witnesses the violent event or the processes that lead up to it. And even when he or she does, the experience disorients just as often as it offers special insight. Is this the man who raped you? We know that witnesses can be both convinced and wrong. In any case, violence has the inherent tendency to create uncertainty about cause.[23] After the most thorough attempts at understanding, most accounts of violence—including this one—retain some degree of murkiness.

If such uncertainty presents an uncomfortable situation for analysts, it often does so much more acutely for persons actually involved in a violent episode. With so much more at stake than "analysis," participants often feel compelled to narrate.[24] And in such situations it is not uncommon for simplified plots to become widely shared. When this happens, cross-checking across sources will not provide the usual guarantees of accuracy in reconstructing how an instance of violence has occurred.

Because it creates unusual degrees of uncertainty about causality, violence establishes conditions in which people can change their attitudes, commitments, and identities. In this way, it can "speed up" history, creating new kinds of apparent clarity. Narratives created after violence, particularly by victims, can therefore unconsciously project back onto the past attitudes and identities that were in fact created by the experience of violence itself.[25] In such narratives, the "projected" past marches toward the present, as what are arguably outcomes come to be understood as causes.

The tendency to read the present (after violence) into the past necessarily overemphasizes and overplays the role of hatred of the other. Nothing "primordializes" identity more efficiently than the experience of violence, especially violence that appears to have been directed at one's group *as* a group. After the ethnic aspect of one's identity becomes literally a matter of life and death, that which may once have been lightly worn—"I am a Xhosa," "I am a Zulu"—can become far more determinative. As it does, the transformation of the present requires for many people a reorganization of the past, as events and incidents are renarrated and fit into new narrative constructions (which, of necessity, are not recognized as new at all).

Identity-based conflicts thus invariably produce what might be thought of as obfuscations of the past. Yet such "misrepresentation" is rarely intentional. In the case of the Cinderella murders, newspapers at the time reported that the Xhosas had attacked the Zulus. Reporters did their work. They interviewed laborers and management, critically weighed their findings, and reported the facts. A simplified ethnic version of the story made sense to virtually all social actors. In today's mediated world, one should expect to hear many more such stories, for they are encouraged by the very structure of ever-faster communicative interaction that necessarily abstracts from local contexts.

Historians have long been aware of the problems of reconstructing events on the basis of found data, but many anthropologists and political scientists—not to mention policymakers and ordinary citizens—remain unaware of the challenges posed. For example, in a 565-page book, *The Deadly Ethnic Riot*, the political scientist Donald Horowitz spends approximately six pages on the nature of the data from which he will generalize: 150 riots in 50 countries, virtually all of which took place after the Second World War, the majority from 1965 to 2000.[26] Any exercise that accepts reports after violence more or less at face value will almost certainly mislead. One must understand exactly how any particular conflict became "ethnicized" to appreciate what it was about.

It is important to read ethnic violence critically not just to better understand, but because simplified stories created after the fact often suggest that cultural difference itself was somehow the cause of conflict—and that separation is therefore the only solution.[27] The track record of partition, from India and Pakistan to Ethiopia and Eritrea, has hardly been successful. Instead, the consequence is often more violence, since the root causes of the conflict have not in fact been addressed.

What I offer in this book is a restoration to view of the politics that drove some black workers at Cinderella to murder others in 1994. Coming to the study of ethnic violence from topics like economic organization and political history, I was struck again and again by just how difficult it was to reconstruct violent events. The perpetrators of the killing at Cinderella continued to work at the mine and to live in the compound. They and those they could intimidate had every reason to cover up what had occurred. Interviewees sometimes opened up with statements, but it often took me years to understand what they had said. To reconstruct what had happened, I had to match narrative against narrative and those against isolated fragments of information. Finally, all I had to offer was another narrative, albeit one that I hope is true to the situated narratives of social actors themselves. In that sense, an analytical narrative can "join" a conflict. That is, an analyst can become virtually indistinguishable from a participant, as his or her account becomes only another way of pursuing a conflict.[28] Such heightened stakes, along with the inherent uncertainty of what could safely be said about a case in which no one was ever tried, much less convicted, presented unusual concerns to me during the long gestation of this book. I have written on demanding topics before, but none imposed quite the political and moral burdens that this book has.

What if I have gotten things wrong? What if I have misrepresented what happened? Most of the actors are still alive. I can disguise their identities, but I cannot change the identities of the organizations and institutions involved. My response is to make the inevitable uncertainties of evidence clear to the reader, even as I follow the direction in which my information leads. Each so-called ethnic conflict is different, and I do not wish to proclaim a general theory of ethnic violence. I believe, though, that appreciating how collective interpretations of the conflict were socially established in this case, how (sometimes misleading) narratives become credible to actors in the unexpected turns of events, offers a critical mindset for approaching other examples of violence for which actors' stories are today made to travel ever farther and faster.

1

PICTURING A
SOUTH AFRICAN GOLD MINE

AS I BEGAN FIELDWORK AT CINDERELLA, I was struck by the visual element of apartheid. The very notion of race in an everyday, if not a legal, sense assumed that race could be visually determined. And the separation of races across space instituted a social order that was unusually susceptible to being captured by visual means.[1] This was nowhere more evident than in the segregated compound for black workers at Cinderella, which was something of a cross between a college dormitory and a prison, but perhaps most like an army barracks.[2] Even in 1994, the vast majority of black workers, who numbered nearly 400,000, on the twenty-six gold mines in South Africa, lived in compounds—or hostels as they were increasingly called.

As I documented the mine and its compounds, it was my good fortune to work with the South African photographer Santu Mofokeng.[3] Santu and I made several trips to Cinderella, and this experience, more than any other during my research, revealed the tensions between white and black that lay just beneath the surface. When Santu and I went underground, a white worker in the cage that carried us into the earth, began the rhyme "Eenie, meenie, maynie, mo," leaving the next verse unfinished: "Catch a nigger by the toe."

I had hoped to include photographs of both white and black workers in this book; after all, their changing relationships were crucial to the wider transformation of 1994. Only the lowest levels of formerly "white" jobs, mostly supervisory positions, were being performed by blacks. In assuming that Santu could photograph white workers as easily as black, however, I had not given enough thought to the social interaction that taking a picture presupposed. There is perhaps an irreducible element of power involved, as is manifest in the basic terminology of photography: we "take" a picture; those depicted are "subjects." When the photographer is black in a context like South Africa in 1994, the power dynamic that plays out in the photographic encounter inevitably exposes social contradictions. There are therefore fewer images of white workers than I would have liked. Significantly, most of the exceptions involve work in the stopes, the cramped underground workplaces where the rock that contains the gold is drilled and blasted, and where the (common) danger of working two miles beneath the earth's crust suspends, at least to some degree, racial tensions.

In the all-black compound, the tables were turned, and I was the one who was constantly reminded that I was out of place. Santu's ability to connect with the workers in that context allowed me to look over his shoulder, as it were, and his sensibility allowed me to see the built environment and social relations of the compound in deeper ways. Far East Hostel at the mine, for example, was a recently constructed structure that housed about five hundred workers (figs. 3 and 4). Whether the wrecked truck in the field outside Far East had simply been abandoned from the nearby motorway, or whether it had once belonged to a particularly successful black worker from the hostel, I was never able to determine. In any case, the new at Cinderella was never separate in its newness; it seemed always linked with the cast-off debris of some past disaster, decaying in the present.

One such ruin was an abandoned mine compound at Cinderella, dating probably from the 1920s (a corner of which had been taken over by squatters and their laundry. See fig. 5). Viewed from the higher elevation of a nearby mine dump's hill of sand, composed of ore that had been pulverized to extract its gold, the compound's close and rationalized spaces become visible. In some areas of the United States, such as California, such a structure might have housed migrant farm workers during a certain historical period. In South Africa in the first half of the twentieth century, this particular compound had accommodated black mine workers. How had those men experienced their lives? Could an archaeology of a ruin be made to tell their stories?

Such relics of the mine's past highlighted the modernity of structures like Far East Hostel. The first photograph that Santu took at the mine was a kind of still life of a mine worker's room and belongings (fig. 6). The manager at Far East, a black man who had recently assumed a position formerly reserved for whites, had prepared for our arrival by asking a Mozambican worker to ready his room for visitors. The man's shirts had been ironed. Curiously, the sheets on his neatly

3. *The new dormitory-style at Far East Hostel*

4. *Mozambican workers at Far East Hostel*

made bed bore the mark of the South African railway, but our encounter took place in a setting so determinedly proper that I did not feel free to ask how they had made their way to a mine hostel. On the bed lay a framed picture of the worker's absent wife, a Bible, and two bars of soap. More than a little of South Africa's colonial history had been staged for this photograph, which presents, perhaps, a black interpretation of what whites want to see.

5. An abandoned compound from the 1920s

The reality was quite different for most workers—specifically the five thousand or so black workers housed in the other compound in operation, which I call Cinderella. Built in stages, with some sections likely dating back to the 1930s, Cinderella did not look like the typical South African gold hostel in 1994. It was much older and more dilapidated. Formed by a maze of six interconnected rectangular blocks—the rooms, with their rusting, corrugated roofs, facing inward—the open spaces of Cinderella were larger than those of the abandoned compound (see fig. 7). In the open areas in the middle of the rectangle were located the toilets, showers, and facilities for washing underground gear, as well as the cafeteria. The windowless backs of rooms formed a continuous wall around the perimeter of the compound. There was only one entrance, close to the compound manager's office, and at the back of the compound, a fenced and covered path led to South East Vertical Shaft.

For the photographic gallery that begins on page 25, Santu took the first five images just outside the compound gate, which was manned by mine policemen. The social concentration of the compound—

6. A staged room at Far East Hostel

7. *Cinderella compound as seen from the toilets located in the middle of a rectangle of rooms*

representing close to five thousand regular salaries—attracted to the vicinity all manner of nonworkers, from visiting wives and relatives, to girlfriends, to any number of sharks, toughs, and sex workers. Not only was sex for sale, but also beer, dagga (marijuana), haircuts, and vitamins. Near the gate was the tribal dancing arena in which whites had been entertained by troops of black mine dancers until the late 1980s. Farther away, not shown, was the Chinese butchery from which the numbers racket, fah-fee, continued to be run.

Succeeding photographs take the viewer inside Cinderella compound itself, including an image of two workers newly arrived from home stays in one of the compound's open spaces (gallery 6). After each twelve-month contract, migrant workers had to return home for an unpaid period (that, for Cinderella workers, because it had an oversupply of black labor in the early 1990s, could last for up to six months). Each man had just been issued a mattress, a plate, and a cup.

In most rooms, mine-issue mattresses were placed on concrete bunks, upper and lower. The upper bunks were unpopular since it was too easy to fall out of them after an evening spent drinking in the compound bar. Compound clerks arranged for injured workers to be transported to the mine hospital, and an examination of the log kept by clerks demonstrated just how frequent such accidents were.

Given its density and design, the compound was a social space in which it was impossible to do anything unobserved. Men ate, showered, shat, and slept together in public view. The packed, all-male environment created an edginess that sometimes flared into arguments about noise, petty theft, or rudeness. But the compound offered as well the possibility of male camaraderie, sometimes even homoerotic pleasure. During the height of apartheid, as Dunbar Moodie's research has shown, "mine marriages" between older and younger black workers were publicly celebrated. Some white compound managers not only turned a blind eye to these relationships, but also encouraged them as a way of preventing the disruptions that competition for local township women typically provoked.[4] According to Isak Neihaus's research, romantic relationships among black workers could be quite intense in the compound—an environment that daily foregrounded the male body.[5] One of Neihaus's informants recalled, "Every Saturday there was a wedding. The Xhosa and Pondo sang and danced in front of our rooms. They would dance, jump up and down, and would pull their blankets so that their buttocks and genitals stuck out. They only covered it with the shell of the *maraka* fruit."[6]

Asked about mine marriage ceremonies in an interview in 1995 (such rites no longer took place publically), an older and successful Sotho-speaking black worker at Cinderella recalled,

> Yes, indeed. How else would others know that that one belonged to you? You had to respect [*hlompha*] him [the boy]. On the day of the ceremony all these men with their boys [*kocha*] would meet. They would go out and buy food and other things for the ceremony. They would dress them up like a wedding. They would sing there, play the wedding ceremony. They would have these tee shirts and tennis balls. You fasten the tennis balls here [on the breast] and then put the tee shirt over them. Then the men would start playing, squeezing the tennis balls. [Laughs.]

The most intimate forms of sociality, such as these, have always been conditioned by economic structures. Capitalism as we usually think of it—that is, capitalism in the context of a liberal state—involves an opposition between public and private, work and home. To simplify, home is precisely the space in which market relations do *not* operate. Home constitutes a haven in an otherwise heartless world.

South African mine compounds were part of a different kind of capitalism, protected by a different kind of state. During the contract period, there was little oscillation between work and home for most black workers at Cinderella. Home, until the closing years of apartheid, referred almost exclusively to foreign countries like Lesotho, Swaziland, or Mozambique, or to the distant rural reserves of South Africa, each ethnically defined and presided over by chiefs, which were the only places that black South African mine workers had legal rights to live. Subject to apartheid's "pass" laws until 1986, black workers had to carry an identity document that demonstrated to the police that they had employment in a "white" area like the mine (where they were housed in black compounds). At the end of the workday, black workers returned to the compound—a space in which the state and the company remained ever present.

In white mythology, the compound protected black rural migrants from the corrosive effects of an unregulated capitalism which threatened to destroy black "tradition." Hence, it was not unusual for the white compound manager to see himself as a kind of "chief" or *ubaba wetu*, "father of all."[7] But this was paternalism with a (capitalist) bottom line. In many ways, the compound functioned as a labor machine, as a way of controlling and renewing black labor on a day-to-day basis.[8] Loudspeakers woke up workers well before dawn. At Cinderella, the first bell was at 3:15 A.M., the second at 4:15, the third at 5:15. Cafeterias provided the protein needed for the workday as determined by Chamber of Mines studies, and compound bars sold the alcohol required to numb.

Nothing sums up this totalizing plan better than Moodie's schematic of a typical South African gold compound, circa the 1950s (fig. 8). As Moodie argues, however, this plan, in its stark simplicity, was a kind of white fantasy. In many ways, black workers at Cinderella made the compound their own; not only did they conduct marriage ceremonies, but in their off hours they operated knitting machines and resoled shoes inside the compound. Indeed, the lines of control contained in the layout of the compound went only so far. Mine workers, even under the most oppressive of conditions, had a finely tuned and constantly renegotiated sense of what was their due, and when management stepped across that line, workers could resist, often effectively so.

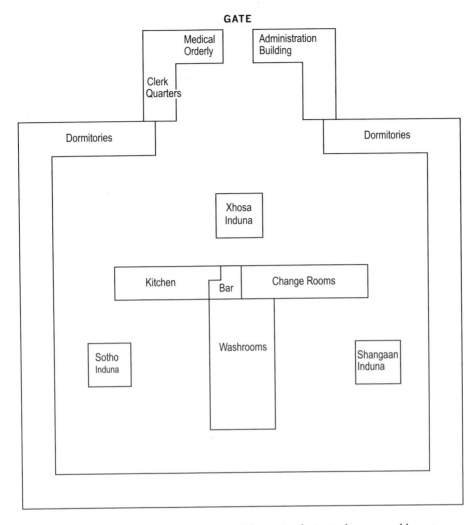

8. Schematic of a typical compound layout, c. 1950s (after T. Dunbar Moodie, Going for Gold, *79)*

According to Moodie, writing of the 1950s: "Workers expected food of a certain minimal quality, as well as wages comparable to those at other mines, a limit on the amount of personal assault underground, fair adjudications of personal disputes, equal treatment for each 'tribal' category of workers, and a considerable measure of latitude in allowing workers private lives of their own in regard to matters such as homosexuality, beer brewing, hospitality for visiting friends, dagga smoking, and other 'forbidden' practices."[9]

If capitalism and the definition of the private in South African mine compounds were different from what one normally assumes, so was ethnicity. Ethnicity was not simply a cultural identification focused within a private sphere, outside the formally instituted relation between labor and capital, in which case it would be possible to speak of class and ethnicity as independent, interactive factors. Rather, ethnicity—or, in South African phraseology, tribe—was itself a part of the way that black labor was structured in this form of capitalism, in which laborers could go home only to ethnically identified reserves or to a foreign country.

At Cinderalla, ethnicity and nationality *were* class to the degree that they were fundamental parts of the way that black labor was defined and regulated. Different ethnic and national groups in the mine could therefore have different class interests, depending on their relative degree of proletarianization, of separation from means of economic survival at home.[10] That meant, for example, that a black worker with access to land and to the possibility of supporting his family via *some* involvement in subsistence agriculture was in a different class position from a worker who had no such access. During the twentieth century, due to overcrowding in the black reserves, subsistence agriculture all but collapsed in South Africa, but this process took place unevenly across space and time. By 1994, for many but not all black workers at Cinderella, subsistence agriculture was only a memory.

Other photographs move the viewer into the compound bar during a cold night on the Witwatersrand, capturing both the comradeship and the anesthetized character of drinking at Cinderella (gallery 16–18); alcohol and marijuana prepared the men to work two miles underground the next morning. There, darkness, heat, and humidity made taking photographs difficult, but several of the succeeding images nonetheless illustrate much of the eeriness—if not the quiet terror— that underground workers faced every day. One of the last photographs is an (exceptional) image of a black worker interacting with a white higher official at Cinderella. It was that relationship, above all, that was transformed by the NUM's presence at the mine (gallery 24 and 25) and by the ANC's assumption of state power.

In the confined context of the compound, it comes as little surprise that fights occurred, sometimes between large groups of black workers. Records of such confrontations extend back into the nineteenth century.[11] Rural fighting traditions played into these contests, which became known as "faction fights." In most areas of southern

Africa, herd boys learned the art of stick fighting, and rural institutions among Xhosa-speaking groups, for example, celebrated stick-fighting contests.[12] Until the early 1970s, faction fights on the mines typically had the controlled and staged quality of these rural contests, resembling ritualized games. In such play, putting oneself and one's buddies on the line was precisely a part of the masculine appeal, as Robert Gordon has argued.[13] Risk to life deepened the game, but murder per se was hardly the object.

From 1947 to 1972, few faction fights were recorded in newspapers and mine records, though it is possible that some simply did not rise to the level of being written about. To most whites, after all, black faction fights were as expected (and as unremarkable) as mine tremors. They simply reflected the nature of things. In fact, the relative calm of the compounds during the 1950s and 1960s may have reflected black memories of white violence—particularly the viciousness with which the 1946 black mine workers' strike had been put down. That year, sixteen hundred white policemen had been called into the compounds to end the strike; in the aftermath, nine black workers lay dead, and more than a thousand were seriously injured.[14]

According to Kent McNamara and Dunbar Moodie, the frequency and character of faction fights began to change in the early 1970s. Raw murder became far more common. In 1973, violence in the mines burst into national consciousness with the "Carltonville shootings." In September of that year, a work stoppage led to an intervention by the South African police in which eleven workers were shot dead. Five months later, Orange Free State mines became the site of confrontations among black workers themselves—between Sotho and Xhosa workers. That conflict left thirty-five dead, not from police bullets, for the most part, but from the homemade weapons of black workers themselves. Company property was destroyed. Production was put in disarray. Millions of rand were lost.

Ironically, the early 1970s was a period in which black mine wages rose dramatically—after having been virtually constant in real terms for much of the century. Conditions were suddenly improving, but as de Tocqueville noted in the nineteenth century, marked improvement after a long period of oppression can be intensely destabilizing.[15] In a counterintuitive development, mine wages shot up precisely at the moment that the wider South African economy transitioned into a period of increasing black unemployment.[16] A mine job began to mean much more than it had before, both because of the increased wage and because of the more intense competition among blacks for all jobs in South Africa.

From 1974 through 1994, an estimated 155 clashes occurred among black workers on South African gold mines, leaving 490 black workers dead.[17] Such confrontations no longer had the character of rural games of masculine honor. Murder could now be used strategically to transform the ethnic mix of the workforce and to provide work to unemployed brothers at home in the reserves. It could also be used to control and profit from the various illegal rackets of compound.

Finally, murder could occur during strikes. Writing about the climatic 1987 strike by NUM, Johan Liebenberg, an industrial relations advisor at the Chamber of Mines, could barely contain his dismay:

> During the recent strike in the mining industry, in the month of August, the following incidents were reported. On August 9 at Vaal Reefs, two non-striking employees were necklaced. On August 10 at Blinkpan, one non-striking employee was strangled with a wire coat hanger in his bed. On August 13, five non-striking employees were poisoned with insecticide, one of whom later died. At Leslie on August 16, a non-striking employee was found stabbed outside the hostel where he lived. At Winkelhaak on August 20, a striking employee was shot dead by a non-striker. Also on August 20 at Libanon, an employee was shot by mine security when a group of 250 wishing to bring Libanon into the strike launched a particularly vicious attack on mine security. At Western Areas two days later, two strikers were stabbed by non-strikers while picketing. At Stilfontein on August 23, a non-striking worker was murdered by strikers when he attempted to go to work. He was stabbed and then strangled to death. At President Steyn on August 24, an employee was killed at No. 4 Shaft in a clash between strikers and non-strikers. He was a non-striker. At Kinross on August 26, a non-striking Mozambican employee was stabbed at the hostel when returning from work, and again at Kinross on August 28, two strikers were shot by mine security after a group of about 200 employees had attacked mine security and hostel personnel. Also on August 28, an employee was stabbed and burnt to death during picketing at the shaft. The employee was a non-striker.[18]

Two traditions of violence came together at Cinderella in the early 1990s. Gold mines had seen three decades of fights in which factions of the workforce asserted themselves through murder. While this scenario was well known on all the gold mines, at Cinderella, because of its location just east of Johannesburg, this mine tradition was overlaid with a new trend after the early 1990s. In the East Rand War, Inkatha Zulus came into increasingly bloody confrontation with other black ethnic groups in townships and shantytowns, as negotiation over the shape of the new South Africa dragged on.

After violence in the local mine tradition changed character in the mid-1970s, management was utterly baffled. One officer of the criminal investigations department examining the Free State riots was quoted as saying, "I don't know why they are beating each other to death. Management doesn't know, and I'm damn sure they don't know themselves."[19] Collective violence always provokes this sense of bafflement—even when it is not allied, as it almost always is in colonial situations such as apartheid South Africa, with notions of race, the inherent savagery of natives, and their primordial attachments to ethnic identity. Postcolonial critique easily exposes these distortions.[20] But, after a thorough deconstruction of the terms in which such conflicts have been represented, a disturbing question remains: black workers killed other black workers. At the end of the fight, corpses lay on the ground. Why?

PHOTO GALLERY BY SANTU MOFOKENG

*Gallery 1. A tough outside the gate
at Cinderella, probably selling marijuana*

Gallery 2. A man by the road selling vitamins

Gallery 3. Open-air drinking at Cinderella

Gallery 4. The card game just outside the gate

Gallery 5. Open-air barbering, with the tribal dancing arena in the background

Gallery 6. Two workers just arrived from home stays

Gallery 7. A man on his way to the shower in the middle of the compound

Gallery 8. Changing clothes after work

Gallery 9. A man preparing to go out after work, as seen through hanging clothes

Gallery 10. Workers eating in their room

Gallery 11. *Two workers chatting*

Gallery 12. *A man eating in the cafeteria*

Gallery 13. A worker repairing his bicycle, with the author and a compound official in the background

Gallery 14. A worker knitting in his off hours

Gallery 15. A worker resoling shoes in his off hours

Gallery 16. Empty beer bottles in the compound bar at the end of a night of drinking

Gallery 17. The coldness of a night at the bar

Gallery 18. A toast

Gallery 19. The heat of rock at two miles deep

Gallery 20. A moment of rest underground

Gallery 21. A white miner and his black team leader at the workface

Gallery 22. A driller with his pneumatic drill pointed upward toward the seam of gold-bearing rock

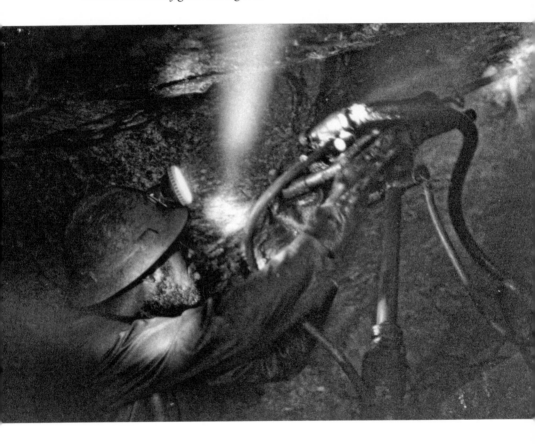

Gallery 23. A section manager after work underground

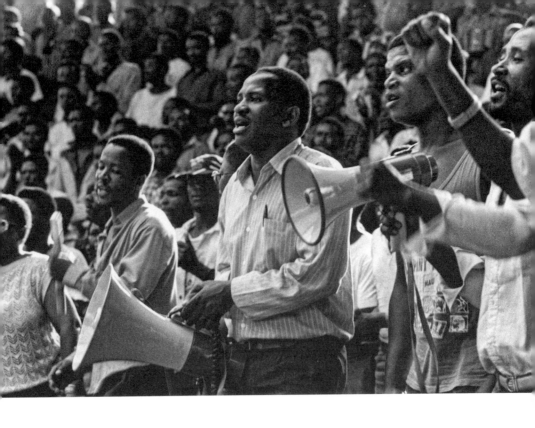

Gallery 24. An NUM rally at Cinderella in the tribal dancing arena

Gallery 25. An address by a leader from the NUM head office

Gallery 26. An NUM *shaft steward in his office*

2

The "underground" people we knew—shift bosses and mine captains and surveyors—had one advantage over us. They were very much luckier with garden boys than my father was. All had their own teams of boys working for them underground; they could detail one, often two or three, to spend a day working in the gardens of their homes. My father had more difficulty. The clerks and errand boys at the office could speak English and write, and were rarely willing to spend their Saturday afternoon off working in our garden, even for money. And they did not belong, the way the Mine boys belonged to their white bosses underground, to my father. He could not send them off to dig a sweet-pea trench or clip a hedge, any more than he could give them a hiding now and then to keep them in order. The underground people found that an occasional good crack, as they put it, knocked any nonsense out of the boys and kept them attentive and respectful, without any malice on either side.

— Nadine Gordimer, on growing up on a South African gold mine in the late 1930s and early 1940s, *The Lying Days*

IN THE EARLY EVENING of 16 June 1994, the first celebration of Soweto Day, Zulu workers at Cinderella were attacked—two were murdered, and another thirteen were injured, five in life-threatening ways.[1] There was no neutral and omniscient observer in the mine compound that evening to record what occurred. We have only variously placed accounts at varying distance from the events.

The first, indeed contemporaneously recorded, description of the violence occurred in the logbook of the mine security force. Like so much other documentation on gold mines in South Africa—where by law, until 1988, the color bar confined black workers to the lowest levels of skill and pay—the log recorded events from the perspective of white, mostly Afrikaner, employees. Cinderella contracted with Gold Fields security to provide police services at the mine, so the keepers of the log were technically Gold Fields employees, who compiled, with a kind of droll breathlessness, most of the log entries, in Afrikaans-inflected English. Functioning as police in the area covered by the mine's claim (on a map, the area beneath an irregularly shaped diamond, at times as much as twelve kilometers across), these white officers rode in armored vehicles when they had to, shot into crowds, and turned over bodies to the South African Police. The log was designed, among other things, to protect security officers from any future charges (which did occur) of improper conduct.

I quote the log at length not only because it was the first recorded description of the violence (and, therefore, occupied a strategic position afterward), but because it enables the reader to enter the white world from which these events were observed.

19:50   A report was received from the hostel that the Xhosa attacked the Zulus who came back from leave.

20:20   Security Manager and General Manager at office.

20:35   Departure of Security Officers Potgieter, Klynsmith, Archer, Alberts, Chorley and Macu to the hostel with crowd control vehicle.

20:40   Departure of Security Officers van Zyl, van Loggerenberg and Newman to hostel with crowd control vehicle.

20:45   Security Officer Potgeiter reported that about nine hundred people were gathering in front of the hostel manager's office. Heavily armed with pangas, kerries, etc.

20:50   Security Manager reported to Potgieter that the Hostel Manager, Mr. Robinson, was still in his office and that he should assist to bring him to safety.

20:52   Security Officer Potgieter then verbally address the crowd and told them to go back into the hostel. They rather threw kerries, spears at the vehicle. Two 37mm gas shells were fired into the crowd. This had no effect on the crowd for they continued throwing objects to the vehicle. It was decided by security officer Potgieter to make use of plastic shot and fifteen 37mm plastic shot were fired into the crowd. This had the necessary effect, for the crowd moved away from the office to the hostel gate.

20:55   Security Officer Potgieter moved to the front of the hostel gate with his crowd control vehicle parked between the hostel gate and the offices.

21:00   A heavily armed group gathered in front of the hostel gate, dancing, singing and throwing objects at the crowd control vehicle.

21:05   Security Officer Potgieter reported that Security Officer Chorley reported to him that somebody in the crowd had a petrol bomb in his hand and attempt to throw it at the vehicle. Twelve 37mm plastic shot were fired out of Security Officer Potgieter's vehicle into the crowd.

21:07   Security Officer van Zyl fired two 37mm plastic shot over and in front of the crowd from the Hostel Manager's office direction. The whole crowd then went into the hostel.

21:08   Arrival of the Internal Stability Unit at hostel gate.

21:10   Vehicle of South African Police and crowd control vehicle of Security Officer Potgieter went into hostel.

21:11   Crowd control vehicle of Security Officer van Zyl followed the other vehicles into the hostel. The whole crowd was dispersed on this time. Security Officer van Zyl reported a body lying on the ground on the right hand side just as you enter the gate and asked for an ambulance.

21:15   The crowd control vehicles slowly drove through the hostel and a dead person's (Zulu) body was found between Block A and D in the entrance. On this time most of the people were in their rooms.

21:20   Security Officer van Zyl reported a fire at the back of the hostel, but on the outside. Security Officer Potgieter to investigate.

21:30   Security Officer Potgieter reported back that it was only a veld fire [a grass fire] and simultaneously reported that a group of people with pangas and kerries are busy intimidating people who are on their way to work in the gangway to South East Vertical Shaft. Two more 37mm plastic shot were fired and they ran to their rooms.

21:31   The South African Police took over the scene where the body of the deceased was lying.

21:40   One security crowd control vehicle carried on with patrols inside the hostel and the other vehicle was stationary at the hostel gate. Security members were posted at both gates to perform access control.

22:00   Security Officer van Zyl visited hospital. Particulars of injured:

Nos. 167452, 29572, 57177, 65609, 168572, 127110, 22691, 48771, 89028, 18244, 59854, 39527 (Zulus), 250187 (Shangaan), 86185 (Sotho). Three of these people was taken to Rand Mutual Hospital.

22:15 Situation Report to Security Officer Schoeman.

01:40 Internal Report no. 5376/6/94 to Gold Fields Security Head Office.

02:30 Situation Reports from crowd control vehicles; all quiet in hostel.

03:20 Security Officer van Loggerenberg reported that little groups of people armed with pangas, kerries, etc. are moving into the hostel. No violence. It is suspected that these people fled the hostel last night and is returning to get ready for work.

03:40 Security Manager and Corporeal Johannes reported that the people start leaving through the gangway to South East Vertical Shaft.

04:30 Situation Reports from crowd control vehicles. Shifts are going out well.

06:30 It was established that the one injured person in Rand Mutual was in fact a Xhosa with the name of Petros Mleuzani and that he was shot with a shotgun. After investigation by the security manager it was found that security officer Chorley fired an AAA BR cartridge to the person who carried the petrol bomb last night. Statement of all security officers who was involved will be obtained. Section Manager phones Rand Mutual and his condition was described as stable.

07:00 All shifts went underground without any problem.[2]

It is striking how much the writer of the log, like virtually all whites on the mine, ethnicized black workers, even in death: "A dead person's (Zulu) body was found between block A and D in the entrance." The injured were identified by ethnic group (Zulu, Shangaan, or Sotho). And the one who had been injured by mine security and sent to Rand Mutual Hospital was "in fact" Xhosa. To an important degree, such ethnicization followed from the initial framing of the conflict: the very first entry reads, "The Xhosas attacked the Zulus." But how could white security agents, located in barracks about two and half kilometers from the compound, have known, from the very first moment, what the outburst at Cinderella compound was about? The log records only that "a report was received from Cinderella hostel." From other sources, we know that Mr. Robinson, the chief hostel manager, had been called to his office at the compound a few minutes before the first security entry.

Andrew John Milner Robinson gave testimony in Industrial Court in January 1995, about seven months after the events in question. Robinson had been employed as chief hostel manager at Cinderella for approximately two years before the Soweto Day murders, but he had more than twenty years of experience in South African mine compounds. Robinson knew his way around. In Industrial Court, the white obsession with black ethnicity starts at the very beginning of the questioning.

PRETORIOUS (advocate for the mine): What was the first intimation you had about a problem in the hostel?

ROBINSON: When my main induna [black official in the compound; literally "headman," a title taken from traditional political organization in the countryside] phoned me and said that there was violence inside Cinderella Hostel.

P: Your chief induna, who is he?

R: His name is Sam, and he's from Mozambique.

P: So is he a Shangaan?

R: He's a Shangaan.

P: Can you remember what time that was when he phoned you?

R: That was about probably twenty past seven, half past seven. I am not sure of the exact time.

P: It was early evening?

R: It was early evening.

P: And what sort of problem was there?

R: A fight had broken out. There was an attack on the Zulu contingent at about that time. We arrived at the hostel and immediately called out security.

P: You say, "We arrived." Who was—

R: It was only myself at that stage.

P: So the royal we.

R: And the night shift induna and the night shift clerk of the hostel at that time.

P: Where were you at that stage?

R: I then—well, after we had summoned security I then went with the chief induna into the hostel to assess the situation.

P: And what did you find?

R: I found that there were a lot of people who had been standing on the verandahs of the living quarters. Just outside the kitchen was a Zulu who had been badly beaten. We then managed to procure a stretcher and then managed to get him outside the hostel. There was an ambulance waiting. We loaded him onto the ambulance and sent him off to hospital. At that stage there were a lot of Zulus who were leaving the hostel and took refuge in the hostel offices. Then there was a contingent of hostel residents who had armed themselves, who then came out of the gate, surrounded the hostel office, and attempted to break into the offices.

P: And you were inside the office?

R: I was inside the office, yes.

P: What was the mood of the people?

R: The mood of the Zulus, very frightened. We managed to hide them away into kitchens and toilets and so on. The mood outside was very ugly, very ugly indeed.

P: What time did you leave the hostel?

R: I must have left about half past eleven that night.

P: Now, there are allegations that the mine security was to blame for what happened that evening. Can you comment on that?

R: The mine security, as we were surrounded—we must have been surrounded about five or six minutes—after we'd been surrounded and people had started pounding on the doors, they had broken into one of the rooms and had beaten a chap of the Sotho nation, mistaking him for a Zulu, the mine security arrived. I am not sure. I was in the hostel at the time. I heard two rounds of gas canisters go off. That didn't break up the mob that was attempting to break in and enter into the offices. Some plastic rounds were fired, and that tended to break that mob up and they went back into the hostel.

P: Now, it's common cause that a number of people were killed. Somewhere I had a breakdown of the ethnic group. Were they all Zulus or were there non-Zulus amongst them?

R: Of the people who were killed they were all Zulus.

P: The injured people?

R: The injured people, there was one Sotho amongst them. That was the chap that we caught in the waiting room and was beaten by the mob. The rest were then all Zulus that were taken to the hospital.[3]

At another point in his testimony, Robinson, under cross-examination by the advocate for the Zulus, captures the high adrenaline of the moment.

ROBINSON: On June the 16th there must have been upwards of about 130 or 140 people surrounding the office trying to break into the waiting, in fact they did break into the waiting room.

KUNY: Yes

R: To identify people in those kind of circumstances you can't coldly and calmly sit down and say, "I recognize you, you, you."

K: Yes

R: It's impossible. In fact I was in the middle of the hostel just before the outbreak of the second wave that surrounded that hostel, myself and the chief induna walked into the hostel, just the two of us alone.

K: Ja

R: And we found one Zulu outside the kitchen. Now we were surrounded at that point, they were standing on the verandahs.

K: Yes

R: It would probably be between 20 and 35 meters from us depending on the buildings, by hordes of people who just stood and looked, and between the chief induna and myself we got our own stretcher and we carried that man out.

K: Yes

R: At the gate, I was personally charged by a man wielding a big knobkerrie and an assegai [spear] made of steel.

K: Yes

R: I didn't have time to sit and try and identify. We disarmed him and after that he fled. I can't identify that man even to today. In those sorts of circumstances at night, it is dark, you can't recognize people.[4]

But, if it was difficult to identify his attacker at the gate, how did Robinson determine the ethnic background of a wounded man lying on the ground? When I interviewed him at his office in May 1995, Robinson expressed himself more freely than in Industrial Court.

On June 15th, 6 to 8 Zulus came back early, but they didn't spend the night in the hostel. The next day, 35 to 50 arrived.[5] It was very quiet; no rumors. Then a group watching TV stood up and said, "Let's go get the Zulus" and that's when it started. At about 7:30, right after the news. I arrived about five minutes after the action started. Sam called me and told me that they were attacking the Zulus inside the hostel. While I was still at home, I called security and told them to get there. They weren't on standby, which I think was a mistake. They weren't really organized; it took them another half hour to get there. I got here [to his office just outside the compound gate] and told Sam, "Right, let's get inside and evaluate the situation." So we went in and the hostel was deep quiet. All the residents were standing on the verandahs. And there was a wounded guy lying just outside the kitchen shouting, "Help me white man, help me," in his language. So I said to Sam, "Go get a stretcher and we will carry him out of here." I then asked some of the cooks to come and help me. They ran. They wouldn't help at all. I then said to the guy, "Hang on." And then I went into the kitchen and phoned the clerk in the office and told him to get an ambulance inside the hostel. As I got to the door of the kitchen, there were a couple of these guys whopping him again with sticks and pangas. When they saw me coming, they just left him and went and stood back on the verandah. A few minutes later Sam arrived, and we put him on the stretcher and carried him out to the front gate. At the gate, there was a guy with a blanket on and, you know, those pick ax handles with a steel tip, and he had a long spear. The blade was about a foot and a half long, and the shaft must have been another foot and half long. He was intent on sorting out the Zulu. I was armed so I took out my firearm, and I told him to put his weapons on the ground. He put them down, and then I told him to sit down. He turned and ran. He knew that I wasn't going to do anything to him. But if he had come at me, I would have shot him. So I picked up those things.

As I said, the hostel was stone quiet. There was some shouting going on at the back of the hostel, but I wasn't going to go that far into the compound without security. I made up my mind that I wasn't going into any other sections of the hostel, regardless of what was going on there, until security was with me. The ambulance was there and got the Zulu in. I told the ambulance to get the Zulu out but to come straight back with another ambulance. There was a lot of noise at the back of the hostel. The A and B sections were very quiet. I came in and phoned the general manager. The Zulus had been sneaking out of the hostel and about 15 to 20 were inside the main office here. Then the rest of the Xhosas came out, shouting and screaming and waving arms and so on. The night shift clerk was Bernard. I said to Bernard, "Lock every door." I told the Zulus to go into the kitchen [the small kitchen just off the main office] and toilet and sit there and shut up. "Don't make any noise." There was one guy who jumped in just as the others started to surround this block. He ran into my office. I told him to get under the desk. So he went and sat under the desk. Meanwhile, I phoned security and told them, "If you're not here in five minutes I don't think there is going to be an office left." As I said that, I could hear the Casspirs [the armored vehicles that mine security called crowd control vehicles] coming down the road. When the Casspirs pulled up here, they opened up with rubber, plastic shot, and teargas and so on. They managed to drive most of the guys out there toward the gate. They went in after them and sorted them out.

To this day, I haven't found out who organized it. It was very well organized. There must have been a hundred or more involved. To keep that secret among a hundred guys . . . I think it was a very small core. They gave the signal. I don't think it was a huge plot beforehand. It was a small group who knew what they were doing, knew their lines of communication, knew their resources and where they were. One Sotho was standing in line waiting for deferred pay, and he got caught up in the group of Zulus. He tried to jump over the wall and got attacked. What set it off, I have no idea. I am convinced, and I still am, it was political at that stage.

So it all began "after the news." On that first Soweto Day (a regular workday on the mines), the television news was concentrated on the new holiday, with stories of the commemorations of the dead across the country, dead who had sacrificed their lives for the new nation. After participating vicariously in these rites, someone jumped up and began shouting, "Let's get the Zulus." Sam, the Shangaan induna, called Robinson. The other induna, Sidwell, a Xhosa-speaker from the Ciskei, was not on duty that evening.

When the injured man on the ground asked Robinson for help "in his language," Robinson may or may not have been able to identify the language as isiZulu. In the past, compound managers had been expected to be white "experts" on local black cultures, and it was not unusual for compound managers to speak a black South African language (having, for example, grown up on a farm with the children of black farm workers).[6] By 1994, such associations were far from dead, but compound managers were expected to be schooled, as well, in the developing formalities of industrial relations. Robinson apparently spoke no black languages (although he probably understood a fair amount of Fanakalo, literally "Like This," the Zulu-based mine pidgin that whites, particularly miners, used to communicate with their black employees). In his day-to-day interaction with workers in the compound, Robinson relied principally on his staff—indunas, clerks, and compound police—for information and translation, not only linguistic but also cultural. He had, as well, as he put it, his "informers" in the compound. "I always know when something is brewing because I have a half dozen Mozambicans coming to sleep in the garage." (Robinson lived in a company house about five minutes away from Cinderella compound.)

If the role of compound manager was rapidly being reshaped and redefined by 1994, the role of compound indunas, or "headmen," was as well. In testimony to the Industrial Court, Robinson explained the changes at Cinderella.

> KUNY (advocate for the Zulus): Is there one induna or more than one?
>
> ROBINSON: In the olden days they used to have one induna that was elected out of—or appointed out of an official—out of an ethnic group.
>
> K: Yes.
>
> R: To look after the ethnic group on a basis. At Cinderella, we only have what we call two indunas, but they're more like security team leaders. I have one working day shift, one working night shift, and they really just make sure that the gates are being manned, that the security hostel police are in place, at various times, at appointed places in the hostel. They play more of a policing role rather than the old, traditional induna function.
>
> K: Now, what would happen with the other ethnic groups, for instance the Sotho contingent of miners, would they not have an induna?
>
> R: We don't have—as I say, the role of the induna has diminished to an extent that I would prefer to call the present induna a police team leader. He really looks after the sort of security aspects of the hostel, manning gates, clipping meal tickets in the kitchens, running errands within the hostel to go and call somebody for an interview at the hostel offices, manning the bar gates and so on. So the ethnic side of the induna has diminished considerably.
>
> K: Is it not traditional that an induna would represent an ethnic group of people?

R: Up to about maybe ten years ago, yes, but as I say, that role has diminished entirely.[7]

To say that Sam's role as an ethnic representative at Cinderella had diminished "entirely" by the 1990s was undoubtedly an overstatement, one meant to deflect the criticism of activists in the NUM who had long rejected ethnicity as a means of structuring the representation of black workers. To the NUM, management-appointed "tribal" representatives such as indunas were only a part of a strategy to divide and rule.[8] However unpopular compound "headmen" had become in the gold industry (at Cinderella they seemed to carry out their functions in 1994 without much opposition), indunas were a part of a wider, shared white mythology about black ethnic differences that had had a long history on the mines.

J. A. Gemmill, for example, an old-style white expert on black workers and head of the Chamber of Mines recruiting agencies for black labor, contended in 1961,

> traditionally, there have always been certain main divisions of labour within the industry. The Thonga/ Shangaan, no doubt by reason of his long association with the industry has always been regarded as "boss-boy" material and as the "specialists"; the Swazi and Pondo as the "machine-boy"; the Basuto, perhaps because he lives in a mountainous country and is used to climbing and horse-riding, as the "tramming-boy" (especially where this is performed on a contract basis) and as the "shaft-sinking-boy" (where pay is high, in some cases being as much as £25 per month, and the risk greater). In later years these wide generalizations have given way to a more specific approach to the problem and a series of aptitude tests have been evolved, in many cases with the help of the National Institute of Personnel Research, which are applied on most mines.[9]

Gemmill does not mention Zulus in this passage because they were hardly represented in underground work at gold mines at the time. The process of proletarianization for Zulus may have been timed differently compared to areas farther south and migrants from Zululand who did search out work seem initially to have found it closer to home in sugarcane fields and coal mines. In any case, according to the South African colonial imagination, Zulus had always constituted an exception.[10] They were South Africa's martial race, the proud inheritors of the tradition of the famous Zulu king, Shaka, who had won battles, if not the war, against Europeans themselves. The complex outcome of both white and black myth-making, the Zulu aura helped place the few Zulus who ended up at the gold mines before the 1970s in role of compound policemen—a role thoroughly disliked by other black workers.[11]

White views of black ethnic groups at Cinderella in 1994 had not changed much since Gemmill's time. Shangaans still made good boss boys (now mostly called team leaders).[12] Sotho were still the preeminent shaft sinkers. And Swazi (and now Zulus) were good drillers. Kaput Swanepoel, as I shall call him, a crusty Afrikaner section manager at Cinderella in 1994, after cussing about how "kaffirs" were never satisfied these days (*kaffir* being the South African equivalent of *nigger*), added political attitudes to technical skills in his typology of blackness: "Most of the union shaft stewards are young leftists, mostly Xhosa. They blame the older guys for not opposing apartheid. The Shangaans, they are cowards. They side with whichever side they think is stronger. The Zulus are like right-wing Afrikaners: brave but stupid. Even when they are terribly outnumbered, they fight. There are not many Sothos here."[13]

There was, then, a long-standing white view on the proclivities, both in terms of work and of politics, of black ethnic groups, one that extended far beyond Cinderella and much farther back in time than the mid-1990s. Questioned by the Myburgh Commission in 1996, for example, William Eksteen, manager of a Gold Fields platinum mine, unselfconsciously explained the connection between skills and black ethnicity.

> In the mining industry there is a certain job pride that is developed over many years, and if we refer to shaft sinking and to the people of Lesotho, they have prided themselves over many years that they can do that better than anybody else, and therefore they have always excelled in that particular job category of the art of shaft sinking. The Zulu speaking people are production specialists in—like the Swazis, in drilling machines. If we talk about operating percussion machines, they are very good in doing that, and so they have made a mark, they have proven in the industry that that is one of the jobs in stoping on production that they can do very well, like the Swazis have. The Xhosas have also excelled in—in my experience the Xhosas showed that when it came to smelting operations and running furnaces that that they could do very well. They also showed that as operators of scoop trams, in other words drivers of

machines, and in our particular case on the mine that I am the manager of at the moment where they do operating jobs, let us say driving locos, working in development ends. There are those sorts of areas where it is popular amongst them to want to occupy those particular occupations. And we know that the Shangaans are very good mechanical people. When it comes to doing mechanical work that they have a reputation of being good mechanically. So in the industry over many years there is a culture that has been built, and I call it job pride, where people have taken pride in, like their fathers, wanting to do a specific job and wanting to excel in that specific job. It is a culture that has developed. It is not an exact science, but it is a culture.[14]

As Jeff Guy has argued, it would be naïve to dismiss such stereotypes as only white mythology.[15] Middle-class black newsmen reporting on the Myburgh Commission scorned Eksteen's views as nothing but white racism.[16] They were that, of course, but had the reporters interviewed black workers themselves, they would have discovered a black discourse not unlike Eksteen's, at least in certain contexts.[17] After a hundred years on the gold mines, what was black and what was white was not so clear. Many Sothos, in the struggle to compete for jobs, bragged that they were the best shaft sinkers, that others could not measure up. And a few Swazis let it quietly be known that they possessed *muti*, or medicine, that, when applied to their machines, guaranteed them success as drillers. Others could purchase the *muti*. An examination of team leaders at one Cinderella shaft in 1995 revealed that, in fact, Shangaans were significantly overrepresented compared with their numbers in the wider mine population. Of the 176 team leaders at Far East Vertical Shaft, 128, or 72 percent, were Shangaans (who comprised 57 percent of the black workforce at Cinderella). Of the Zulus who had worked on the same shaft, about half (48 out of 97) were drillers. The handful of black workers who emptied toilets underground were all Baca—an association between job and ethnic group that was common on South African gold mines and beyond, in black townships.

In the past, black ethnicity had been ritually celebrated on the mines. The occasions most visible to outsiders were those Sundays on which mines sponsored "tribal dancing" for white audiences.[18] According to Hugh Tracey, it was the compound manager at Consolidated Main Reef Mine, Mr. Hallett, who first built a stadium on a mine for these shows.

It was an immediate success both with the dancers and the audiences; and from that date in 1943, when it was first opened, Mine Dances have been a recognized attraction for European tourists and visitors. It is not too much to claim that it has signally contributed to a better understanding of the African mind on the part of white South Africans and their guests. Inter-tribal dances had been open to the public long before the dance arenas were built, but never upon such a scale or under such favourable conditions. It is due primarily to Mr. Hallet, and to a few other enthusiasts, that the present assured position of tribal dancing [in 1952] as an accredited recreation for native miners has been achieved. He it was who encouraged the use of, and indeed, improvised, many of the dance costumes now commonly associated with the different tribes and thus inspired the dancers to keep their teams together and develop *esprit de corps*.[19]

In 1994, Cinderella still had its tribal dancing arena, an elaborately stone-built and roofed circular structure, just outside the compound gate across from the compound manager's office. According to interviews with indunas, who had previously organized the dance teams, mine dancing petered out at Cinderella in the late 1980s.[20] Ironically, by the mid-1990s, the tribal dancing arena was used for mass meetings of the National Union of Mineworkers. But just a few years before, in the same arena, the same workers had "performed" ethnicity, both for themselves and for white audiences. For white South Africans like Hugh Tracey, the dances revealed the "group souls" of black workers.[21]

A Chamber of Mines playbill entitled "Tribal Dancing on the Gold Mines," distributed to white audiences, started with the admonition: "Dances are arranged to provide recreation for Bantu mine workers working on the mines and not primarily for the entertainment of the public. The privilege of attending this dance is extended to visitors on the strict understanding that no use is made of the occasion for commercial or publicity purposes." Then the booklet reads,

> He has completed the routine check on his diesel locomotive; handed in his miner's lamp for re-charging for the last time this week, put aside his newly acquired T-shirt and transistor radio. For today he will dance.
>
> In loin cloth and jackal skin cape, he gyrates to the sounds of the mwenje wood music, repeating the movement that his ancestors repeated on an unmapped East African coast 400 years before him.
>
> This Chopi tribesman is making a journey back into his past — but it is a journey no longer than the one he made just a few months ago from

his hut beside the Limpopo to his workplace near "eGoli" (Johannesburg, city of gold).[22]

The role of the white manager, Mr. Hallet, in helping to design the loincloths and skin capes of the dancers had been forgotten.

Black mine workers' own (stereotypical) views of ethnicity emerge in a report based on the work of black participant observers at a mine in the mid-1970s.

> Black miners claim that different language groups have different characteristics. For instance, the Shangaans, who seem most prone to this ethnic stereotyping, see themselves as faithful, upright and hardworking (other see them as toadies to management). They, in turn, see the Xhosas as "undignified, thieves, immoral, heathens, an artificial kind of people who do not care about a person as a human being." Xhosas always seem to be in debt, constantly borrowing from the mine. This shocks the provident Shangaans. Basothos are quiet, say the Shangaans. They sit in blankets brooding in the sun; but their brooding is not simple apathy. "It is the dangerous and evil brooding which indicates witchcraft."
>
> What substance is there in such stereotypes? Certainly Mocambicans on the whole are devout Christians, enormously hardworking, very conscious of money. They take in washing from other miners at a large profit, they like to be picannins, and to work in the white man's garden after work. They revel in conspicuous consumption, but tend to be self-righteous. For instance, a field officer reported that while Xhosas accept the charge that they are thieves (although the Transkeians blame the Ciskeians and vice versa), they also point out that the Shangaans, who are so self-righteously opposed to thievery, have no scruples about buying stolen goods.
>
> The Shangaans are in fact a most interesting group. They are regarded by management as the most hard-working and submissive group on the mine. Certainly they are well-behaved and appear eager to please. Visitors (even Xhosas) are made welcome in Shangaan rooms—they will even drink tea and joke with them, but will criticize them when they leave. Likewise, they will listen eagerly to Radio Mocambique, rejoicing in Frelimo's rule and criticizing white management on the mine as colonialist, capitalist and exploitative of workers; yet, their criticism of the mine is restricted to ethnic fellows and room-mates. To people from "outside"—Xhosas or Sothos—they say "the mine is alright, OK." To the whites, they remain very submissive. On Sunday night a Shangaan complained: "Tomorrow is Monday, I'll have to face that bearded

Boer [white miner] again," to which his roommates responded: "This is Johannesburg, you must not concern yourself with that man, you have come to get money."

Thus Shangaans, who are supposedly the most docile of all workers, are also most clearly role-players, doing their time on the mine, submitting to white authority for their own monetary reasons. It seems precisely because their attitude to the mine is so consciously exploitative that they make the most stable component of the migrant labour force.[23]

Whenever mine tables, charts, or graphs depicted black labor, they almost always categorized workers by ethnic group (thought to be related to particular skills). In incident reports, personnel files, and compound entries, blacks were referred to, typically, first by their employment number, then by their tribe. Each time a black worker returned from a few months at home to sign another one-year contract at Cinderella, he was asked to specify his chief, headman, tribe, and district. While the compound clerks in charge of collecting this information often left "chief" and "headman" blank on the form in the 1990s, "tribe" was always filled in. It was as if, from the mine's perspective, black individuality dissolved into ethnic blocks, into "group souls," with individuals identified only by numbers.[24]

By the 1980s, all black workers were classified into skill categories 1–8, with team leaders occupying the highest rating. Given the color bar, abolished only in 1988, no black worker could occupy a job classed higher than 8. For every fifteen black workers at Cinderella, there was approximately one white worker. The passage of black workers across the old color bar had begun at Cinderella only in 1995 (at other gold mines, particularly in the Anglo American group, the process had gone farther). There were, in fact, only four black "miners" at Cinderella in 1995. Ordinary workers were not called miners. Miners had earned basting certificates from the state, and they (and those above them) were the only workers legally empowered to wire up the holes drilled during the workday with explosives. As apartheid came to an end, white miners were represented by the Mineworkers' Union, a group that had associated itself with ultra-right Afrikaner nationalism. Above miners were various kinds of "officials," again each with their legally defined duties and state-mandated tests to pass; the hierarchy went from miners to shift bosses, mine captains, section managers, the manager of mining, and, finally, to the general manager.[25]

The hierarchy among whites was military-like and elaborately formalized. The visible symbol, from section manager up, was the company car. Section managers drove BMWs, and those above them drove Mercedes. (And one always knew where these men were, depending on where their cars were parked—typically in individually reserved parking places.) After coming up from underground, all officials wore ties, and in addressing men higher in the hierarchy, they typically used the Afrikaans *meneer*, "sir." During the late nineteenth century and early twentieth, as the gold-mining industry was created in South Africa, skilled white miners were drawn from Europe. However, as mine owners sought to undermine the strength of white labor and as capitalist development began to push Afrikaner farmers off their land, the latter were brought onto the mines, first as strikebreakers.[26] Gradually over the century, Afrikaners came to dominate the white strata of jobs on the mines. If English continued to be the preferred medium of written communication at Cinderella by the 1990s, Afrikaans was by far the most common form of spoken communication among whites, all the way up to the general manager. Only the board of directors of the mine, most of whom owned shares in Cinderella, continued to be dominated by whites from English-speaking backgrounds.

Only one of the white officials at Cinderella appears in Santu Mofokeng's photographs (gallery 23). To capture something of the spirits of others, Santu and I decided to photograph their houses, which, in addition to their cars, had been provided by the mine. At the top in terms of luxury was the general manager's house (fig. 9). With large gardens (and a gardener provided by the mine shown in the photograph), the general manager's house looked like those found in the wealthiest California suburbs: large and well kept, comfortable and understated. The house of a mine captain, a position two or three steps below the general manager, was still quite a large residence (fig. 10). Another two steps down, to the level of an ordinary miner, involved a significant drop in status, as reflected in the company housing for miners (fig. 11); these were the houses that black miners, recently able to earn their blasting certificates, were just beginning to occupy. Until the early 1990s, only a small number of long-serving black team leaders and clerks were allowed to bring their wives and children to live at the mine; they lived in "black married quarters" (fig. 12). All other black workers had to live in the compounds.

White miners at Cinderella were paid less than miners at more profitable mines, and there was a fairly high turnover. This meant that the lowest level of white staff, just above the highest-paid black workers,

9. The general manager's house

10. A mine captain's house

11. Ordinary miners' houses, with a miner's female relatives in front

12. Married quarters for black workers, with a woman sweeping the street

came from distinctly lower-class white backgrounds. One middle-level management official, Afrikaans-speaking, told me,

> Some of these miners live like kaffirs. Not like blacks. Like kaffirs. Do you know what I mean? Their houses are unkempt. They and their wives are rough. They have tattoos. Come salary day, they go out and buy very expensive things. It makes them feel empowered. But then by the middle of the month, they're broke and don't have money for food so they take the stereo and whatever to the pawn shop. They say that the two most important things around a mine are the pawn shops and the bottle shops.

The wife of a white miner reported being stigmatized in the white community around Cinderella. Her children had been teased in school, and it was difficult to arrange for credit from stores after store-owners learned that her husband was a miner. The abolition of the color bar in the late 1980s was in fact a boon for Cinderella, though one that was just beginning to be realized by the mid-1990s. Now, the mine could attract more dependable, highly qualified black labor into low-paid jobs for which there were not enough whites.

If personnel records for blacks homogenized and anonymized, they did just the opposite for whites, even for lower-class workers. White personal files at Cinderella listed not only home language (never tribe), educational achievements, and churches (from the Pentecostal Assembly of God to Methodist and Reformed Churches), but hobbies as well. This harked back to a time, up to the mid-1980s, when the mine provided for its white employees a golf course, a social hall for dances, and facilities for lawn bowling, soccer, rugby, and cricket. The miner Christo Cecil Owen Wright listed his hobbies as fishing, rugby, and woodwork, while the shift boss André Johan Van Antwerpen enjoyed motor sport and rugby. Shift boss Thomas Henry Birch Peacock's English-speaking background emerged not only in his name, but in his hobbies: tropical fish, cricket, and soccer.

This was the latest generation of white men who supervised black men at Cinderella, the latest in a little more than a century. While apartheid had done everything it could to define whites as separate and as opposed to blacks, in fact there had been (and had to be) much intercommunication. Take only the issue of skill. The whole premise of the mine hierarchy was that those in more superior positions were more skilled, but in fact as the century wore on, whites were increasingly "deskilled" in the actual practice of mining. They became merely supervisors of blacks and of each other; they became part of what Alvin Gouldner called a "punishment bureaucracy."[27]

Supervising labor in a gold mine was, after all, an unusually vexed issue.

> Production in a typical gold mine takes place in 150 stopes. The length of the work face of each stope is about 40 metres. If all the stopes were joined end to end, the total face length would add up to 10 kilometres. This would be difficult enough for management to control and supervise in a well lit, spacious factory or along an assembly line. In the confined space, noise, heat and almost pitch darkness of an underground workplace, the question of control takes on a qualitatively different character.[28]

The manager of mining's primary job was to go underground and to inspect the work of those one step below him in the hierarchy, his sections managers—the same with section managers with respect to mine captains and mine captains with respect to shift bosses. But all these interactions had a distinctly staged quality: the person in charge always sternly admonished and criticized, the person being inspected respectfully listened. After these little rites of humiliation, work went on, often just as it had before. And the way work went had everything to do with blacks who actually possessed the relevant "skills." A study funded by the Anglo American Corporation in the mid-1970s, which utilized black participant observers underground, presents the following (possibly exaggerated) view of white miners:

> A fairly wide range of sources suggests that for most of his time underground, the typical white Miner sits on his box in the haulage, his piccanin on guard, relaxing in the company of white fellow Miners: periodically he sends out instructions and asks for reports about work progress. He appears occasionally at the stope, shouting orders to left and right, "pushing blacks around" and "criticizing them." They give orders without giving reasons, forgetting that blacks do this work most of the time without them. One has the impression that most of the genuine supervision is done by the black team leaders. "Workers discuss work problems with the black supervisors." On the whole, then, the white Miner has very little control in a situation in which he claims to be boss and it is extraordinary how little respect blacks have for him: "They think that the white man is physically incapable of doing hard labour and that

he cannot fight as well as they can do." White Miners with experienced team leaders are able to achieve fairly good production without being involved on the stope — except, one suspects, when the Mine Overseer comes to inspect.[29]

In his study of "pit sense" — the ability to identity potentially dangerous conditions underground — Jean Leger found that more than half of white miners and shift bosses he spoke to in the mid-1980s reported that they had learned their skills from black workers. According to one white miner, "Actually, my whole mining I learnt from the blacks. I was in the Chamber of Mines Training College but there they only gave you the basics. The actual mining I learnt from my black team leaders."[30]

The blurring of the boundaries between what was black and white came with its ironies. Earlier in the century, it seems that white workers commonly gave nicknames to black workers.

> Many of the Africans were named after tools and other utensils, or after distinguished actors, politicians, poets, warriors and musicians. Some were even named, regardless of their sex, after great and beautiful ladies; and the gloom of subterranean life was sometimes momentarily lightened by the sight of a spindle-shanked negro running to answer his piquant nickname, bawled by a raucous voice. In the mine, Shakespeare and Cleopatra, Napoleon and Ramses were all contemporaries, and Whisky, Toffee, Hammer and Cheese mixed and worked amicably with them.[31]

By the 1990s, however, blacks had returned the gaze at Cinderella. How much whites were aware of black nicknames for them is not clear. It was likely to have been obvious for the manager of mining who was known as Satan, for that was not an unusual black nickname for white supervisors on South African gold mines.[32] Jan Killion, the compound manager before Robinson, was known as Weyasola, "Sweeping"; he fired employees at the drop of a hat.[33] Before Killion was Mbawula, "Methane," the gas that could explode without warning, and Mbawula's assistant Spikiri, "Nail." Dankie van Rensburg, a shift boss at Cinderella who was able to earn one of the highest bonuses in 1994 on the basis of the work performed by those he supervised, was known as Matekwane, "Marijuana." Whether Dankie smoked it or provided it to his workers, or both, is not known. Finally, slow, inept, and scraggly Chris van der Merwe, with his unkempt salt-and-pepper beard, was called simply Mhlope Wire, "White Wire"—an immediate deflation of white claims to superiority.

There was not much, then, that was simply black-versus-white on the mine by the 1990s. The history of interchange between the races was far too deep. This was perhaps the secret of apartheid. As lavishly and violently as it attempted to "separate" white and black, it depended for its very existence on the mixing that capitalism required.

At Cinderella in the 1990s, that interaction was given a special cast by the presence of so many foreign workers. Almost 60 percent of its black workforce was classified as Shangaan (no matter whether they were Thonga or Chopi back home), this at a time when Mozambican workers on South African gold mines averaged only 14 percent of the total workforce.[34] With its low wages, its depth, its high rate of accidents, and the heat that workers had to endure, Cinderella was not popular among South African workers (who had any choice about where to work). This may have explained in part the high percentage of foreign labor. But as it resisted black unionization throughout the 1980s, Cinderella's management may also have perceived in a Shangaan majority a pliant black workforce during increasingly difficult times.[35] A Shangaan majority meant, according to mine custom, that the chief induna at Cinderella had to be Shangaan.[36] Induna Sam— large and imposing, the owner of a pickup truck, his hand in various undertakings around the compound, probably not all legal—was the quintessentially successful Shangaan role player. For Sam, (South African) Xhosas and Zulus were not exactly "brothers," particularly after the 1994 transition, when Sam became simply a "foreigner." As fighting began in the compound after the television news on Soweto Day, it was Sam who first cast the conflict in ethnic terms to Mr. Robinson and, hence, to mine security: Xhosas were attacking the Zulus.

It is important to note, finally, just what these identity terms meant. Being a "Xhosa" or a "Zulu" on a South African mine in 1994 did not rest simply on a commitment to a cultural tradition, to a past. Nor was ethnic identification created only in the private spheres of black worker families. Rather, being Xhosa or Zulu was anchored in the present realities of work under a particular kind of capitalist regime— itself in the midst of change.

But more was at stake than a simple channeling of black workers into certain kinds of jobs. To draw an analogy with North American forms of capitalism, it was almost as if black workers' retirement accounts had been made contingent on the continued degree of their ethnic commitment. Without a solid relationship to relatives and to the chief back home, workers in the gold mines could not expect to retire at home. As Leroy Vail has argued, much South African state policy was premised on keeping black workers semiproletarians — as circulating migrants who came to work in white industries, but who went home to their families and to their land when they retired. Ownership of what little land had been allocated to the reserves could not be acquired by buying and selling. Land there was allocated by so-called traditional chiefs on the basis of supposed common ethnic ties.

> Men came to think of themselves as belonging to particular ethnic groups, then, not because they especially disliked their fellow workers, nor because being a member of the group made them feel good, but rather because the ethnic apparatus of the rural area — the chiefs, "traditional" courts, petty bourgeois intellectuals, and the systematized "traditional" values of the "tribe" as embodied in ethnic ideology — all worked to preserve the very substantial interests which these men had in their home areas. Without ethnicity — or tribalism — the migrants would have been less able to exercise the control that was necessary for them to assure the continuation of their positions in rural societies and their ultimate retirement in their home areas.[37]

The organization of the reserves was an aspect of apartheid that was left unchanged by the political transition of 1994. Accordingly, there has been a resurgence of "tradition" and chiefly authority in many rural areas of South Africa in the post-apartheid period.[38]

When Sam told Mr. Robinson that the Xhosas were attacking the Zulus at Cinderella, his terms entered into white stories as self-evident categories. No one questioned them. They confirmed too well an elaborate and long-established white discourse about black difference.[39] But to say this does not mean that black ethnic identities were simply a white invention. Black workers themselves took ethnic identities for granted in many situations. Too much of their material lives had been organized in such terms to do otherwise. "White" stories can therefore be read to reflect on more than whiteness.

3

WAYS OF DYING

For someone who has never been down a mine to get some idea of the working conditions with which those actually mining the gold have to cope, it is perhaps easiest to start by thinking of a road labourer digging up a pavement with a jack-hammer drill. Now imagine him doing that work thousands of feet underground, in intense heat, where he cannot even begin to stand upright, and where the drill is not going with the aid of gravity into the ground beneath, but where it has to be held horizontal and driven into the wall in front. Add to this picture the noise of a road drill, magnified several times by the confined space; dust which, despite strenuous efforts to control it with water, invades the lungs; and the possibility that the roof of the mine might suddenly cave in under the pressure, or that a spark from the drill or a careless cigarette might ignite a pocket of methane gas, and one has some idea of the work of a "machine-boy."

—Francis Wilson, *Labour in the South African Gold Mines, 1911–1969*

WORK BEGAN AS USUAL AT CINDERELLA on 17 June, even though two Zulus had just been murdered.[1] It is symptomatic that in all of the thousands of pages of mine documentation that accumulated around the incident and its aftermath, the names of the dead were never recorded in white stories. All we know is their employee numbers: 68160 and 37338.

For the friends and extended families of those two men, the 17th must have brought shocking news. To understand the effect of the Soweto Day murders on other workers requires additional background, for death itself was hardly extraordinary at Cinderella. South African gold mines were, after all, dangerous places to work. In 1994 alone, 357 men lost their lives in accidents on gold mines; among these,

222 were from pressure bursts and other falls of ground, 53 from accidents in tramways, 42 from falling down shafts, 9 from heatstrokes, 6 from electrical mishaps, 5 from explosives, 3 from slipping and falling, and 1 from burning and scalding.[2] Thus, one out of every thousand gold mine workers died in an accident in 1994. This meant, according to a government commission in 1995, that "at current accident levels, it is estimated that a worker who spends 20 years underground faces a 1 in 30 chance of being injured or killed on gold mines."[3]

The chance that a worker knew someone who had died or had observed an incident in which a death occurred was much higher. Matsheliso Molapo, in her study of Western Deep Levels in the early 1990s, observed a range of responses to deadly accidents, from something like severe traumatic stress syndrome to a kind of hardened callousness. She quotes a black mine worker.

> At Christmas, I witnessed a horrible accident underground in which six people died. Their limbs were cut off and some were buried alive. I could not eat nor sleep that night. You are never sure if you will make it safely back (to the) surface each day you descend.[4]

> I have witnessed too many mine accidents underground. I have seen 40 to 60 people whom I know very well die. Some of them were very close friends of mine. I do not have fear of the underground any more; I am hardened.[5]

Cinderella, because it was older and deeper, was more dangerous than the average South African gold mine. In 1994, eight black workers died in mine accidents at Cinderella. Indeed, it could be said that the mine, like all South African gold mines, depended on the sacrifice of worker lives for its continuance. Every 1.6 tons of gold produced in South Africa in 1994 required one worker's life.[6] Earlier in the century, that number had been substantially higher.

The notion that human blood and gold were inextricably linked was common in black worker thought, as is evident in the refrain of one Sotho mine song: "Liphoro tsa mali, liphoro" (Floods of blood, floods). But blood and gold (or money) had far wider symbolic associations than those conveyed in Chamber of Mines statistics. Isak Niehaus, for example, has argued that blood and money are fundamental notions in many southern African black cosmologies.[7] The ancestors provided the gift of blood and life; their descendants owe them sacrifices of money and other similar objects. By the 1950s, in the eastern

Transvaal studied by Niehaus, this cosmological equation had been transferred analogically to the mines.

> Former migrants [in the eastern Transvaal] believed that the true owner of the earth's wealth was a mystical snake whom they called *mong wa mmaene* (owner/boss of the mine). Though no informant had ever encountered the snake, they described it as half-animal, half-human and capable of metamorphosis. The awesome snake could appear in the form of a man dressed in a beautiful suit. The snake lived in rivers deep underground and was nearly always angry when mining companies violated its earth. It could express its wrath at any time by causing rock falls, making shafts collapse, destroying rails, sending bursts of muddy water to flood the mine, and by causing rocks to emit poisonous carbon monoxide gasses to prevent the miners from extracting gold ore. Former miners said that only if the management made sacrifice to the snake would it allow them to proceed with the mining operations. After new shafts had been sunk they reportedly met the snake and negotiated for a share of its treasure. From then onwards the management periodically appeased the snake with secret offers of coins. Parties comprising the general manager, geological surveyor, engineer, mine captain, and two white women reportedly entered the mine at midnight when it was completely deserted. They were dressed in white overalls, white gum boots and helmets. Underground, the women undressed and scattered silver coins, which came directly from the mint, in the mine-shafts. By the next day the coins would have disappeared. In this way the management honoured and paid allegiance (*go loba*) to the snake. Whenever the snake was restless and desired offerings it would send signs such as powerful hot air, blowing from the mine.[8]

This story (also collected by Moodie and his associates among Sotho miners in the Orange Free State during the 1970s, and by me from various ethnic groups at Cinderella in the 1990s) only makes sense against the background of black South African notions of the "economy" of blood and money. Among Shangaan- and Sotho-speakers, it is women — father's sisters, in particular — who present sacrifices to the ancestors; hence, it seems, by analogy, the presence of the two white women in the sacrificial rite. Niehaus goes on to show how this story, in which management sacrifices coins to prevent loss of life could easily be turned on its head. From using wealth to prevent the loss of life through sacrifice, the equation could be recast to one of taking life to acquire (illicit) wealth. Niehaus argues that, by the 1990s, the latter scenario was the one most frequently featured in black mine stories in the lowveld communities he studied. In that version, management transforms from a benevolent father figure who sacrifices to the ancestors into a horrible bloodsucker—a witch who takes life to accumulate wealth.

The intricacies of how blood and money could be related thus found fertile ground for the imagination on the mines. How many black workers had lost their lives at Cinderella since it had opened at the end of the nineteenth century? Given that the Chamber of Mines had always been obsessively thorough with its numbers, it seems likely that a researcher could come up with an exact count. I never tracked down the exact numbers, but one day in 1994, the ghosts of the dead seemed to gather about me as I stepped out of the mine hospital to squint at a fenced, overgrown, and apparently empty field just across the road. There was an old rusting sign that I could not make out. As I walked closer, the words on the sign became clear: "Bantu Cemetery." Efficiently located just across the road from the hospital door, this segregated graveyard was the final resting place for those black bodies that could not be carried home. This end, not to be given a proper burial by family, was and is the most awful imaginable for most black southern Africans—in a sense, an ultimate denial of personhood. Without a proper burial, one's spirit would never rest.

While mine accidents undoubtedly occupied considerable psychological space among black workers, statistically such deaths represented only a small percentage of the total. The personnel department at Cinderella kept accounts of each death, by employee number and ethnic group. In 1994, sixty-three black laborers died at Cinderella. Eighteen deaths were AIDS-related, and another thirteen were tuberculosis-related (these two causes being connected, since HIV infection, estimated by the mine hospital to be around 30 percent for black employees at Cinderella by 1994, had led to a reemergence of tuberculosis on the mine).[9] These thirty-one deaths far outnumbered the eight who died in mine accidents. Another eight deaths were due to "political violence" or to "factional violence," or were simply "violence related" (these eight included the two on Soweto Day). Five deaths resulted from "personal assaults," two inside the compound, three outside. (How compound clerks distinguished between "personal" and "political" violence is not clear.) And there were singular cases as well: one Shangaan committed suicide; one Swazi died of "old age"; one Xhosa died in an automobile accident; and one Shangaan died, according to the note of a white personnel office, because "the witchdoctor fucked up."

Death had become so routinized at Cinderella that a formal funeral policy had been adopted by mine management.

> Upon receiving notification of the death of a mine employee the follow-ing procedure is carried out:
>
> 1. Notification of deceased to Payroll Administration, Hospital and TEBA Johannesburg.[10] Hostel staff is responsible for collecting the necessary documentation, i.e. death certificate, identity documents etc. and for completion of the necessary documentation for Provident Fund.
>
> 2. An amount of R2,000 is forwarded to the family of the deceased via TEBA.
>
> 3. Relations or friends are paraded and sent to the mortuary with a mine official to identify the deceased.
>
> 4. Arrangements are made for the corpse to be removed from the mortuary to the undertaker for transportation home for burial. TEBA notify the family the date the corpse will arrive home.
>
> 5. In the case of a mine accident the mine pays for the undertaker's costs as transportation are concerned. Cinderella uses the Alpha Funeral Parlour in these instances. Should the relatives decide to use another funeral parlour, Cinderella mine will pay the Alpha Funeral price and the family will be accountable for an excess in terms of the benchmark.
>
> 6. If an employee passes away due to a mine accident:
>
> a. Four fellow employees will be granted paid leave for a maximum of two days to accompany the body to be buried within the borders of South Africa.
>
> b. Four fellow employees will be granted paid leave for a maximum of three days to accompany the body to be buried outside the borders of South Africa.
>
> c. Four fellow employees will be granted paid leave for a maximum of four days to accompany the body to be buried in Mozambique. If an employee passes away due to any other reason, employees accompanying the body will only be granted unpaid leave.
>
> 7. A condolence letter is sent to the family, which is arranged by the hostel staff (see attached).

8. The mine purchases coffins for the deceased but the family has the option to forego the mine supplied coffin.

Attached letter with date to be filled in:

It is with a deep sense of shock and regret that we learned of the tragic and untimely death of your husband.

At times such as these words seem inadequate but, may I, on my own behalf as well as on behalf of all the employees on Cinderella Mines, Limited extend to you and your family our deepest and heartfelt sympathy.

Should you at any time require assistance or guidance please do not hesitate to approach the Personnel Department at the Main Office.

Yours sincerely,
General Manager

Clerks in the compound prepared the letter of condolence to the wife. It is not clear whether they also signed it.

Cinderella workers dealt with stress in a variety of ways. Some turned to religion, often a mix of Christianity and African beliefs.[11] It was not unusual to see Zionist Christian uniforms hanging in the rooms of Cinderella workers (see, for example, gallery 10); some of the workers were themselves Zionist preachers, who met their mostly female congregations in the open fields around the mine. Others were healers and traditional doctors of one sort or another. A Swazi I met in the compound specialized in herbs for venereal diseases. And there was always mail-order *muti*, traditional medicine that could be bought through the post. One circular (one side in Sotho, the other in Zulu) I found in the compound came from Peter's Mail Order House in Dalbridge.

Friends, I greet you. I am grateful to have this opportunity to let you know about the help you can receive from our medicines. I am trained in helping people with effective traditional herbs. If you need help do not waste time. Place your order and R10 deposit or the whole cash price, so that we can post your order immediately. There is no delivery cost.

When you post your money, make sure that you post it with an order form so that we will know what you are requesting. Also, please register your letter so that it will not get lost. We also do examinations. Just send R7.00 and your dirty garment (with your own dirt on it) and specify that you want to be examined. Hurry, early bird catches the fattest worm.

After this introduction followed a list of 110 "medicines," including an arm band "to make one strong and to be able to finish work quicker (R50)," other medicines "to be loved by a white boss (R50)," still another "for waking up the penis (R50)," and, finally, "masterlock—to prevent your wife from sleeping with another man, (R60)."

Marijuana and alcohol also played their roles at Cinderella in 1994. The scent of the first was often so strong in the cage that took workers into the earth at the beginning of each work day that it was possible to get a contact high. Alcohol was available both outside the compound, in the open-air shebeen called "Stagane" (gallery 3), and inside in the compound bar (gallery 16–18). Drinking was *the* pastime on the mine.[12]

When two Zulus died on the evening of 16 June, then, their deaths were not out of the ordinary. After all, the incidents that management typically viewed as accidents could easily be seen by black workers as murder of a sort. And killing in the context of black faction fights, to many in white management, lay within the expected order of things— like earth tremors and the collapse of underground workplaces. If death itself was not unusual, however, the way that Zulus died on June 16th, at the hands of other black workers, called for notice. The murderers, whoever they were, continued to live in the compound and to occupy their jobs. This created unusual anxieties for Zulu survivors.

If white stories, particularly those by mine security, provided a kind of panoramic and distanced view, the Zulus' own stories were much more narrowly focused, sometimes frustratingly so.

In the beginning, I expected that the victims of the violence would, somehow, offer the truest and most authentic insight into "what had really happened." But as I pondered my materials, I realized that this assumption overlooked some of the most essential elements of how the experience of violence affects human beings. Violence overtakes and overwhelms. It disorients and disrupts.[13] And as a consequence, "being there" cannot provide the degree of reliability one might expect in a different context.

Having experienced violence, how did the Zulus themselves narrate what had befallen them on Soweto Day? Their stories emerged only slowly and uncertainly, in the days after the violence. Almost a year later, in May 1995, when I caught up with some of the dismissed Zulus who were still living in Injalo squatter camp, not far from the mine, I was struck by how one-dimensional their stories had become: the Xhosa had attacked the Zulus. When pressed to say why the attack had occurred or to identify which Xhosa had perpetrated the attack, none of the Zulus I talked to could.[14]

This standardization no doubt reflected multiple factors. First, there was the initial difficulty of registering events with accuracy at a moment when one's very life was threatened. Furthermore, some Zulus with pertinent information moved out of the area, went home, or found jobs elsewhere; those left in the Zulu squatter camp constituted the only local social container for memory. Finally, there was the inevitable process of forgetting. As a consequence, perhaps, of all of these factors, Zulus' stories at Injalo a year after the violence were frustratingly thin: everything had been fine at Cinderella, and then, without warning, they were under attack.

> THEMBA: We were working, we had jobs, and then all of a sudden fire exploded in front of us and we didn't know why. . . .
> DONHAM: I am surprised that the reasons for the conflict are a mystery to you. They are still a mystery to me.
> LEONARD: Yes, it is a mystery what happened. It is difficult to tell what actually happened.

The very first recorded Zulu narratives of the conflict, from almost year before, were, in fact, considerably more specific. For example, in a meeting between mine management and Zulu employees on 20 June 1994, a few days after the murders, Prince Joseph Zulu, an official from the recently defunct homeland government who had been called to Cinderella by the Zulu workers, asked for a description of what had happened on Soweto Day. According to management minutes of the meeting,

> The representative [Prince Zulu] asked Zulu representatives present to explain what happened in the hostel when the Zulu employees returned from home. He stated that some of the Zulu employees were injured in front of indunas in the hostel. He requested two of the Zulu representatives to explain what had happened. [On Thursday the 16th] the Zulu employees asked the hostel manager if they were safe in the hostel—the hostel manager assured them that they were safe in the hostel.

They then proceeded to their rooms. At about 8:00 P.M. that evening attacks started on Zulu employees in the hostel. The Zulu employees were chased out of the hostel and reported the incident to the South African Police. The police contacted mine security to investigate the matter. The security took one hour to arrive at the hostel. The Zulu representatives explained that the Zulu employees were very unhappy that management did not approach them Thursday when they returned back from home. They asked that employees in section "D" be questioned about the attacks because the Zulu employees believe that it is those employees who started the attacks on the Zulu. The KwaZulu representative thanked the two representatives and asked if the Zulu employees could identify any of the attackers. The representatives explained that they could identify the attackers. The [KwaZulu homeland] representative explained that employees did not want to give statements to the mine security because they are part of the problem and asked for the South African Police to investigate.[15]

The attackers were identified not in terms of ethnic group, but in relation to the section of the hostel in which they lived: D section. And people claimed that they could identify the individuals involved—a much more specific story than had congealed a year later, when I arrived at Injalo.

The next occasion on which Zulu narratives of the violence were recorded was in July, when another representative of the old KwaZulu homeland regime, Mr. Mvelaze, collected statements about the violence from Zulus as a part of a mediation effort that was mandated to look into the causes of what had happened and to reintegrate the black workforce. Mvelaze collected seven narratives. According to Bheki Thungo,

I arrived at 7 P.M. with others on the 16th of June 1994. I went to watch TV in the TV room. One man stood up and said, "Let's go get Inkatha." He shouted twice. Thereafter, all the people went out to pick up their weapons, other people marched out of the TV room while others jumped out through the windows. On the way to my room, I saw groups of men toyi-toying.[16] I met Johannes while he was being assaulted. I grabbed him and took him to the Induna Mbhele [the Xhosa induna, Sidwell]. When I reported to Mr. Mbhele, he asked me if I had seen the man who assaulted Johannes, and I said no. He also asked the very same question of Johannes who also replied no. Mbhele told us that our statements were fake because there was no evidence. While we were arguing about this, an ambulance arrived. I did not know who called it but I discovered that Themba Mbatha had already reported the matter to the office.[17]

Like the compound manager, Mr. Robertson, Thungo located the beginning of the violence at Cinderella in the TV room. According to Thungo, after the evening news reports of the commemoration of Soweto Day, one worker at Cinderella jumped up and shouted, "Let's go get Inkatha." Other accounts reported that the attackers simply yelled phrases like "Hit the Zulus," but in Thungo's narrative, the violence was more narrowly focused: of the approximately 350 Zulus in the compound, only an estimated 40 to 50 belonged to Inkatha.

Were members of Inkatha specifically targeted in the attacks? Even though Milton Ngema, the branch chairman of the IFP in the compound, denied in Industrial Court that such targeting had taken place (the attacks, according to him, were directed at Zulus, as such), there is some evidence to suggest the reverse. First of all, Ngema himself (who was not in the compound on the 16th) received a tip afterward that his life was in danger. After having been prominently involved in Zulu affairs in April, he went into hiding in June, while most of the rest of the displaced Zulu workers stayed on at the mine, hoping to go back to work. As the head of Inkatha, he seems to have felt more vulnerable than others. Also, in the narrative above and in the one below, it is clear that some of the attackers were after specific persons, including James Zwane, who other sources indicate was a member of Inkatha. According to Bekubaba Ndlanzi,

> I arrived with another group on June 16, 1994, and I registered accordingly. I was allocated Room 75. After I prepared my bed, I went to visit Joseph Mdluli in Room 70 at about 7:55 P.M. On the way, I saw Nicholas Dlamini being assaulted by a group of people. When I arrived at Mdluli's place, I informed him that I had seen Nicholas being assaulted, and we decided to run away in the direction of section F. On the way to section F, we were trapped by a huge fence with barbed wire that Mdluli and others managed to jump over, but I was too short and the fence was too high so I failed to jump over. While I was trapped there, I saw that the attackers were coming, and I ran away and entered a room to hide myself. When I was there in the room I heard people shouting "Open, open." One of them pushed the door in, and he came in with the others. Then they asked me where "Intshebe" ["Beard"] was (meaning Mr. James Zwane). They asked me why I ran away and I replied because I was scared. One of them stated that I was running away because I was Zulu. I denied that

and stated that I was Swazi. Another insisted that I was Zulu and they assaulted me until one of the men decided that I should be taken to the Swazis to state whether they knew me or not. They decided to take me to the beerhall and on their way I was threatened and told that today was my last day because I was going to be killed. On our way to the beerhall, we met another Zulu man who was injured and was trying to run away to safety. It was then that the group chased that man and left me. I got the chance to run away and went to the office of security where I reported that there was trouble in the hostel, that Zulus were being killed by other hostel residents. The security men arranged for an ambulance and I was taken to the hospital where I was admitted.[18]

Evidence given in Industrial Court indicates that both Dlamini and Mdluli were Inkatha members. Nicholas Dlamini's own story was as follows.

We were allocated rooms and I was placed together with Mr. Julius Gumede in Room 78. At about 6 we went for supper and returned to our rooms. I decided not to sleep fast that night because I wanted to be on alert all the time. One Pondo man, known as Fox, came in and asked if there were Zulus in this room. A Shangaan man answered, "Yes." I realized then there was something going wrong, and I decided to dress and leave the room. As I went out, I saw many people outside and asked them what was wrong. Instead of answering they beat me with sticks and I ran away. As I arrived in B section, I met another man who beat me on the thigh with a stick, but I continued to run until I arrived at the police station where I reported the matter to the police and thereafter was taken to the hospital where I was admitted.[19]

In Industrial Court on 24 March 1995, Dlamini related much the same story, but clarified that after the Pondo man Fox had left, another, named Vice, had entered his room and had begun to assault him.

Round about half past seven, Mr. President, I went to bed to take a rest. Round about quarter or ten to eight, a Xhosa-speaking person [Fox] came into my room. He asked, "Are there any Zulus here?" And one Shangaan in the room answered, "Yes, there's a Zulu here." After Fox left, another Xhosa by the name of Vice came in, and he was carrying a kerrie and a pipe. I got up on the bed, and I asked what was wrong. But he didn't answer. He just began to hit me with the kerrie. That's when I got an opportunity to run away. At the door I found a group of people. They were also carrying kerries and pipes. Mr. President, they hit me on the head, the neck and the back by the shoulder blade. But I managed to flee.[20]

If the Inkatha core were the favored targets, as far as they could be identified, it is also clear that, eventually, any Zulu — or, indeed, anyone who could be mistaken as Zulu — became fair game on the evening of the 16th. One of the seriously injured was a Sotho caught running away with Zulus near the compound manager's office. According to Zulu Alfred Ndlovu,

> I arrived with others on the 16th of June 1994 at about noon and registered accordingly. I was told to come back at about 2 and then I was allocated to room 165. I then decided to go to the beerhall where I wanted to spend some time. While sitting there, I saw people wearing blankets entering the beerhall. I therefore became suspicious that there would be trouble and I went out. On my way out of the beerhall, I saw another group of people also wearing blankets and one of them shouted, "Here is another Zulu." They then started to beat me and I ran away. While running, I looked back and one man hacked me with an axe on the back of my head and I fell down. I tried to get a look at him, but I couldn't. After a few minutes a couple of mine security arrived and one of them said, "Here is another one." His partner said that they should not move forward but should wait for the ambulance to arrive, and then I was taken to the hospital where I was admitted.[21]

If the category of those attacked bled one into another — a political group, Inkatha, into an ethnic group, the Zulu — apparently only a portion, perhaps a fairly small portion, of the Xhosa attacked. Other Xhosa attempted to assist Zulus with information about what was happening. According to Gubungu Mpontshane,

> I arrived at 11 A.M. on the 16th of June 1994 and was allocated Room no. 14. I went to sleep at 7 P.M. One Pondo man came in and informed me that there was a big fight outside. When I looked outside, I saw many people wearing blankets, and I too went back into the room and put on a blanket [as a disguise]. While I was going out, one man saw me and shouted, "Here's another one." They started assaulting me with an axe, and I fell down, and they beat me until they were satisfied. Later on, I regained consciousness and proceeded to the gate. I arrived at the office where I met Nhlanhla Sibiya who informed me, "Our people are being assaulted in the hostel." I was transported to the hospital.[22]

Pondo help for others went even further, according to Erick Nciki.

> Pondo Khwesube arrived while I was about to sleep and he greeted others who were in the room. He saw me and said to me "Mzala" which means cousin. He asked, "Mzala, are you still sleeping here?" I asked what was going on. Khwesube told me to get up and that he would take me out of the compound, as there was trouble outside. As we were leaving, we met a man carrying a bundle of spears, and that man threw the spears on the floor. Kweshube told him that we had to go, as we were on our way to pick up some guns. When we arrived at the gate, I saw a man wearing only underwear and a t-shirt trying to escape. I recognized the man as Alpheus Zindla Dludla. I heard people shouting "*vimba ngaphambili*" which means "stop him from running away." One of them came and attacked him with a pick handle, and Alpheus fell down. A group of people attacked Alpheus and killed him. I proceeded with Kweshube, and when we were outside the gate, Kweshube told me to run away. The man who initially attacked Alpheus Dludla was Jonathan Giyose. I didn't know the other people who were among the group.[23]

How different from any story that I could collect a year later! We learn, finally, the name of one of the Zulu dead: Alpheus Zindla Dludla. And the person who attacked Dludla first was not simply a Xhosa-speaker or, more specifically, a Pondo, but Jonathan Giyose. After witnessing Dludla's death, the narrator of these details escaped under the ruse that he was a Xhosa running out of the compound to get guns to attack the Zulus—aided in this deception by a Pondo man.

It may have been that even the security force—after it finally arrived—inadvertently put Zulus at risk by not uniformly controlling the compound. According to Amon Nkosi,

> I arrived at 7 on June 16, 1994. I was allocated a room. While I was in bed, one security man by the name of Maxwell entered the room and asked if there were Zulus around here. I said that I was one of them. The security man said that I should follow him to see my induna. On the way to the induna by myself, I was attacked by a group of people. I went unconscious until I discovered that I had been admitted to the hospital.[24]

Chaos reigned for about an hour after the television news. Blood flowed. Men died. And in that moment of high adrenaline and life-threatening blows, it was not unusual for those attacked to be unable to identify their attackers.

The next occasion on which Zulu narratives of Soweto Day at Cinderella were recorded was in Industrial Court, first in March 1995 and again in September. Most of the Zulu witnesses had been involved in negotiations with management after the violence, and many, like Milton Ngema, belonged to Inkatha. In court, these men were evasive when it came to any detail that might place Zulus in a bad light, and, consequently, their testimony did not inspire complete trust. Most of their stories had become formulaic, as if repeated telling had drained them of specificity: as they described it, the conflict was simply Zulus versus Xhosas. Little blurring of ethnic boundaries occurred in what they related, and none could identify actual perpetrators.

Occasionally, however, the messiness of Soweto Day reemerged, for example, in the testimony of Daniel Nkala. Humorous and straightforward, a member of a Zionist Christian church (and, therefore, as he said, not an IFP member), Nkala more than held his own with white lawyers. When the advocate Pretorious attempted to engage Nkala about his knowledge of South African politics, Nkala fended him off.

> Normally as a person who is a religious person, I normally don't entertain these discussions. When a person comes to me and tells me about all these political parties and that and that, I normally don't listen to that person and also on the radio when I hear about these fights of parties, you know, I just switch it off, because I don't like hearing, listening to the news that tells me somebody has died. You know, I'm a religious person, I listen to a religious program that will cheer me up spiritually and give me comfort in that.[25]

Christian Nkala survived the attacks of Soweto Day with assistance from his Shangaan friends.

> NKALA: We were given cutlery and the mattresses [on the late afternoon of the 16th]. Then from there we went to the kitchen to have food there. Because I was tired then I thought it would be good for me to go and lie down in my bed.
> KUNY: Did you do that?
> N: Yes.
> K: And what happened?
> N: We, when I was about to really fall asleep I heard noise in the hostel. Well, normally there is noise in the hostel, but what

surprised me after hearing a commotion was, there is a certain man called Mr. Nkosi, he came inside my room and he dropped and fell down, and when I looked at him, he was covered in blood.

K: You say he dropped and fell down?

N: Yes, he came in and then he fell down.

K: What did you do?

N: When I rushed to this man to try and find out what happened from him and tried to assist him because he was bleeding, one of the Shangaan men from the room said "You Zulus are getting killed. You better run for your safety. Get out. We will attend to this person."

K: What did you do?

N: At that time then there was another Shangaan guy who was coming from the bar. He came in and said, "Because you are a Zulu take this blanket and wear it," and he gave me a copperhead to put on and he said, "Now wear this copperhead as a disguise so that they won't be able to see you."

K: What did you do with the blanket?

N: He said I must take this blanket and wrap it around, just like the Xhosas.

K: What did you do?

N: Then I tried to find a way out.

K: Did you find a way out?

N: Well, I did manage after a big struggle, you know, trying to break this "stop nonsense" fence so that I would be able to get out.

K: Trying to break what?

N: There is this cement wall which is called a "stop nonsense" fence.

K: Stop nonsense. Did you notice anything? What was going on around in the hostel on your way out? Did you see anything?

N: It was like I was in a dream because at that time when I look back, you know, there were people carrying these big knives and they were busy, you know, slashing everything across, and as I was running, there was one guy who was badly injured, lying there like a corpse, then I realized that I was really in danger.[26]

Like a nightmare, the memory of the killings—directed at any Zulu, not just the Inkatha core—remained in Nkala's mind. But given that he had been focused on escaping with his life, he could not identify any of the attackers.

My own interviews of Zulus took place still later, in May 1995, at Injalo. I got to know one former worker, whom I shall call Themba, well
enough to learn about the existence of his Xhosa boyfriend. By 1995,
Themba lived with a woman in Injalo, but he had had relationships
with other male mine workers. As it happened, Themba was with his
Xhosa boyfriend when the attacks on the Zulus began.

> Usually there is a procedure when you are admitted back into the com-
> pound. You get sleeping equipment. They give you a section and room
> number. Some of us found that the rooms that we were living in before
> were full. Well, some were allocated their old rooms. I was one of those
> who didn't get my room back because it was full. I was allocated to an-
> other room. I found that I was the only new person in the room.
>
> We were told that we would go back to work and some people went
> to the kitchen to eat. At about 7:30 to 8:00 when I was making tea (I
> was actually not in my room but I was visiting a friend because I didn't
> know anyone in my new room), we heard a noise outside and while we
> were listening, someone ran into the room with a weapon. It was a sharp
> weapon like an axe. He said something is going on outside. We were
> shocked and looked at him. And he shouted back, "Why are you just sit-
> ting there?" And then he ran out and we stood up to see what was going
> on. We saw people running up and down shouting, "Grab the Zulus,"
> "Grab Inkatha," "Grab the Zulus," "Grab Inkatha."
>
> Ah, so we realized this is the time because I had heard that we were
> not welcome. So we were being killed. I left the room because I was
> only visiting. I told my friend that it would be better if I died in my
> room. When I got there all my roommates had sticks. Ah, luckily what
> saved me is that I spoke other languages. They were speaking Xhosa
> and I asked them what was going on. They said that they were beating
> the Zulus. So I couldn't ask what the Zulus had done because then they
> would find out that I was a Zulu. None of them knew that I was a Zulu.
> That was different from the room that I was living in before; there they
> knew that I was a Zulu. So I said, "Ah, I've just arrived. I don't have any
> weapon. Just give me one stick." They gave me a broom stick. When I
> went out of the room, everyone had a weapon and they were wearing
> blankets and sheets. So I suspect that they had met beforehand and de-
> cided what they were going to wear.
>
> So I took my own sheet so that they couldn't identify me as a target.
> And then while I was wearing my sheet, I realized that this wouldn't
> work because I had been on the soccer team and most of them knew me

very well. So I stayed in the room and I discovered that everyone had gone out. Something quickly came into my mind. If they find me here alone they will ask what was I doing here. In that room there were two passages. I realized that taking either of them I would end up in their hands. I thought what am I going to do? I said a short prayer like a man would usually do when he is in deep trouble. Tears were running down my face and I said, "Lord if this is the time, it's fine with me." I went to the toilet but I couldn't piss. I asked myself then what am I going to do? When I looked across, I saw someone whom I knew very well, and he was saying, "Yes we are finished with the Zulus." He said, "Now we are waiting for the Zulu top officials so that we can kill them all here inside. Now the next thing to do is to go from room to room. There must be a few cockroaches left.[27] We haven't finished with them yet."

Eh, now I realized that they were going to find me, because they were going to go from room to room. Just about then another group came up and with them was a guy with whom I had just come from home. From where I was, I couldn't tell what was happening, whether he had been killed or was just injured and lying on the ground. By then I couldn't see any way of escaping. I just told myself that I would stay in the room and die there. Just when they were talking about going room to room, I heard a noise from the gate. I didn't know whether it was a gun shot or not. Later I realized that it was tear-gas because I had smelled it and saw the crowd dispersing. Some were running to their rooms; others were running to the bar. From the station side, I saw a Hippo [another term for Casspir, an armored vehicle] coming and it was firing tear gas. The crowds were dispersing. Even in my room, they came back but not all of them. They said that we must shut off the lights and sleep because this thing of killing the Zulus will cost us our jobs. After the lights were switched off I could hardly sleep. I was scared. And I didn't want them to see that I was crying.

I just got under the blanket but I didn't sleep. I just sat while the others slept. I heard a knock from the room three down and a voice asking if there wasn't a Zulu here. I couldn't hear the reply from the people inside. And then I was scared again but I didn't know how they could be searching for Zulus even after the police had arrived. When they knocked on the room next door, I realized that it was the hostel police. And they were looking for Zulus. They were with the induna called Samuel and they were asking for Zulus. And the reply was "No, there are no Zulus here." They came to my room and asked again whether there were any Zulus here. At first, I was afraid to say anything. I just didn't know how the people around me would respond. I was afraid that they might all jump on me. I waited for all of the police to come inside the room and there were also soldiers with guns. I said, "Yes, I am here." When I said that, they all propped themselves up on their beds. It was as if they thought that they had missed their prey and now it was too late. The security man among the police said, "Oh, it's you, Mr. Majola." I took my bag because I hadn't unpacked when I came in. I had simply put the blanket on the bed. When I took the mattress and the blankets, he said that I must leave them and take only the bag.

When I went out of the room, the Hippo was standing outside the door and when I got into the Hippo I found two other Zulu guys. The Hippo went from room to room collecting all of the Zulus. When we were going around collecting people we saw one of our brothers dead. They asked me to jump out and to identify him. I didn't know his real name with which he was registered but we called him Zinja ["Dogs"] Dludla. They insisted that I must look at him thoroughly, and I confirmed that it was him. The ambulance came to take him and as we were driving past the gate, we saw blood all over the place. We concluded that all of the Zulus were dead, because it was only us three in the Hippo. We didn't know what happened to the others. I didn't know whether they had died or what had happened to them.

They dropped us next to the bus and we found that the bus was full of other Zulus. We got into the bus and they took us to the place where they used for accommodating the security officers. They called it Blue Sky. Then we started asking each other where so-and-so was, because we knew each other, having just come back as a group. Some of the responses were that some were killed and others injured. And luckily I was clear-headed. I wrote down the names of those present and also those who were missing. I got the paper from the security. They called out to me who was present and who was missing. Then the security came, this black sergeant, and he asked if there was anyone missing. We told him that some were missing. He said they would go back and look for them. They managed to come back with a few others. They managed to find them at the police station and the mine security. Until the next morning, they were busy going back and forth looking for the missing men.

Beyond the mine, the murders at Cinderella were quickly forgotten. There were so many other examples of violence on the East Rand that competed for attention in South Africa during the 1990s. And at the mine, the culprits were never identified. An investigation was never completed. Until the mine went bankrupt, in 1999, management continued to employ workers whom it knew had murdered other workers inside the compound.

There were many ways of dying at Cinderella, but the Soweto Day murders were a public, almost ritualized form of killing, one with its own theater designed to threaten those who observed and to empower those who performed.[28] That it took time to kill was perhaps an essential feature. Two or three thousand workers, maybe more, witnessed a gang of maybe a hundred slowly hack two Zulus to death.

4

GOOD FRIDAY AT CINDERELLA

TELLING A STORY ALWAYS INVOLVES the question of where to begin. Change a beginning and much else is changed. I now retell what happened on June 16th from a different starting point. From Soweto Day, I move back a couple of months, to Easter—another ritually marked day with a complex congeries of meanings. For Christians (most black workers at Cinderella considered themselves Christians), Easter is the quintessential new beginning, commemorating Christ's triumph over death through resurrection, and the establishment of a new religion.[1]

June 16th was not the first time in 1994 that Zulus had clashed with other workers at Cinderella. Earlier in the year, tensions over the national political campaign had come to a boiling point at Cinderella on, as it happened, Good Friday. No one died then—on the day that Christ was crucified—but the attacks were serious enough that on Easter Sunday, the chief hostel manager, Mr. Robinson, evacuated all Zulus living in the compounds. Shortly thereafter, management sent the Zulus home on (paid) leave during April and May, for a "cooling off" period that encompassed the elections that ended apartheid.

The religious timing of the Easter events was most likely a coincidence.[2] The violence could have occurred on perhaps any holiday (when remaining workers drank more than usual and when the numbers of a minority group such as the Zulus were further diminished and so presented an easy target). However, an element of sacrifice was certainly involved in the attacks on the Zulus—sacrifice not so much in a religious as in a political sense, in that some actors decided to take Zulu lives and livelihood in service of what they considered the greater good of the nation.

If Easter was a powerful instance of a new religious beginning, it did not constitute the only breaking point that seemed imminent in South Africa in 1994. A new nation was being born. Four years before, in a move that had electrified the world, the National Party government had released Nelson Mandela from prison. From that point onward, it was clear that a new dispensation was in the making. For nearly four decades, the ANC had been banned in South Africa. The leaders in exile had, in many ways, brilliantly orchestrated international pressures against apartheid. But in the late 1980s, the ANC was hardly attuned to the quotidian struggles of black migrant workers in South Africa. To ANC modernists, the sex-segregated compounds exemplified by Cinderella represented only a hated and "unnatural" creation of apartheid: what they were fighting against. By the late 1980s, they announced that ANC policy would be to dismantle the compounds; workers should bring their families to the sites where they worked.

What this overlooked was the actual material and symbolic stakes for black migrant workers themselves—a significant portion of whom retained commitments to the countryside. Not only did workers have to have access to compounds if their true home was in the countryside, but in fact black migrant workers had long since created a rich associational life in the compounds, even in the heart of apartheid darkness. As the ANC became a legal opposition, in 1990, rumors spread among migrant workers that it would clear the compounds to house its own returnees and exiles. Having inadvertently attacked the foundation of migrant life for many, the ANC created an opening for Chief Buthelezi and Inkatha, who capitalized on migrant fears that they would lose the urban work that made possible their lives and their families' lives in the countryside.

Inkatha—the word for a sacred crown worn by Zulu kings before the European conquest—had been an early-twentieth-century cultural movement, Inkatha kaZulu. Buthelezi reestablished the group in 1975 as Inkatha yeNkululeko yeSizwe, with ANC blessing. Among its stated goals were the mobilization of rural groups against apartheid and the abolition of racial discrimination. Unlike other black homeland leaders in the 1960s, who accepted nominal political independence offered by Pretoria, Buthelezi, as chief minister of KwaZulu, refused. However, it was not long before the ANC in exile accused Buthelezi of being interested only in his own power and Inkatha as being a puppet of the apartheid regime.

The political split grew violent, as Inkatha espoused free-market economic policies and as Buthelezi became one of the few black South African leaders to speak out against the international campaign for sanctions and disinvestment. As surging black labor unions sided with the ANC in the 1980s, Inkatha established its own, more accommodating union, the United Workers Union of South Africa, UWUSA. And when the ANC was legalized, in 1990, Buthelezi transformed Inkatha, whose members were dominated by the rural poor, into a political party, the IFP.[3]

In the buildup to the elections of late April 1994, workers at Cinderella — and at dramatic moments, viewers from around the world — watched television news that reported the progress, or the lack thereof, of the negotiations among the National Party, the ANC, the IFP, and others: high drama with high stakes. For many, the IFP was a spoiler. In an act of brinkmanship, Chief Buthelezi boycotted the upcoming elections, demanding that Zululand receive autonomy and recognition for its king. To those who had fought in the struggle against apartheid, this position seemed nothing short of traitorous. Apartheid had been organized around the supposed cultural distinctiveness of black ethnic groups and their attachment to — or, more precisely, their containment within — "homelands." The IFP, at the moment of liberation, appeared to betray the new nation.

While the formalities of the negotiations continued, with speeches and rallies by de Klerk, Mandela, and Buthelezi duly reported, some segment of the National Party government or independent elements within the white police and army structures — what the ANC eventually labeled a "third force" — began to foment clashes by supplying Inkatha with tactical support, arms, and military training.[4] The intent of this mayhem was to divide what would soon become the black electorate and to position the National Party as the only bulwark against social chaos. The effect was just the reverse, to push the National Party and the ANC closer to holding elections, whether Inkatha participated or not. Waves of violence occurred on the East Rand — with random massacres on trains and taxis and with pitched battles between black South Africans in municipal hostels, squatter camps, and townships.[5] All in all, an estimated 14,000 South Africans lost their lives in the violence between 1990 and 1994 — more than at any other period in the struggle to end apartheid, as Stephen Ellis emphasizes.[6]

As the killings continued, the terror they inspired resulted in the ethnic purification of black urban locations around Johannesburg. The IFP took over various municipal hostels that had formerly been ethnically mixed, while the ANC, based largely in the townships, began to dominate certain squatter camps. By early 1994, thousands of people on the Rand had been displaced in the clashes, each instance of which encouraged further ethnic separation: apartheid effected by means of fear.

New nations (like new religions) are not created easily. Each night, along with the pictures of leaders like de Klerk, Mandela, and Buthelezi, the news also broadcast the results of violence and chaos. In an earlier day, such images and stories would have been communicated across social space more slowly, but in South Africa in 1994, narratives of atrocities, told from one side or another, traveled almost instantaneously.[7] In these conflicts, the IFP was often understood simply as "Zulu" (even though many Zulus were members of the ANC), and from the opposite point of view, it was usually possible to label any ANC group as "Xhosa" (Mandela and other prominent ANC leaders had came from Xhosa backgrounds, even if they eschewed ethnic politics).[8]

These tensions, with Buthelezi and the IFP resisting the formation of a new and modern nation, reached a white-hot pitch on the Monday before Easter 1994, which was to become known as Bloody Monday.[9] On that day, the IFP organized a march through downtown Johannesburg to demand its own kingdom, its own homeland as it were. Accounts of what happened, like nearly all examples of collective violence, differ. Bloody Monday, March 28th, generated an explosion of stories.[10] The police estimated that the march included approximately 10,000 IFP supporters, and at the end of the day, more than 50 were dead, including 8 Inkatha demonstrators shot by ANC guards at Shell House, the ANC headquarters in downtown Johannesburg. To many South Africans, the country seemed on the brink of civil war.

Bloody Monday—with its images of death and destruction—flashed across the screen in the television room at Cinderella. These images reached workers who had seen nearly four years of violence on the East Rand, in the black communities surrounding Cinderella. At the height of apartheid power, though mine workers had always been connected to black townships beyond the compound, such ties were intermittent. From the early 1980s onward, in contrast, many black workers at Cinderella had girlfriends, sometimes wives, and often relatives in the surrounding communities. A few men even lived in squatter camps nearby or in black townships, using the compound simply to change clothes. By 1994, the plotline of Inkatha attack and then revenge (or the reverse) had been condensed and standardized at Cinderella. It was the default schema into which most black South Africans fit new instances of violence on the East Rand.

In Industrial Court, all of the Zulus testified steadfastly that there had been no trouble between Zulus and others before Easter. When I interviewed him in Injalo squatter camp in 1995, however, one of the Zulu witnesses in the court case, Thembinkosi, offered a beginning that reached farther back in the year.

> What appeared to be the problem, just before the elections, there were people who were teaching people about voting. I remember that at that time Chief Buthelezi had indicated that he was not going to participate. Yet in the hostel we were all of us being taught how to vote. So everybody was taught. Those who were on night shift, when they were coming back, they were taught, and so on and so on. The arrangement was that before you sleep, you had to report to the hall where they were demonstrating voter education. So I think the problem started there when management invited people from outside to come and demonstrate voter education inside the hostel. It is when the matter started. There were others who said that those who didn't want to vote should be assaulted.

Other workers I interviewed claimed that some of the Inkatha core in the compound had attempted to disrupt the voter-education program in the compound, dancing and singing and waving sticks. According to Odysseus, a full-time NUM steward in 1995, "They [the Zulus] came there singing their war songs, kicking around the table, saying things like, 'Fuck off, fucking asses, they come to teach us about the ANC.' You see, it was just chaos." The education program was conducted between 22 February and 1 March by the Independent Mediation Service of South Africa, the Home Affairs Department already having issued voter identification cards on 15–16 February (foreign workers such as the Mozambicans at Cinderella voted in the 1994 election).

Even before February, there were longer-standing political tensions that had come into focus, once again in the television room. When prominent political leaders appeared on the screen, it was not unusual to hear jeers from the other side. "What's that [directed at Buthelezi]? He says he's representing the Zulus. He's talking nonsense. He's a puppet."[11] Sometime in 1993, compound clerks recognized the problem and brought it to the attention of the compound manager, Mr. Robinson. Notice how political party turns into ethnic group in Robinson's recollection.

About a year before [i.e., a year before Easter 1994] I got a peace committee together—the union [NUM], the IFP, and the ANC together. The union and the ANC bowed out because they said it was a matter for the hostel residents themselves. And we got a forum going between Xhosa and Zulu, primarily Zulu, and Sotho and Xhosa on the other side. And we solved that problem around the table. We decided we wouldn't have insulting songs and so forth.

The forum included Thembinkosi from the Zulu side, who recalled,

When you were sitting around watching TV and maybe the induna mukulu [the big chief] appeared on the screen, maybe Buthelezi, or maybe it is an ANC person, the clerks said that we should go and address that matter. We formed a committee of five who went from room to room. I was one of those chosen for the committee. We were going to each room and every block. We were trying to explain to the people when they see our leader on TV they must not talk about political issues inside the hostel. It is not allowed. That was from the hostel manager. So we went about talking to the people and it appeared that they understood. And that passed. It appeared that it had stopped. Before the 7 o'clock news at about 6:30, we would rush to the blocks and speak to the people, telling them not to say things that were going to upset others. So people were really listening to us. They respected us.

So a series of tensions had existed at Cinderella well before Easter, indeed well before the voter-education program in February, even if compound leaders thought that they had successfully dealt with them in 1993.

How, then, did Bloody Monday affect Cinderella workers? Images of Zulu death must have immediately struck fear in the hearts of Inkatha members in the compound, a tiny minority of Cinderella workers. There they were, surrounded by political enemies. Their sense of estrangement must have been highlighted, in an altogether tormenting way, as some Cinderella workers laughed when they saw the Zulu dead on their television screen Monday evening. But non-Inkatha and non-Zulu workers were caught up in fear as well. Given the paradigm of attack and revenge, they began to worry about an Inkatha counterattack for Bloody Monday. The ecology of distrust grew as people's attitudes changed in basic ways—in how quickly they were prepared to jump to conclusions, in how convinced they were prepared to be of rumors.

By the middle of the week, a rumor circulated through the compound that a group of Inkatha workers had stormed out of the compound gate, vowing to return: "We'll be back!" In the context of the time, "We'll be back" could only be interpreted to mean that this group had gone to recruit Inkatha confederates to help them attack other compound residents over the Easter holiday, when many would be gone.

The (illiterate) Sotho worker mistakenly attacked as a Zulu recalled the idea of a planned Zulu attack in quite concrete terms, as involving a written and posted notice.

> They [the Zulus] wrote something and stuck it onto the notice board. At the manager's office outside. In that note, they said that people inside the hostel must be ready and wait for them. "We are coming back." They wrote that paper. And they were not afraid to show that it was Zulus who wrote that letter. They didn't say it was this person, that person, but "We the Zulus." They put the paper on the notice board. The manager saw that. The police saw the note. Those people who could read saw that. Like this paper, when I look at it, I see what is written. So they told other workers that there is a certain paper outside the hostel manager's office. So other workers also went to see it.

Nothing in management or security records at the time or in the interviews of management and security personnel afterward confirms the idea of a written threat. (The notion of "posting" probably came from management practices that attempted to make policies official by posting them in Fanakalo.) It seems, rather, that *after* the conflict—which had produced Zulu dead and a mistaken attack on at least one—workers, consciously or not, felt a need to "inscribe" a certain beginning to the story, a beginning that inevitably shaped whatever narrative followed, a beginning, that is, that implied Zulu guilt for their own dead.

If such a note had not been posted, did some Zulus nonetheless make threats before Easter? Certainly, the compound manager, Mr. Robinson, did not believe so. When he heard the rumors midweek through his underlings and informers, Robinson called in Milton Ngema, the chair of Inkatha in the compound, and asked him whether such threats had been made. Ngema said he did not think so, but would investigate. In a second meeting, he reported to Robinson that the rumors were absolutely untrue. Afterward, in Industrial Court, every Zulu witness testified that there was no truth to the rumors, and, indeed, the court case (and my research) presented no evidence to substantiate the notion of a planned Zulu attack. And in the event, no Zulu assaulted another worker. All of the dead and injured were either Zulu or mistaken as Zulu.

In an interview in 1995, Mr. Robinson was confident: it would make no sense for a minority as small as the Zulus to attack other workers at Cinderella. The expert witness in the Industrial Court on behalf of the Zulus, the social anthropologist Kent McNamara, a scholar who had spend his career studying violence in the mines of South Africa, was of the same opinion.

> Not only were they [Zulu at Cinderella] a minority prior to that event but they were an even smaller group at the time of the Easter weekend because many of them, in fact, had left the hostel. What is important for the Court to consider is that there are some very striking parallels with other cases. The investigations I referred to earlier and others that I've done show that when a group becomes shrunk down to those kinds of numbers, it does represent a tactical opportunity for other groups to expel them. In the many cases that I've looked at there are almost no examples of a minority group taking on the majority directly. I don't know how many rumors were floating around at the time but the rumor that the Zulus would attack the majority group is not sustained by the pattern of violence on the mines over the last fifteen/twenty years.[12]

What was the source of the rumor that the Zulus would attack? Given the nature of collective violence, it is not possible to know with certainty. When all the evidence is considered, one possibility that cannot be excluded is that the enemies of the Zulus made up such stories in order to cover up their own planned attack. This stratagem, according to McNamara, was present in other examples of collective violence on South African gold mines, and according to the Goldstone Commission, it occurred in townships on the East Rand as early as 1991.[13] With this possibility, one has entered a true hall of mirrors in which the image that one first takes as reality may turn out to be a reflection from the opposite direction.

The possibility of a plot against the Zulus is strengthened by an anonymous telephone call to mine security during the week before Bloody Monday. According to the logbook at the compound,

MARCH 20, 1994

9:45 pm Nimrod [mine security] phoned asking about the situation in the hostel because of the man who phoned to them at about 9:40 telling them of the rumors of Pondos who might attack the Zulus tonight. The man refused to give his name.

11:50 Mr. Potgieter [security] also phoned about the same incident mentioned above.[14]

The heightening of tension after Bloody Monday may have presented an auspicious opening for a plan that was already being mooted. What is beyond doubt is how effectively the rumor of a planned Inkatha attack mobilized other workers against the Zulus. One Sotho worker, interviewed in 1995, boasted, "We are the people who chased the Zulus away from the hostel. We chased them away, and we showed that if we found them in the hostel we going to cut their throats. The truth has to be told." A Shangaan informant was just as proud of his participation in actions against the Zulus.

In the end, Zulus did not initiate an attack in the compound on Good Friday. On the contrary: other black workers attacked the Zulus. Many workers had already gone home, but men in blankets went from room to room, asking whether Zulus were inside. Thembinkosi recalled,

When people were going home [for Easter] I was working afternoon shift. So I knocked off on Thursday night. On Friday morning someone waked me and told me that the situation outside [the room] was tense. Then somebody came into the room and told us that if there were any Zulus in this room it would be better if they left now because the Zulus were going to be killed in the compound. I got up then, put on my clothes, walked toward the gate, and got out of the hostel and went until I came here [Injalo]. I slept here and the following day, Saturday, other Zulus came to Injalo.

The events of Friday evening were documented in the logbook kept by the night-shift induna at Cinderella (whether these entries were made by Sam or Sidwell is not known. See table 1). Amid the routine assaults and sickness, something else was taking place on the evening

TIME	INCIDENT	ACTION
17:15	14140, Shangaan, Room 42, assaulted by known person inside hostel, argument over moneylending business	Ambulance phoned, sent to the hospital
18:40	120845, Sotho, Room 20, assaulted outside hostel	Ambulance phoned, sent to the hospital
19:30	592986, Room 39, reported sick	Ambulance phoned, sent to the hospital
19:44	36617, Zulu, Comet Married Quarters No. 5, assaulted by unknown person inside hostel	Ambulance phoned, refused to go to hospital, left the office and went away
19:45	592986, Room 39, reported sick	Ambulance phoned, sent to hospital
	129372, Swazi, Room 36, assaulted by unknown person outside hostel	Ambulance phoned, sent to hospital
24:35	203513, Room 35, reported sick	Ambulance phoned, sent to hospital
02:15	273860, room 213, reported sick	Ambulance phoned, sent to hospital
02:30	Phoned security. Zulus went out of the hostel with their weapons. Proceeded to Cinderella West Shaft	
02:50	Phone Mr. Allen	Informed him about the hostel situation. Arrived at 03:35 and went to security office.
03:00	Phone Mr. Robinson	Informed him about the hostel situation. Mr. Robinson was stationed in the hostel.

Table 1. *The compound logbook at the end of Good Friday*

of Good Friday at Cinderella. At first, the night-shift induna did not recognize it. At 7:30 P.M., a Zulu visiting from married quarters was attacked and came to the office, but refused to use the ambulance when it arrived. From other evidence, such as my interview with Thembinkosi, we know that systematic intimidation of Zulus had commenced. By 2:30 in the morning, Zulus who remained in the compound were so frightened that they assembled for safety in block A and proceeded outside as a group, most heading to the Inkatha squatter camp, Injalo. The mine apparatus immediately responded. The night-shift induna telephoned both the assistant compound manager, Mr. Allen, and the chief compound manager, Mr. Robinson. Allen went immediately to the mine-security office, and Robinson remained at the compound.

Under heightened security, with Casspirs posted at strategic points, Cinderella remained calm on Saturday. Mine security took a statement from a Zulu employee, who claimed that he had been assaulted by Xhosas on Friday evening at about 10 P.M. Mr. Robinson attempted to set up a meeting between Zulu and Xhosa delegates, but the Xhosas did not attend. At 10 P.M., security received a report that "Xhosas are shouting and asking, 'Where are the Zulus?,'" and about five hundred Sotho were singing and dancing, first in block A and then in D. At 1:30 that morning, two gunshots were fired near the compound; according to the Gold Fields security log, "They could not establish from which direction. Patrolled around hostel. No reports of any injuries or damages."

Easter Sunday dawned at Cinderella. The Zulus who had left the compound for the Inkatha squatter camp had to return if they were to go to work on time early Monday morning. Dumagude, the Inkatha headman of Injalo, phoned a contact in the Internal Stability Unit of the South African Police (widely rumored at the time to be the "third force" aiding Inkatha violence on the Rand). An armored vehicle from the unit led a group of about fifty Zulu workers—many of whom probably constituted the Inkatha core at Cinderella—as they proceeded back to the compound. The choice to involve the Internal Stability Unit was a fateful one, since it made plausible stories of how the Zulus were being used by apartheid agents against the new nation.

In this instance, at least, there is no evidence to suggest that the police or the Internal Stability Unit provoked or armed the Zulus. Behind the armored vehicle, the frightened Zulus attempted only to go back to work. According to Thembinkosi,

An elder whose name is Dumagude, he arranged that we should be safe on the way back to the hostel. He arranged that the Internal Stability Unit should escort us. He had their telephone number. He phoned them and asked them to come down. So the police were informed this way. Other police were there. So we went with them through the town. When we got near the police station, we stopped again there. We told the police that we were going to the hostel. They said, "Okay, we will also escort you." So they got out and accompanied us. There were two Hippos. Three police vans.

By the time the group had rounded the bend in the road to the compound gate, over a thousand workers from the compound had poured out of the gate with their weapons — machetes, homemade iron instruments, and wooden sticks of various kinds.

Gold Fields security, with its technology of surveillance and control, began videotaping in the middle of the confrontation. In the videotape, Cinderella workers are dancing and singing in a menacing way. It is impossible to tell their ethnic background from the tape. Some had covered themselves in blankets and sheets. Singing in Xhosa can be heard, and several men are inciting the crowd by blowing whistles. One man yells out a taunt to the Zulus: "You picannins!" Another runs toward the Zulus, strikes his machete on the pavement setting off sparks, and then retreats. One panicked Zulu worker, coming out of the compound gate, behind the lines as it were, attempts to run through the crowd to reach his compatriots and is struck and injured before he can reach the police line separating the two sides. After a break, the security tape pans back and forth over the marks made on the ground by the rubber bullets and teargas that had been used to control the crowd — all evidence that could be used in any future proceeding that might question whether Gold Fields security had used excessive force.

In a move that is often celebrated in colonialist rhetoric — when it is successful — Mr. Robinson, the compound manager, strode between the two sides.[15] This must have taken some courage, for Robinson had four years before witnessed a white subordinate killed and almost dismembered by black workers in a similar moment of confrontation in the Orange Free State. Now, in front of the compound gate, over a thousand Cinderella workers were threatening battle. Down the road was the much smaller group of Zulus (about fifty of them, scared by the confrontation, according to the voice of a policeman caught on the security tape), who stayed behind an Internal Stability Unit Casspir. According to Thembinkosi,

> Then we saw people from inside the hostel coming out. They were all coming out and they were all running. Then the police stood in front of us. They told us, "Wait, wait, wait, we want to see what these guys are trying to do." Then we could see that they wanted to come toward us and unfortunately we were very few. Then the hostel manager came out and he went to speak to the police. He then came to us, "Men, these people are going to kill you. Remember you are very few. So I would advise you to go back. Go to the mine security offices where they will make arrangements for you to get food."

So the Inkatha contingent retreated. And on Easter evening, Mr. Robinson ordered police and security at Cinderella to go through the compound and to remove *all* Zulus to temporary accommodation at the training center. Henceforth, no Zulu would be allowed to stay in the compound or to go to work.

It is essential at this point to pause and reflect on the nature of compound architecture, the forms of sociality that it encouraged, and the ways that the built environment conditioned conflict. It was hardly an accident that the Easter confrontation took place just in front of the gate — the single point of entry to a fenced and policed square dormitory, itself composed of six internal squares.

By the 1990s, South Africa had been housing black migrant workers in similarly confining spaces for more than a century. So-called closed compounds — in which workers were basically imprisoned — emerged in the early days of the diamond mines. The ease of diamond theft motivated such arrangements. When low-grade gold ores were discovered on the Witwatersrand toward the end of the nineteenth century, the same square compounds — albeit ones in which workers could move in and out, usually through a single point — were built next to the mine shafts. As mining expanded into the Orange Free State in the 1950s, the mines built huge new circularly arrayed compounds that eerily replicated Jeremy Bentham's panopticon, with all of its functions of control and surveillance. Style changed once again by the early 1980s, as mine compounds, built of smaller units separated by open spaces, came to resemble North American college dormitories, as was the case with Far East Hostel.[16]

13. *The gate to Cinderella compound (photo by author)*

In many ways, stepping into Cinderella was stepping back in time. Outside the gate, to the right, was Mr. Robinson's office. To the left were a few shops and the tribal dancing arena. The gate, as the single point of constriction for all comings and goings (see fig. 13), functioned as a form of company power: control the gate, control the people inside. But, of course, the interaction of space and power was rarely so one-sided. If the gate ordinarily conferred power on the company, it offered the same potential to any group of workers—even relatively small groups of workers—who could, if only momentarily, capture the gate. At the end of the day, the company held the upper hand—by the 1990s, the compound manager could call in armored vehicles from Gold Fields security, as both the gate and the compound had been designed to allow the entry and movement of Casspirs or Hippos—but such exertions required organization and the expenditure of resources, fiscal and otherwise. The everyday operation of the compound, if it were to be effective, had to take place at considerably lower levels of coercion.

This led to an ongoing, low-intensity conflict between management and workers that focused on the gate. Inside the gate was an extremely concentrated, all-male society. Such social density ordinarily fulfilled management goals of efficiency and cost reduction, but it also made it easy to rally resistance to the company. News and rumor traveled swiftly. Workers could be mobilized at the drop of a hat. And any small group of workers, if organized and motivated, could intimidate and exert power considerably out of proportion to their numbers. In this context, the performative aspects of threat—which almost always involved song and dance for black mine workers—grew luxuriant.

By Saturday of Easter weekend, what mine security interpreted as "self-defense units" patrolled and looked out for the rumored Zulu attack.[17] When the Inkatha core appeared down the road on Sunday afternoon with an Internal Stability Unit Casspir, the rumor appeared to be amply confirmed. Within minutes, over a thousand workers grabbed their weapons and streamed out of the gate to prevent the Zulus from entering. Mr. Robinson, the compound manager, could do little but recognize the situation. The crowd was eventually dispersed by the Internal Stability Unit, who fired shots above workers' heads, but Mr. Robinson made no attempt to return the Inkatha Zulu to the compound.

Rather, he evacuated *all* Zulus from the compound. In view of what followed—from Easter onward, no Zulu would ever again be able to claim a place in the compound or to take up his work—this decision was weighted with consequences. Even though a confrontation had taken place between Inkatha and many of the rest of the workers at Cinderella, the separation that resulted was effected by the bureaucracy of the mine, not by the process of the conflict itself. While there is no way to know, there may even have been Zulus in the crowd outside the compound gate who threatened to attack the Inkatha core. Certainly Zulus remained inside the compound while the clash occurred, confident in the support of their non-Zulu roommates.

Rather than the clash itself, it was Mr. Robinson—in the name of preventing further conflict—who separated out not political but ethnic groups. According to his reasoning, he was preventing further violence. Given the complexities of the situation, it is impossible to say with confidence that Robinson was wrong. Nevertheless, his intervention was based on an assumption that black ethnic identity had a propensity to trump political alignments on the mine. Moreover, Robinson's intervention accomplished a kind of self-fulfilling prophecy: what had been a political clash between the Inkatha core and others at Cinderella became—through Robinson's own preventative intervention—an ethnic confrontation, between all Zulus and everyone else.

When I interviewed him, in 1995, Hudson, a Xhosa NUM shaft steward, was critical of Robinson.

HUDSON: So people say that Mr. Robinson intervened there. He told the workers, "Don't fight, leave them. I am going to expel them. And the people went back inside the hostel. And the Zulus [in the Inkatha core] left with the police. Then Robinson told his hostel police that all the Zulus inside the hostel had to leave. When I inquired how many Zulus had been accompanied by the police, I was told that there were about twenty [there were probably up to fifty]. But Robinson withdrew *all* the Zulus inside the hostel. Those who didn't have a problem with the people.

DONHAM: Do you think that was a mistake?

H: That was a big mistake.

D: Do you think they were safe?

H: Yes. Yes.

That some of the evacuated Zulus themselves considered the compound safe is suggested by their return the following week to drink with buddies in the compound bar. This behavior was amazing to Mr. Oosthusizen in Gold Fields security, who commented on it with much emphasis during an interview in 1995.

What determined who counted as a "Zulu" in this conflict? Mine records. When a black mine worker returned from home stay to begin a new contract period at the mine, he was interviewed by a black clerk in the compound, who filled out a card, which called for the worker's "tribe." Those who answered the question "What's your tribe?" with "Zulu" were those separated from the compound after the events of Good Friday—eventually to lose their jobs.

The relationship between black clerks and mine workers had long been conflicted on southern African mines. In his study of a copper mine in Namibia in the 1970s, Robert J. Gordon wrote, "Of all the occupational groupings, the clerks form the most distinctive group. They clearly differentiate themselves from the other workers. They see themselves as self-reserved, health-conscious, tidy, liking privacy, and leading a more 'developed life' than the other workers whom they believe to be untidy, dirty and ignorant."[18] Figure 14 shows one of the clerks at Cinderella compound—well-dressed, two pens in his pocket, leaning over old-fashioned files. Unlike the newest hostels, Cinderella was still dependent on paper files. Only at the entrances to the shafts had computers been introduced, to keep track of workers' hours (fig. 15).

The nature of the encounter between compound clerks and workers is significant, for an examination of compound records revealed that certain workers, particularly in transition zones or in ethnically heterogeneous areas, answered differently over time to the question "What is your tribe?" For example, Thulani Gamede, a driller from Umzimkhulu, listed himself as "Xhosa" as he began a contract period in 1994. But in his three previous contracts, in 1990, 1991, and 1992, he was listed as "Zulu," and in an even earlier contract, in 1989, as "Baca." Because he was listed as a "Xhosa" in 1994, he was not evacuated from the compound, and he kept his job. Had the conflict occurred two years earlier, Gamede would have taken his place among the "Zulus."[19]

Tsebetso Selai, a stope team member, a "Xhosa" from Matatiele in the Transkei in 1994, had a similar background. In 1985, he had claimed "Sotho" as his ethnic identity; in 1987, "Hlubi"; in 1988, 1990, and 1991, "Sotho" again; in 1992, "Hlubi"; and finally, in 1994, "Xhosa." Joseph Magadla Maphasa, a driller from Mt. Fletcher in the Transkei claimed to be "Hlubi" in 1984; "Xhosa" in 1986, 1987, 1990, and 1991; "Sotho" in 1993; and, finally, "Xhosa" in 1994. Finally, Vuyisile Joja, a lasher from Mt. Frere in the Transkei claimed to be "Baca" in 1984; "Xhosa" in 1986, 1987, and 1988; "Hlubi" in 1990; "Xhosa" in 1991; "Hlubi" in 1992; and "Xhosa" in 1994.[20] It is notable that in each of these four cases, the worker had come to identify himself generically as "Xhosa" by 1994—a direction that may have been encouraged by the ANC's assumption of power during the 1990s and the popular perception among many workers at Cinderella that the ANC was a "Xhosa" organization.

These cases—which happened to appear in a systematic collection of the records of four work teams that were composed of a total of 74 black workers—were the exceptions. Most workers replied in the same way over time to the question about their tribal affiliation. Nonetheless, such exceptions are powerful indicators of the bureaucratic logic that identified Zulus in this case. Zulus were those for whom a clerk had recorded a reply of "Zulu" in the blank space after "Tribe." Whatever affected that short social and linguistic interaction—however the

14. A compound clerk at Cinderella with old-style paper files

15. A clerk working at a computer at the entrance to a shaft

question was posed, whatever mistranslations occurred, whatever mistakes in recording the responses made—these determined Zuluness, not the lines of opposition drawn in the clash on Easter Sunday.

After numerous meetings, the Zulus separated out from the compound were finally persuaded to accept a two-month paid home visit. After this "cooling off" period—during which the 1994 elections were scheduled to occur, at the end of April—the Zulus would return to their places in the compound and to their jobs. The hope was to reintegrate the workforce at that point.

Behind the April compromise lay the reality that mine management was barely in control of the situation. Non-Zulu workers had claimed the gate. Even though mine security had returned to formal control by late Easter Sunday, it was clear to everyone that if the Inkatha Zulus had been allowed to return to the compound in the context of the fast-approaching elections, other workers might well have attacked them. At the very least, it was clear that other workers would have gone on strike—and a prolonged and disruptive strike would have put Cinderella out of business.

It took more than two weeks of meetings with workers before the April compromise could be reached. On the Monday morning after Easter, management organized a meeting with NUM shaft stewards—representatives of the union who had recently received official recognition by the company. By that time, two unions were on the mine: the ANC-aligned NUM, and a much smaller but older union, United People's Union of South Africa (UPUSA), informally linked with Inkatha. Even though these two unions replicated the split that was so violently being played out in national politics, it is essential to understand that, before Easter, ethnicity did *not* map onto union and political alignment at Cinderella. In fact, of the Zulus who belonged to a union, the largest number, 85, belonged to the NUM (which had a total of 2,686 members at Cinderella by April 1994). Even Milton Ngema, head of Inkatha in the compound, was a paid NUM member before the conflict. In contrast, only about 50 Zulus belonged to UPUSA—which had a total of 147 members. Before the conflict, then, the majority of Zulu union members belonged to NUM, and the majority of UPUSA members were non-Zulu, even though it had links with the IFP.

It was the process of the conflict itself that was to change all this, that was to destroy cross-cutting ties and to "ethnicize" local social groupings among the mine workers. And what is perhaps most striking about this process, as with so many other cases of so-called ethnic conflict, is that the result of the process was read back into the conflict as its explanation, as a cause for what had occurred. This was true for both black and white participants and observers. Zulu victims almost universally framed what had happened to themselves in ethnic terms — the Xhosa had attacked them — and mine management did the same. One of the few newspaper accounts of the conflict, in *Business Day* on 14 July 1994, trumpeted a headline that read, "Ethnic Strife Could Cost Jobs." But what had become "ethnic" by July did not start out as such in April. It became so only through a complicated series of events that depended on company actions as much as those of workers.

If Mr. Robinson's separation of the Zulus from the compound on Easter was one turning point in the process of transforming a political into an ethnic confrontation, another crucial juncture was reached on the Monday after Easter when the NUM washed its hands of its own Zulu members. Recorded in the minutes of the meeting, the NUM representative explained, "Zulu employees cannot be allowed back into the hostel as their safety cannot be guaranteed by the union. The representative requested that the Zulus be informed about the dangerous situation in the hostel and the workplace. The representative suggested that management talk to the Zulus, to try and find a solution for their problems."[21] The NUM was hardly in the habit of suggesting that management, on its own, solve black workers' problems, and the NUM official's words made clear that the local shaft stewards no longer considered themselves representative of the interests of Zulu workers. For the stewards, the politics of nationalism (and the NUM's alliance with the ANC) trumped their interests as workers. In the acute tensions leading to the elections, all Zulus — even Zulu members of the NUM — had become suspect national subjects. Ethnicization was now virtually complete. Abandoned by the NUM, the Zulus whom Mr. Robinson had separated out of the compound, even the majority who previously had nothing to do with Inkatha, now had to turn to the Inkatha-dominated KwaZulu government and to the Inkatha-aligned union UPUSA for support.

After the meeting with NUM, management convened a meeting with the Inkatha representatives of the Zulu workers. There, management quickly came to the position that it held in all succeeding meetings in April: either the Zulus could end their employment at Cinderella with a separation package, or they could go home for a "cooling off" period and come back after the elections scheduled for the end of April. Management's position was related to the fact that the Zulus were only a small minority on the mine, only about 350 out of a little more than 5,000. Had Zulus represented over half of the black workforce—as did the Shangaans—the mine could not have pursued such a solution.

By the end of the day on 15 April, all of the Zulu workers had been forced into accepting the cooling-off period and had boarded buses for KwaZulu. Not quite two weeks later, at long last, on the 27th and 28th, the national elections took place, and images of liberation went out to the world—black voters waiting patiently in line to become citizens rather than subjects. The ANC won an overwhelming victory, but the IFP managed to scrape by with a win in what became KwaZulu-Natal. Buthelezi and de Klerk formed a coalition government with Mandela in what seemed like a miraculous outcome.

The process leading to the elections had had, however, darker consequences at Cinderella. What might be called the tyranny of numbers had played into local contests in a way that encouraged the ethnicization of social relations.[22] Before, ethnic identity, union membership, and political identity had crosscut one another to some significant degree. After Easter, and especially after the Soweto Day murders, these ways of identifying "lined up" to produce much more clearly defined and antagonistic social groups.

As these events churned through the lives of individuals, many Zulus came to think of their Zuluness in a new way. What had been lightly worn, particularly for those Zulu who belonged to the NUM, now became more consequential. Being a Zulu had become, in fact, a matter of life and death. For other black workers—a few of whom were literally to get away with murder—the triumph of expelling the Zulus from the mine encouraged further action. About a year later, the rumor went around that the Shangaans—foreigners now to the new South Africa—should be the next group to be expelled. To black nationalists, there were too many South African brothers sitting at home without work. But the mine could not survive with literally half of its labor force gone, and management immediately and forcefully let it be known that any attack on Shangaans would bring suspension for the workers involved. No attack occurred.

New beginnings contain their share of ironies. At a moment when change is celebrated, old and deep continuities go unrecognized. In this regard, the South African transition of 1994 can hardly be de-

scribed as a revolution. What happened in 1994 looks rather like a continuation of the process of capitalist restructuring that had begun at
least as far back as the 1970s. Conversely, the really new in moments
of self-proclaimed change can be experienced as only more of the
same—as the product of what is assumed to have always been. But
this sense of the "always has been" was in fact produced at Cinderella
over a remarkably brief period of time. Resulting from a complicated
set of interactions, ethnic feeling (the supposed constancy of opposition between Xhosas and Zulus) was read back into the past to provide an explanation for the conflict. In fact, what it was to be Xhosa or
Zulu—much less Shangaan—was changing as a new nation was being
created.

5

FREEING WORKERS
AND ERASING HISTORY

LABOR UNIONS PLAYED A KEY ROLE in the events at Cinderella. More specifically, the reluctance of local NUM shaft stewards to become involved in the Zulu matter in April was critical to what followed. To interpret the NUM's stance, I turn to the history of black labor in the mining industry in South Africa and to the relatively recent history of black labor unions.

In the classic formulation—in both Marx's formal analysis and in standard neoclassical theory—workers are "free" under capitalism. They are, first of all, socially and legally unconstrained in their choice of employer (and, hence, differ from slaves, serfs, or dependents in patriarchal households). And they are "free" in a second, ironic sense in that they are separated from the means of production (and therefore must work for *some* employer). These two senses of freedom, under liberal forms of the state, result in a recognition (however grudging) of workers' rights to organize vis-à-vis their employers. Unions represent workers' interests, and through law, the state develops a more or less elaborate apparatus for regularizing conflicts between employers and employees. In the ideological framework that results, everyone is seen as having something to sell (and buy), which concentrates efforts on encouraging exchange, the underlying assumption being that everyone benefits from smoother and ever more extensive exchange.

South African capitalism departed in fundamental ways from this model. Indeed, as Susan Buck-Morss has recently argued, perhaps all existing capitalisms do.[1] Systems of bound labor, such as plantation slavery in the New World, were, for example, created by global capitalism (as Marx himself emphasized). In other words, free labor does not exist in pure form; moreover, there are systemic connections between bound and free labor. But if so, it is probably correct to assert that over the broad sweep of world history, free forms of exchange have penetrated ever more deeply into spheres of production formerly associated with bound labor. It is against this broad outline that South African capitalism became such a flagrant exception in the last decades of the twentieth century. As dominant ideologists in other capitalist societies began to question racial and gender barriers in labor regimes (at least as legitimating ideologies), South African political leaders took the opposite tack, particularly after 1948, erecting an ever more elaborate array of separations and exclusions based on race and tribe.[2]

In the apartheid view, black inhabitants of South Africa were not individual citizens with universally defined rights. They were, rather, massed members of tribes, each enveloped in its own tradition, subjects of chiefs presiding over ethnically marked homelands. The stated purpose of racial separation was not just to maintain white purity and privilege, but also to protect black workers from the corrosive effects of market exchange, particularly in a world in which, as jural minors, they were seen as incapable of protecting themselves. Thus, after 1948, the leaders of the National Party often presented themselves as father-like figures to the black population, fathers who held the responsibility of determining what was desirable for their erstwhile children.[3]

It is difficult at this point in time to interpret assertions such as these as anything more than the crassest forms of ideology, and ones that no one actually believed in or felt bound by. But we should reflect for a moment on this interpretative difficulty. Why is it easier to "see" ideology in forms of labor control other than so-called free exchange? Does it not reflect a certain naturalization of wage labor itself—in fact, an inability to see the complex mix of truth and falsehood, of ideology and reality, in all forms of labor control? Apartheid politicians, like others, were certainly capable of lying. But what might be called paternalism in South African labor relations in the 1950s—the construction of a bound, quasi-parental relationship between white superiors and the black men in their charge—was more than a lie. It motivated men, white and black, and it held the power to organize a significant portion of economic life on the mines, which like white farms, were quintessential sites for South African paternalism.[4]

As befits both the notions of blacks as jural minors and as temporary sojourners in white areas, there were no unions on the mines to represent black workers in the 1950s. The Chamber of Mines had actively rejected unions for black workers, even though white miners' unions had existed since the 1920s. Rather, African workers were deemed temporary inhabitants, "boys," whether "machine boys" or "timber boys," or, that contradiction in terms, "boss boys." And all "boys" should ipso facto be under the authority of a father figure—underground, a white miner with a blasting certificate, and in the compound, the compound manager.

> Although paternalistic attitudes predated and became part of class and industrial relations of the developing gold industry in the late 19th and early 20th century, a coherent managerial discourse was elaborated only in the 1940s and 1950s, when apartheid thinking was on the ascendance. A response in part to its repressive management of the 1946 African miners' strike, the Chamber of Mines felt compelled to account to unsympathetic constituencies why it refused to recognize emergent African trade unions. African workers were "tribal," it was explained, too unsophisticated and uneducated for modern trade unions, and lacking in any elementary sense of responsibility needed to manage an advanced system of industrial relations. In the language of the time, the Chamber held up a philosophy of "trusteeship," where African workers were depicted as "wards" of management, who on the workers' behalf made all the important decisions affecting their lives.[5]

Rather than the abstractness of exchange, it was the enduring connectedness of a parent-like tie—one that could turn on a dime from benevolence to violence—that organized labor relations. "Boys," after all, had to be disciplined from time to time, and as Nadine Gordimer related, it was often claimed that "an occasional good crack, as they [white miners] put it, knocked any nonsense out of the boys and kept them attentive and respectful, without any malice on either side."[6]

Paternalism was not just a white ideology. Black workers themselves came from deeply patriarchical cultures in which fathers had to be respected. Amos Bam, a Xhosa-speaking boss boy on the mines before the Second World War, interviewed by Keith Breckenridge in the early 1990s, reported, "If *umlungu* [a white man] says to me—as big as I am—I must stop so that he can beat me, I stop and he beats me. I could beat him, but we were respectful [*sahlonipha*]."[7] Breckinridge goes on to interpret what Bam meant by "respect."

> The term that the migrants used to describe their refusal to respond to white violence in kind was *ukuhlonipha*. It is one of a number of related words that can be used to convey respect or deference, but it has specific

associations. The abstract noun *hlonipha* is used in everyday speech to describe the proper relationship between a wife and her husband. But the idea of *ubhlonipha* is central to the relationship between generations of men. For very old male informants, to show respect in this way is a very powerfully valorized expectation of their sons. The use of the term *hlonipha* to describe restraint in the face of violence (where the word for fear — *ukwesaba* — might seem more appropriate) suggests that it was seen as sign of moral and physical strength.[8]

Being a boy vis-à-vis a black father was, of course, a different matter than being a "boy" in relation to a white employer. In the context of rural black cultures, boys eventually became men and fathers. Indeed, migrant mine work was understood precisely as a way of accomplishing that transition, of building a household with the worker as head. In the mines, however, boys stayed boys forever, at least in relation to white supervisors, and even if black workers interpreted their restraint in this situation in terms of their own cultural idioms of moral strength, it is clear that the absence of any alternative to accepting the white man's *klap* (Afrikaans for "smack") and retaining one's job was also a part of the situation.

The legal contrast between black and white, the so-called color bar, persisted until 1988. By law, black workers could not rise above the highest grade of unskilled work (category 8). Only whites were permitted to earn the blasting certificates that gave them responsibility for explosives. Only whites, at the end of the workday, could charge up the holes that blacks had drilled. Apart from the political significance of preventing black access to explosives, the sexual symbolism was perhaps lost on few, especially in the hypermasculine world of underground work: drilling, charging up, and blasting. While white men carried out the climax of the work process and controlled it because of their purportedly inherent mental superiority, blacks symbolically remained forever "boys." For all their muscle power, their sweat and blood, black workers were rendered symbolically ineffectual without white supervision.[9]

The crucial interface between white and black occurred in two relationships. The first was that between white miners (including the white officials above them) and their piccanins — literally small black children, but more specifically, black servants underground. The piccanin carried the miner's or official's gear, water, and whatever else was needed. He was a source of information and cultural translation vis-à-vis other black workers, could stand guard to warn that supervisors approached, or be a life-saving source of help during falls of rock. At the end of the workday, as miners and officials came up the shafts, tired and wet from the heat underground, but soon to reach the sometimes cold winds of the Witwatersrand, it was customary for piccanins to help dress their white masters in new, dry overalls. A miner sat down and as he extended his leg, the piccanin took off his boots and handed him dry overalls as the miner undressed.

The intimacy—and absolute inequality—of this relationship provided, as apartheid came to end in the 1990s, one of the most charged symbols of the inequities of the past. The freedom contained in wage labor often gains its symbolic charge and allure precisely from such contrasts with bound labor that has become economically dysfunctional. Strikingly, of the many issues of concern to the NUM at Cinderella during 1994 and 1995, no topic recurred more consistently in the meetings between management and shaft stewards than the question of piccanins, or as they were called then, personal assistants. The union argued that personal assistants should be banned as relics of the racist past, while management replied that they were required for safety in certain situations. In any case, very few were left at Cinderella by 1994, though some did exist for the higher-level officials. For example, when I accompanied the manager of mining—Satan, as black workers called him—on his rounds underground, a tall black personal assistant stood discreetly in the background to hand knee pads or a pen and paper or water at just the right moment, like a server in an expensive restaurant (see fig. 16).

The other key patriarchical relation was that between white miners and their boss boys. According to Keith Breckenridge's interviews, white miners in the 1950s had relatively few boss boys over the course of their careers.[10] (Gallery 21 shows a white miner with his black boss boy at work underground.) The long-term relationships that developed—in which boss boys took on as nicknames the black vernacular translation of the white miner's surname, for example, Oosteesh for Oosthuisen—involved a complex flow of favors, with white miners providing, at various times, rides to black workers' homelands, illegal liquor, extra employment on the weekend, and the ever present South African recreation of the *braai*, or barbeque.[11] In return, boss boys did much of the actual work of supervision, of making sure that holes were drilled on time, that rock was transported, and that the face advanced.[12] With white miners behind them, boss boys could be just

16. A black personal assistant waiting for his white boss outside the door of the mine overseers' changing room (each level of mine official had its own changing room)

as arbitrary with black workers in their charge, just as violent, just as demanding. They could, for example, use their power to coax and to coerce attractive young men into mine marriages.

How exactly paternalism came unhinged in the mines—as it did, beginning in the mid- to late 1970s—is a story yet to be fully told.[13] In general, it can be said that bound forms of labor subsist and are "naturalized" only in relatively stable niches within the wider flux of capitalism. The mark of capitalism—what distinguishes it in relation to other economic systems—is surely what Schumpeter called "creative destruction," the ways in which competition continually undermines stability and thereby produces technological progress and productivity. Less efficient companies die. They go out of business.

Marx's famous phrase "all that is solid melts into air" does not apply to the production of all commodities. Gold was, after all, precisely the commodity that did *not* melt into the air. For most of the twentieth century, it was the assumed standard, the uniquely trusted store of value against which all other commodities were measured. From the

1930s until 1972, the price of gold was fixed by international agreement, so that, unlike the case of diamonds, for example, South African companies, despite their impressive share of world production, never exercised much influence over the price paid for their product. Prices were set by world power, agreements among states, not by markets.

With the price of gold fixed for much of the twentieth century, all that South African capitalists could do to assure profits was to control the costs of production. This meant, above all, the necessity of cheap black labor.[14] This requirement had, indeed, been built into the very beginnings of the gold industry in South Africa.[15] Had such deep-level and low-grade deposits as those in southern Africa been discovered in a context in which labor could not be obtained so cheaply, the gold would have stayed in the ground.[16] It would have been "uneconomic" to mine.

In many ways, the maintenance of cheap black labor for the gold mines furnished the "bottom line" of southern African history in the nineteenth century and the early twentieth. State power in southern Africa operated with an unusual forthrightness in this respect. Its motives were visible for all to see.[17] J. A. Hobson, the famous liberal theorist of imperialism, writing in 1926, maintained, "Nowhere in the world has there ever existed so concentrated a form of capitalism as that represented by the financial power of the mining houses in South Africa, and nowhere else does that power so completely realize and enforce the need for controlling politics."[18]

Rather than compete against each other and thereby bid up the price of black labor, the mining companies, through the device of the Chamber of Mines, banded together at the end of the nineteenth century to form centrally directed monopsonist recruiting agencies for black laborers, first for workers from outside of the country and then from inside. This arrangement was justified on the basis that black workers were not maximizing individuals in the modern sense; they were members of tribes, target workers, who had to be supervised and looked after. By the 1920s, the chamber had driven private entrepreneurs out of the business of recruiting black laborers to the mines.[19] Even though periodic crises occurred in the form of labor shortages, some severe, these were neutralized by aggressive recruitment in ever more distant and impoverished zones of southern Africa over the course of the twentieth century.

Despite the consolidation of cooperation among mining houses to prevent competition over black labor, mining capitalists wanted yet more. At the end of the nineteenth century, many yearned for a new kind of state. At that point, the mining areas of the Witwatersrand were contained in the Zuid Afrikaansche Republiek, still ruled mainly by agrarian interests. To the Afrikaner farmers who dominated the Volksraad, the Transvaal legislature, Johannesburg and the mining towns thrown up by the gold rush were often seen as dens of iniquity dominated by Uitlanders, foreigners, not as industries to be embraced and supported by arms of the state. The republic itself was not yet a modern bureaucratic state; it floated on the top of the economy with limited powers to penetrate social communities below, white or black.[20] "By 1895 the managements of most of the [gold mining] companies—French, German, and British—had come to the conclusion that the republican government [of the Transvaal] was an obstruction. Similarly, the American engineers who predominated in many of the companies came to identify 'Britain with economic opportunity and the Boers with economic restriction' and to favor 'a British take-over' of the Transvaal in the interests of economic development."[21]

Just why imperial Britain stepped into the breach to create, through the South African War (1899–1902), a new and enlarged, unified state in southern Africa—now known as South Africa—is a complex matter.[22] Whatever the mix of motives, the outcome was a much stronger state, and one more attuned to the needs of mining capital. In 1913, the new state passed the Native Land Act making it illegal for black peasants to buy land outside of the roughly 7 to 8 percent of the land that was designated as reserves at that time. Even if black South African workers had originally entered the mines for reasons other than those of sheer economic compulsion, they would eventually be caught up in its necessities, as subsistence farming declined in the overpopulated and overworked reserves, particularly after the mid-1950s.[23] The object of the Native Land Act had been precisely to create the conditions for white enterprise, to provide cheap black labor to the mines, and to undermine competition peasant agriculturists might pose to white farmers.

As a measure of just how successful the mines were over the twentieth century (with mining providing a large portion of state revenues and the state creating the conditions for further capital accumulation), real wages for black workers remained roughly constant from 1897 until 1970.[24] By then, wages offered by the mines to blacks represented only about a third of what was paid to black workers in industrial production. No wonder then that the great bulk of black workers on the mines at that point came from outside the borders of the country, in a network of administered recruitment that had extended as far north as colonial Tanganyika.

Gold mining in South Africa was a branch of capitalism created and maintained by political power — not by so-called free markets. In that environment, not much changed during the early to mid-twentieth century, at least in outline. For example, "lashing," the backbreaking work of shoveling and loading ore into railroad cars, continued well into the twentieth century. Given abundant supplies of inexpensive black labor, it often made more sense to hire more workers than to invest in improved technology. This was the world in which paternalist work relations were made to make sense to both whites and blacks.

The 1970s began, unevenly and incompletely, to bring this world to an end. Since the 1930s, the international price of gold had been fixed at $36 an ounce. In 1972, the United States went off the gold standard, and the price of gold was left for world markets to determine. By 1980, the price had shot up to about $600 an ounce, but in the 1980s and early 1990s it declined to between $350 and $450 an ounce (although the rand price of gold continued to escalate because of the widening gap between the dollar and the rand).[25] This windfall in the freeing of gold prices was the first factor that unhinged the paternalistic system of South African mines.

The second was the sea change in the interstate system in southern Africa. After decolonization removed racial restrictions for much of the rest of the continent by the 1960s, South Africa was increasingly isolated. It stood out more and more. In April 1974, after a plane crash that killed many mine workers returning home, President Hastings Banda, of then independent Malawi, ordered the complete withdrawal of 120,000 Malawian workers from the South African gold mines — approximately a third of the labor force at the time. The same month, a coup in Portugal led to a series of events that would quickly free its colony Mozambique under a socialist-oriented independent government. Seen in retrospect, the late 1970s were the high-water mark of what has been called Afro-Marxist regimes on the continent, and South Africa, whose wealth had been so obviously produced through the capitalist exploitation of black labor, became a target.

Before the withdrawal of Malawian labor, a little more than three-quarters of the labor force in the mines had come from outside the borders of South Africa, most of it from Malawi and Mozambique.

Planners in the Chamber of Mines quickly discerned that dependence on concentrated pockets of foreign labor was far too precarious in a postcolonial world, and it committed itself to a steady reduction of foreign workers. To do so, it had to compete internally for South African black labor and thus to raise wages. In most capitalist economies, mining wages are higher than manufacturing wages, but in South Africa the reverse was true. The rise in gold prices after 1972 provided the opportunity to raise mine wages, and the chamber began to do so, dramatically.

Between 1974 and 1983, the chamber raised black wages roughly 200 percent in real terms.[26] Black inhabitants of the homelands—who were increasingly proletarianized—responded enthusiastically. By 1977, there appeared in the homelands seasonal surpluses of men looking for mine work, and by 1980, there was a "highly visible reserve army of unemployed workers at mine recruiting offices country-wide."[27] By then, it was clear to the Chamber of Mines that if, for some reason, its supplies of foreign labor were completely cut, it would have no difficulty in recruiting within South Africa all of the labor it needed. Thereafter, into the mid-1990s, the percentage of foreign workers stayed constant, at around 40 percent (a reflection perhaps of the mines' need to keep relatively experienced workers).

Rather than depend, however, only on the homelands traditionally involved in providing labor to the mines, such as the Transkei, the chamber actively sought new sources in areas relatively untapped in the past, such as KwaZulu. In the 1960s, the number of Zulu workers in the gold industry was less than 5,000, a tiny fraction of the total. Work in the gold mines was unpopular among Zulus, given their alternatives on local sugar plantations and in coal mines. This was to change in the 1970s and early 1980s, as unemployment in the homeland became increasingly dire. Even so, some Zulu workers did not adapt easily to the rigors of mine employment. Some broke their contracts, and, in one case, workers deserted en masse.[28] Nonetheless, by the 1980s, Zulus appealed to the management of some mines because of "their conservative reputation and presumed immunity to modern labor radicalism."[29] Many of the Zulu workers at Cinderella had, in fact, first come to the mine during the chamber's drive to diversify its labor supply.

After a period of relative peace on the mines during the 1950s and 1960s, the 1970s saw a series of deadly conflicts, both between black workers and white management and among factions of the black workforce. Where the mines had once used ethnicity to communicate with the black workforce—via an array of indunas, tribal representatives, and so forth—now the violence, costly not only in terms of labor lost but also in property destroyed, was being expressed through those very same forms, typically as Xhosas versus Sotho. It was not unusual, for example, in the conflicts of the late 1970s, for one induna to lead a fight against another.[30] The evident cost of the destruction and killing for the mine owners—the lack of any workable process of negotiating with their increasingly politicized black workforce—led some, particularly the leadership of the large and influential Anglo American mining house, to conclude that a new system of labor relations was needed in the gold mines and that black unions should be legalized.[31]

But not all of the mining houses agreed. Some, like Gold Fields, persisted in paternalist relations right through the end of apartheid. And within each house, particular mines had their own local histories. Nonetheless, when the South African state appointed the Wiehahn Commission, in the late 1970s, to examine labor relations, Anglo American went around the divided Chamber of Mines to make its own argument to the commission, that all black workers on the mines should be allowed to unionize. By 1981, the commission formally adopted such a recommendation, fearing that black unions could not be stopped in any case. The founding of the NUM followed, in late 1982, and, from the very beginning, the organization of the union owed much to the encouragement of Anglo American management.[32]

One might say that in the atypical world of South African gold mines, capitalists—as much as workers—spurred the creation of nonracial (effectively black) unions in the early 1980s. But what such capitalists wanted was not so much the welfare of their workers; in fact, the NUM was unable to raise wages during the 1980s, at least in real terms, and Anglo American would adopt a particularly unyielding attitude during the NUM strike of 1987. (That year the NUM formally allied itself with the ANC and called for the nationalization of the mines.) Rather, what the managers at Anglo wanted was to delegate the responsibilities of paternalism in a world in which they no longer made sense—economically or ideologically. Black workers by that point were caught in the snare of the market. Even though they lived in homelands and had limited access to livelihood there, they had to work in wage labor to support their families. They had become career miners who returned, one contract after another, to the same mine and often to the same work group.

Over the 1980s and into the early 1990s, beginning with Anglo American and extending unevenly to other mining houses, mine owners would increasingly reject the paternalism of their own past practices — that the mines should provide housing and food for black workers, or that the color bar should define what work they did, and so forth. Boss boys became team leaders. Tribal representatives became hostel policemen. And piccanins, if they survived at all, became personal assistants. In these changes, black personhood was being officially redefined. Now, black workers were being hailed as modern individuals. They were "free." They had their labor power to sell. They should be allowed to organize with their fellows to pursue common interests.

This pattern — hardly unique to South Africa — in which fractions of capital reject and attack the very forms of labor control they themselves formerly pursued, goes toward the heart of how capitalism is continually relegitimated. Capital "frees." It is progressive. Critically, in the process, it erases any appreciation of the past in the past's own terms. Paternalism, for example, becomes opaque, difficult to credit as a way of life. The present turns into a celebration of the *end* of "backward" practices, which in turn obscures the coercive underside of freedom. This process of relegitimation furnishes perhaps the greatest irony in the transition that occurred in South Africa in 1994.

It is true that black and white now entered the market as formal equals. But how was it, exactly, that black workers had come to the point that they *had* to sell their labor power? Once upon a time, black peasants had possessed land on which they produced surpluses for sale.[33] They had commanded herds. It was precisely mine capitalists, including those at Anglo American, who had done more than any other historical actors to create the conditions in which such alternatives had been eliminated. These aspects of freedom, that workers had been "freed" from other alternatives they might have preferred, never came into focus during celebrations of the end of bound labor.

Granted, not all mine managements encouraged unionization. Some clung to paternalist rhetoric. For example, the manager of the Kloof gold mine in the western Transvaal asserted in a deposition during the mid-1980s,

These people [black workers] are mostly illiterate and uneducated. They are hundreds, if not thousands, of miles from home. They are superstitious and fearful. They are a tinderbox waiting only for the appropriate spark to send them into a surging flame of unrest and devastation, spreading even to other mines with consequences too horrific to contemplate. Every mine management is alive to this. Its only weapon is effective and speedy disciplinary procedures that strike quickly and efficiently at agitators who make it their business to promote these evils.[34]

In this, one detects little change from the 1950s and before. But such opposition served only to emphasize how progressive other mine capitalists, such as those at Anglo American, were. By providing such a cogent reminder of the past in the present, it made the progress of the present all the more commendable.

With access agreements that allowed NUM organizers into Anglo American compounds, with lenient criteria for recognition (33 rather than the usual 50 percent plus one worker), and with the company bureaucracy processing so-called stop orders to provide dues to the union head office out of wage payments to workers, the NUM exploded on the scene in the mid-1980s. Once allowed inside the compounds, labor organizers found an ideal social setting for their activities: thousands on thousands of workers, all housed together, accessible, easily called to meetings (and during strikes, easy to control). In five years' time, the NUM became the fastest-growing union in South Africa (and possibly in the world) representing, by 1988, roughly 60 percent of the entire black workforce in the South African gold mines. That percentage was concentrated on Anglo American mines, but had begun to extend to mines within other houses as well.[35]

In retrospect, the strike of 1987 represents the high-water mark of NUM assertiveness; that year the union officially called for the nationalization of the mines. What had been given (by Anglo American) could be taken away, however. And that is precisely what happened. A week into the strike of 1987, Anglo American imposed a lockout at Vaal Reefs and began mass dismissals of striking workers. Fired workers were easily replaced with unemployed work seekers—many recruited, as it happens, from Zululand. The NUM was soon forced back to the negotiating table to accept the wage offer, unchanged, that the chamber had offered two months before.[36]

Given the increasing competition from lower-cost gold producers abroad (in Canada, the United States, and Australia) and given the declining role of gold reserves in backing up currencies into the 1990s (more and more central banks began to sell off their reserves as gold became a mere commodity), the price of gold steadily declined from 1987 until 1992, to improve only slightly by 1994. South African gold mines went into an extended period of crisis as a result, shedding labor at an alarming rate, just as it became clear that there would be political transition in the country.

In 1987, the gold industry employed roughly 531,000 workers, whereas by 1994, that number had dropped to 391,000.[37] Mines were closed. Shafts within mines were closed. In this environment, the NUM accomplished relatively little for its members in economic terms, even as it increasingly committed itself to the struggle for black liberation. The growing success of the latter may, indeed, have covered up the limitations of the former for its members. In any case, black nationalism had always been an important component of unionization. According to Dunbar Moodie, the strategy of the NUM by the late 1980s "expanded beyond unfair dismissals and safety and even wages (although these issues remained fundamental) to highly symbolic acts that sought to restore the integrity of black mine worker manhood through direct racial confrontations."[38] By 1991, the general secretary of the NUM, Cyril Ramaphosa, resigned to become a central figure in the negotiations that would lead to the democratic transition, and others in top positions at the union would be taken up into the new government. The political negotiations that led to democratization took place on the heels of an epochal shift in world history. For whites, the fear of black political empowerment had always involved the fear of communism. By 1994, however, the Soviet Union was no more, and Marxism was dead as a political ideology (even if the Communist Party of South Africa survived). Some Western writers proclaimed the "end of history": the market constituted the only way to organize modern economic life. Sensing the new playing field, the ANC jettisoned its call, made just a few years before, to nationalize the mines. During the last half of the 1990s and into the new millennium, South Africa would hew about as closely as any country in the world to the celebration of the market expressed in the neoliberal "Washington consensus." Meanwhile, members of the "struggle elite," men like Ramaphosa and a few others, would join the ranks of the captains of industry.[39]

In late April 1994, black South Africans were freed. They became equal citizens before the law. But the underside of this triumph was that it became virtually impossible to recall the process that created this state of "freedom" — how enormous wealth had been produced for a few while the multitude had been reduced to the status of workers (if they were fortunate) or to the ranks of the reserve army of the unemployed (if they were not).

As capitalists themselves attacked forms of bound labor that had once produced their wealth, the ideological effect was overpowering: the present became a spot in time detached from the past that had produced it. And as time collapsed to a moment, social classes dissolved into autonomous individuals. Now, poor black South Africans — whose material lives were hardly to be affected by the transition — were just like everyone else. They had things to buy and sell. Never mind that the only thing that most of them had to sell — if they were lucky — was their capacity to toil in places like Cinderella. This denouement was all but covered up by the celebration of black liberation.

6

UNIONIZATION FROM ABOVE

HOW DOES CINDERELLA'S STORY FIT within the broad outline of the "modernization" of labor relations in South African gold mines? If Anglo American mines represented the leading edge of change, Cinderella lay at the opposite end of the spectrum. When Mr. Robinson, the compound manager, arrived in April 1992, from a gold mine in the Orange Free State, he was struck by how "backward" Cinderella was.

> People [at Cinderella] were still doing in the 1990s what had been done in the 1970s. Some of the forms still referred to Bantus, and so forth. Some of the forms went back to the 1950s. We didn't have an industrial relations department. It was just Peter Allen and myself. The industrial relations way of doing things was fire them now, and we will sort them out in court in two years time. The philosophy then was to use the process of conciliation as a shield. Use it to buy time. The kind of industrial relations philosophy that Gold Fields is using now was very prevalent at that stage. The general manager was "up and at them." His famous saying was "Let's rubberize them and we will have them back at work," which was another way of saying he was going to shoot them with plastic and rubber bullets.

As Santu Mofokeng's photographs show, stepping into the compound at Cinderella in 1994 was like stepping back in time. The door to the *stokisi*, the holding cell, in which errant workers had been imprisoned and sometimes made to stand naked in water up to their ankles, was still visible as one walked into the center of the compound. The visibility of the past in the present must have continually reminded workers—many of whom, by the 1990s, had worked at Cinderella for decades—of how they had been treated in the past. One Sotho worker I interviewed recalled how he had been put in the stokisi for arriving late for work one Monday morning in the 1970s.

I came here late. Then I was staying in Room 141. But when I got here I was fortunate in not being hit. There was a Xhosa policeman. He came and grabbed me. I was being kicked. So you would run when you were taken to the stokisi. When I got there, one of them said that I must take my clothes off. So inside there were already three people standing. They had been arrested before me. So our Sotho induna at that time was Shadrack, the light-skinned one. So he told the police to let me keep my clothes on. So the other policeman who was a Tswana pushed me inside the stokisi. Then inside I arranged this little dam [to keep the water away]. I was there inside from 6 [am] until 1 [pm]. No food is brought there. Nobody comes to visit you. So you'll only be taken out when people come up from underground [thus workers had a choice between being on time for work or spending the work day in the stokisi]. Then you are tired and hungry. Because you have loafed, that is why they have taken you to the stokisi.

While things were changing at Cinderella by the early 1980s — the stokisi had apparently fallen into disuse — management did not foster a relationship with the NUM.[1] In its annual report for 1985, management noted the growth of the NUM at other gold mines and the industrial unrest that had occurred, stating, "Although the NUM approached the mine for access to recruit, very few employees have joined the union." The next year's report was similar: "Although the National Union of Mineworkers was granted access to recruit at the mine in October 1986, there has been no sign of NUM having made any significant progress in recruiting members." In 1987, the year of the climactic strike for the NUM, the report noted, "Despite a somewhat turbulent industrial relations climate at the time of the National Union of Mineworkers strike, the company maintained normal operations. Both management and the employees of the mine are to be commended for the mature and constructive way in which they have promoted sound industrial relations." By that point, management used consultative councils on which more senior and influential black workers were called on by the company to represent the views of their fellow workers.

Zamakile, or "Killa," one of the early stalwarts of the NUM at Cinderella, recalled that the head office of the union had sent an organizer to the mine in 1986. Zamakile himself joined the union that year. But the "stop order" system, in which the company deducted union dues from workers' paychecks and automatically transferred the monies to the head office of the union was not yet in place. Instead, people were collecting dues and giving receipts on the spot. Bengo, who was a shaft steward in 1994, recalled that in 1987 the organizer from the head office, a man named Mlungisi, was collecting the dues: "When he realized that he had enough money, he took it and disappeared. That was a lot of money because there were 20,000 workers then, and we were giving 1 rand a month. After two months, that was a lot of money. The company was happy about what this organizer did."

The memory of the corrupt NUM organizer would inhibit unionization for years to come.[2] Whatever small beginning had been achieved in the mid-1980s was completely wiped out when the mine began reducing its workforce in 1988. Soon, all of the NUM committee that had been elected at Cinderella would lose their jobs. Whether this represented a deliberate company policy (as almost all union members in 1994 believed) or whether it was simply the result of the "last in, first out" principle of retrenchments is not clear. In any case, after the layoffs began, most workers were afraid to be associated with the NUM, for fear they would lose their jobs.

The retrenchments at Cinderella were extensive by the end of the 1980s. Already one of the deepest mines in the world, Cinderella had more or less reached its limit by the mid-1980s. Its hope for the future lay in sinking a new and modern shaft, in the corner of its claim area, that would allow it to reach higher-bearing reefs. With yields steadily declining, the mine hired more and more black labor to hoist more and more ore that contained less and less gold. Black employment reached a peak of approximately 20,000, in 1986, but that same year, the mine went into the red. It would not declare a profit again until 1994. As gold prices declined, after 1987, the financial pressures grew, with the mine desperately trying to stay open long enough to make the capital investments necessary to reach areas of higher yield. To this end, the mine restructured its debt more than once, appealed for government assistance (which was given), and, above all, effected massive reductions in black labor. By 1990, the labor force of black workers had been reduced to about 5,500.[3]

By then, the NUM was dead in the water at Cinderella. "From there," according to Zamakile, "nobody was saying anything about the union. It was simply quiet." The end of retrenchments in 1990 created an opening for a colorful Zulu operator, Mr. Nxumalo, to begin to organize another union at Cinderella, the United People's Union of South Africa (UPUSA). Unlike the NUM—which had openly allied itself with the ANC by the end of the 1980s and with, at that point, a socialist future — UPUSA presented itself as a nonpolitical, free-market alternative. It was a labor union that did not take up "politics."

In fact, UPUSA, like its better-known cousin, the United Workers' Union of South Africa (UWUSA), had informal ties to Inkatha, and Inkatha apparently received support from the apartheid government to organize unions in South Africa that would undercut the radical politics typical of black South African labor unions by the late 1980s. According to the UPUSA shop steward in 1994, a Sotho worker named Mpho, "In organizing UPUSA, people didn't go from room to room in the compound. The people who were retrenched explained UPUSA to us. The organizer [Nxumalo] gave us rules that we had to follow and said that we should elect our own leaders: one, that we should not fight; two, that we should not participate in a strike outside the law; and three, he was going to talk to the *babaholo* [the big ones]. He warned us that we must never make a strike."

Hudson Bunzi, an early NUM activist (who by 1995 had earned a blasting certificate and had become one of the first black miners at Cinderella) recalled Nxumalo's coming.

> When Nxumalo came, a number of people went to see him because they thought he was an advocate [a lawyer]. They didn't go to him because he was a union [man], but because they thought he was an advocate. Then he came to the mine. So his union got to be established here, after he had already met the people. I myself nearly joined. Because I remember the day I saw him at the main office. I was really impressed with his eloquence. I would have joined if I had had the money that day.

If Nxumalo could impress black workers, he was sometimes less effective with whites — for example, on the day he showed up in Industrial Court in Pretoria, to represent a retrenched mine worker from Cinderella, wearing a wig and a gown. Not even judges in the Industrial Court wore gowns, much less wigs, and the judge demanded that Mr. Nxumalo remove his. At Cinderella, the compound manager, Mr. Robinson, thought that UPUSA lacked professionalism. "You fired somebody, and he [Nxumalo] got very emotional about it, and you went to court. Not matter what you did, you ended up in court. Well, you ended in conciliation. And as I said, we used the conciliation process as a shield, to put something into limbo in the court."

In the vacuum that existed at Cinderella in the early 1990s, substantial numbers of black workers began to turn to UPUSA for help with their problems. According to mine records, the number of members fluctuated significantly from month to month, but during both 1991 and 1992, UPUSA had more members than the NUM — which had only a little over 300 by the beginning of 1993. At that point, UPUSA had a core of Zulu members, particularly those in Inkatha, but it always had significantly more non-Zulu than Zulu members.

As the political transition picked up speed in the early 1990s and as the issue of home-stay durations began to affect the Cinderella workers who had managed to retain their jobs — to reduce costs, the mine was giving black workers extended home stays — a small core of mainly Xhosa activists, among them Zamakile and Madiba, continued their efforts to organize workers for the NUM at Cinderella. Zamakile recalled,

> In 1990 I left here for home. I was given nine months to stay at home. When I got home, I was telling this to friends at home that my mine had given me nine months. So friends asked me, "Is there a union on your mine?" "How could the mine give you nine months if you have a union?" This made me feel bad. We had a union but it got lost and we didn't know how it got lost. The organizers disappeared. When I got back in December 1990, they were still deducting a stop order for me. I was a member. In January, it was when this thing started worrying me, seeing that I was not safe in terms of job security. My friends had advised me that if I had a union, my job would be safe. I tried to find the office where the NUM was. I didn't even know where it was. I went to look for it in Johannesburg.

Recalling the same trip to the NUM headquarters in Johannesburg, Madiba said,

> When UPUSA came here, I was a member of NUM. I had signed a stop order in 1989. When we were busy watching that, I met Zamakile Nombali. He asked me what I thought about UPUSA. We discussed it. I said to him UPUSA isn't going to deliver. I said that because of my knowledge of the unions. Because I got the information from those more senior than I. I said that I knew that UPUSA was being led by the IFP. They were just hiding its real name; the real name was UWUSA. They were simply using UPUSA as a name to mislead people. We watched this thing as it was going on. Zamakile said to me we had better go to the NUM head office and find out from them. We went to the NUM head office, myself, Killa, and Sipho. We had invited Sipho to come with us so that he

could hear for himself. We wanted to know, since we were members of NUM on the mine, what was going on. Our members had signed stop orders. We wanted to know what they were doing since they were getting money from stop orders signed by the people. They were receiving these monies, but they were not coming to the members. They said they couldn't come to us. Everything, they said, depended on us. "If you want to have power, you must make workers join your union."

Madiba and Zamakile brought back forms for membership in the NUM and began to encourage friends in the NUM to recruit room to room, but their friends were afraid to store the forms in their rooms, which they felt put them at risk of being caught by management and losing their jobs. At that point, most workers at Cinderella interpreted mine regulations as preventing union organizing on mine property. Madiba recalled, "Now, what were we going to do with these forms? It appeared as if we would have to throw them away. I said, 'OK, bring all these forms to me.' I told them what they could do for me: they should go and speak to the people and tell them that I have the forms with me in Room 36. They should ask for Madiba, and I would fill out the forms for them. We agreed on that. But I didn't see people coming. Days were going by."

It so happened that two doors down, in Room 38, there were a core of UPUSA leaders, including the Sotho, Mpho, and a Xhosa man named Mtembu. Madiba quickly came into conflict with Mtembu, who demanded, "Can't you see that UPUSA is here? Why do you come with NUM? Don't you know that the NUM has eaten the people's money?" And it was not long before Zamakile was taken to the compound manager's office for questioning about handing out NUM leaflets: "I [Zamakile] was afraid because I knew that they didn't want the union on the mine. But I tried. When they caught me busy handing out pamphlets, they took me to the manager's office. Asked me many questions. And they tried to influence me to forget about the union. Because the union just took people's money. There was nothing that it could do for me they said. They said they were calling the general manager and security [about me]." Zamakile recalled how few gains he and others had made in 1991 and 1992.

ZAMAKILE: People didn't want to listen to me about the union. They didn't want to listen to me about the union.
DONHAM: Which language were you speaking?

z: With a Shangaan, for example, I would speak Fanakalo. With Sotho, I would try to speak Sotho. Xhosa no problem. Zulu no problem. Swazi no problem.

d: Which were the hardest groups to reach?

z: Ah, especially the Xhosa, it was very hard to get them. They gave me a lot of problems. Because all the time they said to me, "You are a tsotsi" [a thug, a criminal, from the township as opposed to the compound]. This is the group that gave me lots of problems.

d: Why did they think you were a tsotsi?

z: Because I was working for NUM, and NUM was a tsotsi. Me also I was a tsotsi.

d: Why did they associate NUM with tsotsis?

z: Because NUM came here and then they disappeared [with people's money]. And the deductions continued.

d: They thought it was just stealing?

z: Yes.

d: How did you get over people's resistance?

z: Ah, I can't really tell you. In truth, even I, I don't know. Everyday I asked God to help me make these people understand. Luckily, in 1992 I heard there was a fax from NUM that had come through the manager's office. This fax wanted me to go to the manager's office. When I got to him, he asked me if I was a member of the union. I said yes. And he asked me many things about the NUM. Thereafter, he said to me, "Here is your fax. You are wanted in Johannesburg. Tomorrow at three o'clock." He just left it.

A new manager, Charles du Toit, had taken over the human-resources department at the head office in late 1992. Due to his background as a student anti-apartheid leader during his college days, du Toit had probably been held back in his career during much of the 1980s, but by the early 1990s, apartheid was ending, and those who had stood against apartheid became useful in mine management. Given the dire economic straits of Cinderella, it was clear to du Toit, and then to others, that the mine could survive only with the support and cooperation of the black workforce: workers at Cinderella were going to have to accept lower pay and lower pay increases than those who worked on richer mines. This meant developing lines of communication. It meant teaching workers about the financial conditions of the mine. Everyone's future at Cinderella depended on it. And the only union with the organizational capacity to effect such agreements was, in du Toit's (probably correct) estimation, the NUM. On the surface of things, Inkatha-related unions like UWUSA and UPUSA were more pro-management, but they did not enjoy wide legitimacy among black workers, nor were they—at least UPUSA—professionally organized.

In other words, what Cinderella needed in the context of the early 1990s was a black union with political credibility that would help management manage. The fax that Zamakile received in late 1992 called him to a meeting with du Toit and the higher echelons of the NUM at the mining house's richly furnished head office in Johannesburg. There, du Toit set out his vision of a partnership between Cinderella management and the NUM.

The only problem was that the NUM did not exist as a local organization at Cinderella. At the beginning of 1993, NUM members represented only about 4 percent of the workforce—less than UPUSA members. In a move that replicated the transformation in management philosophy at Anglo American mines in the early 1980s, du Toit set about creating the conditions that would encourage union formation at Cinderella. Interviewed in 1995, he was clear about what role he had played: "I got the union recognized. I brought in full-time shop stewards.[4] And I set up collective bargaining funds.[5] The latter two were firsts in the industry." He then emphasized, "The mines are very military-like. So if you tell them to march in a particular direction, they march. And they march very well. The trick is to get the support of those on top."

To obtain that support, du Toit approached the executive committee of the mining house and got agreement that Cinderella would recognize the NUM when its membership reached approximately 35 percent of the workforce (previously, 50 percent plus 1 worker had been the standard). In addition, he transformed the culture of how stop orders were dealt with at Cinderella.

What was happening before is that stop orders would be handed into management. Management would handle them in a very slipshod way. Lose them. Call employees and demand to confirm signatures. And they would refuse to count stop orders for those on home stay when calculating the percentage of union members. That meant that it was very difficult to get a critical mass going. I went to meetings between management and the NUM on the mines, and if the union guys complained about stop order being messed around, I would tell the industrial relations manager that if I came back and heard the same stories that he would be out of a job.

But perhaps the most critical thing that du Toit did was to assign a mine-owned office—located just outside the compound—to NUM workers at Cinderella. The symbolic significance of that move, as far as black workers were concerned, cannot be underestimated. At that point, there was no question of reprisals against workers who joined the union. According to Zamakile, "They gave us an office there. That was when people started coming." Indeed, before the end of the year, the NUM would gain official recognition from Cinderella management. What had taken two to three years on some Anglo mines in the early 1980s was compressed into the dizzying space of about nine months at Cinderella in 1993, and against the background of the protracted national negotiations about how apartheid would end.

With management philosophy having reversed 180 degrees, an event occurred early in the morning of 4 April 1993, a Sunday, that was to catalyze the transformation already in motion. It did so by dramatically, almost mythically, portraying for black workers the past in the present. An onsetter (the person who operated the cage that took workers up and down the mine shaft), Johannes van Zyl, one of the lowest-paid white workers on the mine, whose job was to be quickly occupied by new black workers, pulled out a 25-gauge Baby Browning pistol, then shot and wounded a black worker in the cage. (See figs. 17 and 18 of workers arriving at the shaft and coming up from underground.) The black man had allegedly pressed too closely against van Zyl as the cage ascended at the end of a shift. Coming up from underground at the end of a shift is always a moment of tension. Having survived another shift underground, everyone wants to get out, but given the inevitable bottlenecks introduced by getting men and materials down and up, and ore out, there is usually a wait. One of the rituals of apartheid had required black workers to climb stairs to take a separate cage, above the one white workers entered. By 1993, such rites were passé. The white workers most threatened by the passing of old racial hierarchies were, of course, those in jobs soon to be occupied by upwardly mobile black workers. (In early 1994, the union activist Zamakile had already become an onsetter.)

One detail of the incident shaped its aftermath: the black worker shot was a Mozambican. Some NUM activists at Cinderella had de-

17. Workers transported to the shaft from the compound

spaired of ever reaching recognition for the union, since a majority of the workforce at the mine was Mozambican, and Mozambicans were notoriously difficult to convince to join unions, at least from the perspective of some NUM activists. According to Madiba, before the April event, Mozambican workers,

> were always saying that they couldn't understand. "We did not come here to fight for this country. We have our own country." After that man was shot, it appeared that nobody did anything about it, especially the whites. To them, it was only a dog that had been shot. Then workers immediately came together. They tightened and stood together. After the strike started, NUM people came from head office and tried to show people how to proceed so that things would go well. Right, we all understood. So after that visit, and after people had understood the union better, we started getting people.

It is noteworthy that the interim branch committee of the NUM did not organize the strike. The head of the NUM committee (who did not

18. Workers clocking out after an underground shift

live in the compound) learned about the strike only when he arrived for work on Monday morning. By 2:00 P.M. on Sunday, mine security, through their informants, had received news of a "possible strike." Security had already handed van Zyl to the South African Police, who arrested but then released him on his own recognizance, with an order to appear in court. (After two postponements, the charges against van Zyl were dropped, in mid-May, on the ground of "insufficient evidence"; van Zyl claimed that he had drawn the gun in self-defense and that it had gone off accidentally.)

Whether workers in the compound heard that van Zyl had been released on Sunday is unclear. In any case, they felt that white authority did not take the shooting of a black man seriously. By 7:00 P.M. on Sunday, groups of workers had taken over the gates of the compound and had begun to threaten any of their fellows who attempted to go to work. With workers having claimed the gate, the power of apartheid architecture had been inverted. Entries in the security logbook went as follows:

19:12	A report was received from Cinderella that four employees were stopped at the walkway by another employee and sent back to the hostel and told not to proceed to work.
19:28	Intimidation: Workers are still being intimated at the shaft walkway. Riot sections are busy trying to eliminate these intimidations.
19:48	Report: Security Officer Newman reported that the workers are toyi-toying in front of the shaft lamp house. + 20.
20:00	Report: Security Officer Potgieter reported that + 1800 workers are in front of the hostel gate. + 60 are active and the others are just spectating. They want to be addressed by the General Manager in the entire group and not in groups of ten.
20:04	Mr. Williams informed of the workers' request and he proceeded to the hostel and was escorted by security.
20:18	Report: The General Manager is going to address the workers in front of the hostel from inside the Casspir.
22:20	Report: Mr. Williams is trying to address the people in front of the hostel offices.[6]

The general manager of the mine, Mr. Williams, could not convince black workers to go to work Sunday evening. It is difficult to say what the distribution of opinion was among Cinderella workers, but given the layout of the compound, it was not difficult for small groups of workers—about twenty at the back entrance to the shaft from the compound and sixty at the front gate—to assert their will over the entire workforce (over five thousand). White violence, after all, had already decreased the differences among black workers at Cinderella.

Van Zyl's shot epitomized the exploitations of the past, a past that was not yet fully past. One might even say that in that moment "exploitation" was defined. What had previously, in the 1970s, for example, been accepted more or less as the order of things, that white supervisors had the right to use physical force against black workers—whether in the stokisi in the compound or in beatings underground—was now rendered unacceptable. In its very exaggeration, the shooting called forth associations in the experience of virtually every black worker at Cinderella, and thus led to an explosion of resentments. Some complained about the racism of the compound manager, Mr. Killian, the disgusting conditions in the compound, and the bad food, while others brought up the issue of van Zyl's white supervisors, Mr. Van Deventer and Mr. Kleynhans. Many white workers, it was asserted, carried weapons underground, and their white supervisors turned a blind eye. Other workers brought up the continued existence of black piccanins underground. Still others talked of wages and the long home stays that Cinderella black workers had to endure.

On Monday, regional NUM organizers from the head office arrived at Cinderella, having been notified by members of the interim branch committee on Sunday. Two organizers were responsible for Cinderella at that point. One was a forthright Xhosa- and English-speaking former mine worker, Madezi, schooled in the ways of mines. Madezi had, in fact, worked at Cinderella for a short period in the late 1970s. The other was a recently returned South African exile, Fabian Nkumane, an Ndebele-speaking communist who could barely communicate in the languages used by most mine workers and who stuttered as his concentration and seriousness grew. It was clear that Madezi, a man from the ranks, looked with more than a little disdain on Nkumane, who sometimes talked in Marxist phrases such as "classes in and for themselves."

Nevertheless, Nkumane and Madezi together channeled the discontents expressed in the April event to focus on two: safety for black workers underground and the larger problem of racism on the mine. Monday began as the general manager, using a loudspeaker, tried once again to address the workers in the compound from a Casspir. According to Patrick, head of the interim NUM committee, the crowd was not listening.

> The people said, "No, we are sick and tired of you management." You know there were a lot of different demands. So I took the loudspeaker. It was something past 8 A.M. when I took the loudspeaker because now I went straight away to the Casspir, and I said to the general manager, "No, give the loudspeaker to me. I'm going to try to speak to these people." So at the end of the day when I took that speaker, then the people started to listen and we went all of us to the soccer field [to elect a committee to negotiate with management].

The committee of workers—elected along ethnic lines, so many Shangaans, so many Xhosas, and so forth—included several NUM interim committee members, but it was not an NUM committee as such. This committee demanded, first, that it be provided transportation to visit the wounded worker in Rand Mutual Hospital, and then in the afternoon, it sat down to talk with management, along with the two NUM regional organizers. By the end of the day, it had been agreed that work would resume Monday evening, that mine security would search all workers (white and black) going underground, and that the NUM would have observers at these searches. Two white workers were placed on suspension until charges of racist behavior could be investigated by an independent mediation service (three months later, these charges were found to be unsupported by the evidence presented).

What was most important about this incident was that the NUM had placed itself in the conflict such that it could claim to represent workers to management. In the words of the mediation report issued three months later, the NUM, for the first time in its history at Cinderella, came "face to face with management regarding a serious problem."[7] This was precisely what management wanted, and the symbolic value of the gaze back and forth across the table should not be underestimated: even if the two controlled resources of incomparably different magnitudes, management and workers now composed two sets of formally equal individuals. This change offered many black workers a certain kind of exhilaration, a hope in relation to the past.

An official narrative of this event formed literally overnight—one that created the NUM as an actor. On 7 April, according to *Business Day*,

> Workers returned to work yesterday after a two-day strike sparked by an underground shooting in which a black worker was wounded by a white colleague.
>
> The wounded man is recovering in the Rand Mutual hospital.
>
> Police said a man would appear in court today.
>
> NUM spokesman Fabian Nkumane said more than 5,000 workers went back to work after management agreed to meet their demands for stricter security checks and a commitment to address alleged racism on the mine.
>
> Nkumane said that at a meeting on Monday night management agreed to step up its searches on workers going underground, and added that workers would be involved in monitoring the process.
>
> Black workers had complained that white workers were exempt from searches.
>
> Management agreed to look into the problem of racism, said Nkumane, who added that reports of racial discrimination had failed to reach the appropriate levels.

An inquiry, headed by an independent investigator, was to be established to address the problems of discrimination and violence at the mine.

There would be no disciplinary action against the strikers, but management refused to pay them for the two days of the stoppage, Nkumane said.[8]

But this narrative is misleading. The NUM had no official role at Cinderella at the time. From the end of December 1992, when management gave them an office near the compound gate, until the shooting in April 1993, the interim branch committee had managed to increase its membership from about 4 percent of the workforce to approximately 9 percent, according to management records. At that point, the NUM was only marginally larger than UPUSA, which had perhaps as much claim to represent workers at Cinderella as did the NUM.

Moreover, the NUM did not organize the strike. When Madezi and Nkumane arrived on Monday, they found the strike already under way. Neither they nor the interim branch had had anything to do with its instigation. So who did rouse workers against mine management that Sunday? Patrick, head of the interim branch committee, asked the same question on Monday morning: "So we asked some of the people, 'Who did this?' And the people told us it was Sakhiwo and some others inside the compound." Sakhiwo was a Xhosa-speaking worker, a tough guy, who had been involved in a number of assaults on workers outside the compound. He would, in fact, in a matter of months, lose his job because of one of these incidents. I was not able to interview Sakhiwo, but I was able to confirm that he was a member of a secret Xhosa-speaking group in the compound, the amabutho, the "regiment." The amabutho was only one of a number of such ethnically organized gangs with a long history in South African gold mines like Cinderella.

To some considerable degree, social groups based on ties at home were built into the system of migrant labor in South Africa. Away from home, in a potentially threatening environment like the compound or the city, black workers often had as their closest friends—those on whom they depended for support and with whom they drank and socialized—those who came from areas close to home.[9] Indeed, an exceptionally rich South African literature documents this pattern, and Xhosa-speaking migrants seem to have shown a special genius for constructing these ties.[10] What looks on the outside like a propensity for ethnic clumping is probably better interpreted as simply the easiest way of coping with migrant labor in the South African context.

But if home-based groups could be used for defense, they could also be used for offense (and the boundary between the two blurs in any conflict). Almost all black male migrants had grown up in rural areas in which they learned the art of stick fighting. Although such weapons were simple, they could wreak havoc when wielded by a skilled and coordinated group. Such organized coercion could be made to "pay" in any number of ways. In truth, the South African state was never excessively concerned about violence—as long as it did not reach white areas. Therefore, a tradition of gangs developed early in the mine compounds and in black townships around them, and in the townships, at least, a series of vigilante groups rose to oppose them. Over time, it was not unusual for vigilante groups to become virtually indistinguishable from the gangs they had originally opposed.[11]

One of the earliest such gangs that grew up around the mines was the Ninevites, documented by Charles van Onselen.[12] By the first decade of the twentieth century, Zulus (and a sprinkling of individuals from other ethnic groups) had organized themselves under an *inkosi nkulu*, a great chief, Nongoloza. Living in abandoned mine shafts and derelict buildings, they took boys as wives and supported themselves through robbery directed mostly against black mine workers.[13] Offense begets defense, however, and it was not long before the threat by Ninevites had provoked a response from Xhosa-speaking Mpondo workers, who organized their own gang, the Isitshozi.[14] By the 1930s, Isitshozi were based not in abandoned mine shafts but in the compounds of the East Rand themselves, including Cinderella. There, Isitshozi asserted their power by monopolizing boys involved in same-sex sexual relationships. Boys who repeatedly refused the Isitshozi could find themselves beaten, even murdered, and men who had boys were subject to having them taken away if they did not comply with the wishes of the gang. By attempting to control sex in an all-male environment, the Isitshozi asserted its power over much more: over flows of stolen goods, the giving and receiving of favors, and general deference from other workers. In these matters, the display and dramatization of violence was critical. It advertised what would happen to anyone who opposed the Isitshozi.

By the 1940s, a Sotho gang called the Russians, the amaRashea, employed many of the same methods, now deployed toward controlling the sexuality of women.[15] In the 1980s, the Russians, who then dominated the mines of the Orange Free State, controlled the squatter settlements that ballooned around the mines as the pass laws were abandoned. If a black mine worker wanted to establish his wife or lover in one of these settlements, he had to pay protection money to the Russians. Again, by controlling sex, the Russians attempted to control much more.

By the 1990s, ethnically organized gangs had existed in the compound at Cinderella for almost a century, and under the surface, they had organized much of the life of the compound. Although both the Isitshozi and the Russians had apparently declined in influence at Cinderella, the Russians continued to work in the lucrative business of moneylending, and there were rumors that some Mpondo controlled the open-field shebeen that had developed just outside the compound gate, in which women sold both bottled beer and sex.[16] There was also the marijuana business, a numbers racket controlled from the local Chinese butchery, and various smuggling schemes, usually Shangaandominated, to and from Mozambique. Many of the AK-47s that circulated in the compound and the surrounding squatter camps had arrived via the last route.

Against this history, the Xhosa group at Cinderella in the early 1990s represented both a continuation and an innovation. Ties to brothers at home still represented the most reliable way of organizing in the compound; if such groups were ethnic, they did not have to be motivated by "ethnic" projects. Yet, unlike the criminal gangs that preceded it, the amabutho saw itself primarily in political terms: as, in fact, freedom fighters for the ANC. One worker maintained that the amabutho had formed secretly at Cinderella in 1989, before Mandela was released from prison, "to bring the NUM to the mine." It was impossible at that time to discuss union issues, much less national politics, in Cinderella and still retain one's job. Others insisted that the group had been organized a few years later, in reaction to Inkatha attacks on the East Rand.

Whatever the timing of its founding, the amabutho mobilized the strike at Cinderella in April 1993. By doing so, it gave expression to many black workers' resentments and grievances, but in a way that also advertised its own power within the compound. Sakhiwo and his friends spread the word on Sunday—always a day of drinking and rowdiness, and the only day on which there was no regular work shift. The decision was that no one should return to work, and the Xhosa gang, dancing and singing with their sticks and knobkerries, were on hand Sunday evening at strategic points to enforce that decision.

It is doubtful that management at Cinderella, particularly at the head office, recognized these under-the-surface connections between gangs and strikes. The man on the ground, Mr. Robinson, understood more than most of the management team; he understood, for example, Mpondo domination of prostitution and open-air shebeens, but in fairly extensive and frank interviews, he never connected any of the gangs to union politics or industrial relations. The official narrative was, after all, captivating, for black South Africans and many whites as well: as freedom progressed, black workers were at last organizing to assert their rights. Management and black unions were working together to erase the apartheid past.

The sense of elation created by this narrative in 1994 is brilliantly captured in Santu Mofokeng's photographs of an NUM rally that took place in the former tribal dancing arena at Cinderella (see gallery 24 and 25). At the very moment of triumph, however, what was actually transpiring was more obscure and, ironically, involved the reinforcement of what looked like some long-standing apartheid patterns. If the all-Xhosa amabutho was not motivated, at least in the beginning, by ethnic chauvinism, that potentiality always existed because of the way the group was organized. And more important, other black workers could interpret the actions of the amabutho as ethnically driven, even when they were not. In forming so rapidly at Cinderella, the NUM had grafted itself onto already existing social structures in the compound, in this case, the regiment. The interim branch committee became the public face of black workers' struggle, but power in the compound in fact rested in the hands of men like Sakhiwo. As company philosophy underwent a sea change in late 1992, relinquishing traditional forms of coercive control over black workers, the Xhosa gang stepped to the fore. By late 1993, it was emboldened enough to organize a land invasion of mine property, setting up a squatter camp called "Ramaphosa," after the former general secretary of the NUM. By then, the political and ethnic separation of squatter camps around the mine was complete: Ramaphosa was ANC- and Xhosa-dominated; Injalo was Inkatha- and Zulu-dominated.

If management was desperately trying to keep its head above the wave of change in early 1993 and only dimly perceived what was happening in the compound, the NUM, for its part, had lost some of its most experienced leaders. The founding head of the union, Cyril Ramaphosa, left in 1991 to take up a position with the ANC, and according to V. L. Allen, who had access to union affairs in the early 1990s, the effect on the head office was marked. Ramaphosa had come from a Venda background, and very few Venda worked on the mines. As a consequence, his decisions were rarely interpreted by union activists as ethnically biased.[17] According to Allen, this began to change in the political jockeying that developed at the NUM head office after Ramaphosa's departure. A fault line developed between members of the South African Communist Party and others, and was overlaid with ethnic differences between Xhosas and others.[18] "The changes in the composition of the secretariat influenced the manner in which the administration in the head office was organised. Ramaphosa had intervened in the details of its day-to-day operations and, through those interventions, had exercised control over it. A relatively stable and committed staff had, moreover, served him. His departure to the ANC created an administrative vacuum that was not filled."[19]

Whether the changes at the head office created a space for regional organizers to take matters in their own hands is unclear. In any case, there was a difference in emphasis between the two regional organizers at Cinderella, though this difference did not replicate the lines of tension at the head office as described by V. L. Allen. The communist Nkumane continually argued against any assumed role for ethnicity. For example, when local union activists despaired of ever reaching Mozambican workers in early 1993, Nkumane got into heated debates with them and with the other organizer, Madezi: "There was a big argument. Some thought that it would be difficult to organize at Cinderella because there were so many Shangaans, and they wouldn't be interested in the union. I argued against that." It is not clear how much even Nkumane understood of the working relationship between the union at Cinderella and the Xhosa gang.

Xhosa-speaking Madezi, in contrast, was frank about the connections. Interviewed in 1995, he explained that there had been three main obstacles to organizing at Cinderella: the already established existence of UPUSA, the lack of facilities to automatically deduct union dues from wages, and the majority status of Mozambican workers. "Those people really were not interested in labor issues." If the last obstacle was nationally and ethnically defined in Madezi's mind, the way around it was as well. According to Madezi, the strategy of the interim committee in early 1993 was to reach out to Xhosa workers. "Our targeted group at that time was the Xhosa-speaking people. We needed to mobilize them to come to our side so that we could be in a position of maneuver."[20]

DONHAM: Why did you target workers from Transkei?

MADEZI: Most of the organization people in the ANC at that time were coming from the Transkei. People who understand how to fight were the people coming from Transkei. Ciskei, you'll find those people are a bit moderate, not so very much aggressive. People of Transkei are *very* militant. They're ready to fight at any given moment if something went wrong. So that was the combination. So it was easy for you if you were an experienced organizer to see what was the easiest way of organizing people.

More generally, the NUM strategy during 1993 at Cinderella, in Madezi's telling, was to identify the structures of power in the compound, to avoid moves that would threaten that structure—while inserting the NUM shaft steward committee over them. "No, let's come together and work with these people because they are the leaders. If we ignore them, we are going to have a problem. That was the process." Interviewed in English, Madezi identified the leaders of the compound as the "amabutho."

There was a ready-made organization [the amabutho]. The only thing you need to do is to give a direction to that organization. *Don't* undermine that organization. Because once you undermine that organization you are creating a situation you cannot control and in which you cannot operate. That is my experience. Once you undermine that organization it's going to be very difficult because they will see NUM as an opponent. So you will be enemy number three. Though enemy number one is management, and enemy number two by that time was Inkatha. So if you're going to organize them, you must be very careful in a select way, when you address them.

The full-time NUM shaft steward Odysseus, a Swazi, first became aware of the regiment in the early 1990s. Loosely related to other such "regiments" in the squatter camps of the East Rand, the amabutho had its own commander at Cinderella, a Mpondo man nicknamed Whitey. The nucleus of the group was housed in Room 201. And they had a traditional doctor, an *inyanga*, who lived nearby and who provided traditional medicine to strengthen and protect them for fighting. Odysseus had first become aware of the regiment when some of its members returned to the compound from fights in nearby squatter camps like Zonkesizwe with black marks on their foreheads.[21] In mine slang, these marks were "numba eleven," the two parallel incisions into which traditional medicine had been rubbed.

According to one Xhosa worker I interviewed who was almost certainly a member of the amabutho,

> The regiment wanted to make something wrong right. If you have a problem in our [Xhosa] culture, you call your relatives to discuss what might be a solution. It's like consulting a lawyer. The lawyer may tell you, "If you kill this person, this will happen to you. You will go down that path. That won't be good. Do it this way." It was that way. You knew someone from home and maybe he knew a third. The group grew that way. Maybe you would visit someone while you were at home and you got to know him better. That was the way that the amabutho was established.

It is difficult to estimate the number of workers in the amabutho. According to the worker, there were at least fifty and perhaps a hundred. The group could be convened through secret signals. All were Xhosa-speaking and included both Mpondo and other Xhosa-speakers.

It was the amabutho who took over the compound gate and declared a strike after the white onsetter shot the black Mozambican worker. The NUM organizers arrived only afterward, attempting to direct and to channel a process already underway. The difficulty was that Whitey's gang was an all-Xhosa group. It danced and waved weapons and sang songs that celebrated Xhosa chiefs' conquests from the past. It shoved other black workers around. As an expression of what others must have seen as ethnically organized power in the compound, it represented a potential threat to all non-Xhosa workers—particularly to the Zulus.

The April strike, according to Madezi, created tensions.

> Once the people were on strike, the people knew very well that the reaction of Inkatha, it may be different on the whole issue, they may attack. During the process of the strike, you would see these people [Zulus], ready, preparing something, cooking themselves [inhaling the vapors from traditional medicine meant to strengthen and protect], and then you would see amabutho on this side starting to do the same thing, and moving around, and then other people observing this would get upset, "Alright, if they start attacking, I'm telling you, these people are

going to have to deal with us." The relationship that we built, the network [with the amabutho] helped us to stop violence, to be in a position of controlling tensions.

The Communist Nkumane was thrilled to see workers revolting against their oppression, but his enthusiasm seemed naïve to Madezi, who understood that what was happening was far more complex.

> It was the first time [for Nkumane]. When we were heading into the strike, he was so [pause] excited such that we had an exchange of strong words between us [laughs]. He said that it was his first time to see workers revolting. He was so very happy. I said to him, "There is no reason for you to be happy because if these people [the Xhosa and Zulu] fight here, you won't be happy. It will be a very big problem. If management fires them, you won't be happy."

But no such fight took place in April, and afterward, Mozambicans and others poured into the NUM at Cinderella. Against the background of the upcoming political transition, black workers' expectations rose. In June annual wage negotiations began, and in July another strike occurred. Management had tabled an offer of a 5 percent increase in wages, but given workers' rising expectations, this increase must have seemed a mere pittance. On Tuesday, 20 July 1993, the night shift struck, and workers would not be persuaded to go back to work again until Sunday evening, 25 July.

This time the strike *did* involve the NUM interim committee at the mine, but the decision to strike was not the result of a collective process among union members. Longtime activists like Odysseus and Madiba had in fact argued against a strike, pointing out that such action would be illegal, that the union was not yet recognized, and that it would be easy for management to fire strikers and to undermine the power of the union during this critical phase of union-building. But the chair of the committee, Patrick, took unilateral action; he may well have been acting under pressure by the amabutho.

In any case, Whitey and the Xhosa regiment once again played a critical role in organizing the strike.

> DONHAM: How did you organize it? How did you get the word out?
> PATRICK: Well, we just organized it with about six people. And those six people had to go straight into the hostel, telling people, "Today we're doing this and this."

D: So I would think that the strategy would be to go to all the important groups in the hostel and get them on your side.

P: No, you know, the group that we were using straight away, it was the group from the Xhosa side. The Xhosa side. We were using Xhosas. [Patrick himself was from a Tswana background.]

D: So you went to them and tried to convince them?

P: I went to them. That time, before Sakhiwo had been dismissed, he was part and parcel of [pause]

D: Was he on the union committee?

P: No, he was not on the committee but he was a guy who was [pause] Sakhiwo was there. He was dismissed after the strike of July.

D: So, did you yourself go talk to him?

P: Yeah, I spoke to him. I spoke to him.

D: Was he willing at that point?

P: To be a leader of the strike? Yes, he was willing.

D: But the danger in using the Xhosa is that then you might provoke a faction fight.

P: You know we were using those guys because at the end of the day we knew that they could persuade other people, even on the side of the Sothos, because we presented a strong presence. The Xhosa and the Sotho, they were against the six-month home stay. But if you were from Mozambique, then you weren't bothered by it. Mozambicans enjoyed a long home stay. Then we have those Zulu guys, you know. They didn't want to have a strike. But we went to them and explained to them, "This is not a political issue, this is our [common] concern because we are working in this mine and we're not getting money. Please, can you join us?" Then they joined us.

Once again, no open confrontation took place between the Xhosa and Zulu gangs, but tensions were raised yet another notch. The interim (soon to be full-time) shaft steward Odysseus observed,

Fine, O.K., we embarked on the strike. Management informed the [NUM] region, telling them, "We have a problem at Cinderella." Now when Nkumane and Madezi arrived, they tried to talk to the people, but the people were so militant, armed with spears, UPUSA pulling this direction, and there was some tribality in it, the Zulus not mixing with the other masses, going their own way, singing their own songs. The people didn't want to listen. You see, the problem we had in that strike was a lot of drinking. That shebeen was operating just outside the compound. It was alive and operating. Whenever we called people to a mass meeting, they came there drunk. They had just one word. "Is money there?" If you talked about anything else, it was "Fuck off." They were threatening the leadership. When we saw that, hey, things were getting out of hand. O.K. We tried to persuade management to just give something, just one percent. They said no, we don't give you anything.

In fact, the strike accomplished nothing for workers. The wage increase for the year remained at 5 percent. Management did recognize the union, soon after the strike, but that would have occurred in any case. Had management not so desperately needed the NUM, striking workers would probably have been fired—particularly Patrick for his role in organizing an illegal action. But after repeated warnings from management and after an address by the president and general secretary of the NUM pleading with Cinderella workers to go back to work, the night shift resumed work Sunday evening.

After some further negotiation, it was decided that no worker would be penalized for the loss of days of work at Cinderella. According to du Toit, at the head office,

> After it [the July strike], there was no acrimony between me and the union leadership [at the head office]. In a way, I think we were both caught up by the pathos of this heavily financially burdened mine and these poor guys who were being paid badly, living in awful conditions, with no alternative, and so when we gave the ultimatum, the general secretary called me and said, "Du Toit, please give me the weekend." He phoned me at home. I said, "O.K., Kgalima, you have the weekend. I don't want to fire the guys, nor do you. You can go in there." And we arranged for them to go into the hostel. I got management to withdraw the ultimatum. And James Motslatsi and Kgalima went and spent the weekend in the hostel. And Sunday night, the night shift went underground. It was no victory for anybody. That's just an indictment of unemployment and an indictment of the fact that these guys really don't have an alternative.

After the union was recognized, the NUM elected shaft stewards, including four full-time stewards, one for each of the three shafts, plus one for the surface workers. These full-time stewards were to be paid by management (at the top of the pay scale) to carry out union business. Two were Xhosas, one was Swazi, and one Tswana. The overrepresentation of Xhosas (who comprised approximately 15 percent of the total workforce) was far more evident among part-time shaft stewards. Of the twenty-six part-time shaft stewards working at the three shafts at Cinderella, fifteen were Xhosas. Thus there was some basis to the charge that the NUM at Cinderella was "Xhosa." Regional organizers like Madezi had, from the beginning, targeted Xhosa workers; Philip, the Tswana chairman of the branch committee, relied on the Xhosa regiment to enforce strikes; and, by whatever means, Xhosas were elected—far beyond their proportion in the general population—to be shaft stewards in November 1993.

Nothing was exactly as it seemed at Cinderella. On the surface, the NUM was a labor organization committed to universal rights for all of its workers vis-à-vis employers, in alliance with the ANC, committed to black liberation. Certainly leaders like Cyril Ramaphosa saw NUM as part of the struggle to restore dignity to black workers. Interviewed by Dunbar Moodie in 2001, Ramaphosa recalled,

> As a young boy growing up in Soweto, I used to see [black miners] at Johannesburg station. They would be huddled up in a corner, holding their loaf of bread. People didn't talk to them. We didn't mix with them. They were a completely different breed of people and they were looked down upon . . . I mean they were treated as the lowest of even us, the oppressed people in this country. For me, the challenge was to fight for their dignity: to get mineworkers to walk tall; to be proud of being mineworkers; to be proud of the contribution they were making to the economy of this country; for mine workers not to feel that they were nothing, nonentities.[22]

Underneath, however, the NUM depended for its power, at Cinderella in 1993 and 1994, on a Xhosa gang, and it appears that this arrangement was not unique. To maneuver in the compound, the union had to become a part—to some degree—of its subterranean world. Undercover amabutho, who could always be presented to the outside as "union marshals," surface in a number of accounts of mine violence. In a case described by Dunbar Moodie, an amabutho turned on the NUM itself in 1985 as a charismatic shaft steward at Vaal Reefs, named Lira Setona, used the regiment to defy head-office leadership. Another amabutho appears in V. L. Allen's history of the NUM.[23] There, when dismissed mine workers from Rustenburg refused to leave the head office in Johannesburg in 1986, some union officials in desperation called in the amabutho from Grootvlei gold mine, "a heavy-handed security service for the union." The Grootvlei amabutho attacked the dismissed mineworkers occupying the head office and forced them to disperse. Finally, the report of the commission of inquiry into the violence at Vaal Reefs South in 1995 — which left 11 dead and 150 injured — concluded that NUM union marshals "appeared to have become a band of vigilantes available to enforce the will of certain members of the shaft committee."[24] "The approximately twenty-three volunteer marshals became a symbol of the lawlessness, lack of democracy and ethnic tension with the hostel."[25] The marshals were apparently Xhosas at a mine at which at least 40 percent of the workforce was from Lesotho and Swaziland (and thus "foreign" by 1995).[26] The conflict broke out as a Sotho gang, the Russians, retaliated against the (Xhosa) marshals for having enforced a bus boycott they did not support. The commission concluded "the marshals must be forthwith disbanded. There must be no 'dogs without owners.'"[27] As we shall see, however, even dogs with owners can bite.

7

MOTIVES FOR MURDER

WHO CARRIED OUT THE MURDERS on 16 June 1994 at Cinderella? In the days, months, and years that followed, no official clarity ever developed in relation to this question. Strangely, the company never initiated its own investigation into the causes of the violence. This was in sharp contrast to how it handled the shooting incident involving the white onsetter a year before, when mine security had immediately taken statements from witnesses, and the accused had been caught and turned over to the South African Police. The company had also suspended those accused of racist behavior until an independent organization, the Independent Mediation Service of South Africa (IMSSA), could investigate.

After the Cinderella murders in 1994, management carried out its legal responsibilities. They asked a local peace committee of clergymen, black and white, to work at reconciling the workforce and through this process to identify the perpetrators. When Zulu workers said that they could identify some of the men who had attacked them, management called the South African Police to take statements. But from the very beginning, the managers must have realized that the peace committee—who did not charge for their services and who were not trained in the law—would have far fewer organizational resources than, say, the IMSSA. Indeed, it was not two weeks before Cinderella management had lost all confidence in the clergymen and their mediation process. After a month—during which time the Zulus were on paid leave—the mediators had yet to present an acceptable solution to reintegrating the Zulus into the compound, and on 18 July management, exasperated, fired all of the Zulus who lived in the compound on a so-called no-fault basis. Although a few Zulus kept their jobs at the mine, they did not live in the compound (even if they worked there during the day or night as clerks and policemen). To the retrenched Zulus, this outcome added insult to injury. The targeted victims of violence now lost their jobs, while the murderers retained both their freedom and work. From the company's point of view, the July retrenchment was all it could do in this situation. The mine was losing money. If things went on much longer, everyone would lose their jobs.

What occurred just after the retrenchment offers the first insights into the identity of the murderers. In a carefully orchestrated action about a month after the Zulus had been removed from the mine premises, three Cinderella workers were finally arrested for the Soweto Day murders—apparently on the basis of statements that the Zulu workers had given to police almost two months before. Mine security worked quietly with the South African Police to catch the three while they were away from the compound. Management was concerned about the possibility of a strike once the workforce heard of the arrests (these worries must have been based on tips from informers in the compound). The accused were taken, not to the police station closest to the compound, but to one farther away. All three, according to my interviews, were Xhosa-speaking Mpondo.

Whether management also worked with the head office of the NUM in this action is not clear. In any case, according to Odysseus, a full-time shaft steward at Cinderella, the NUM head office in Johannesburg soon sent one of its white employees to the police station to provide bail for all of the three arrested—a total of R9,000. At least one of those arrested was not an NUM member, since he was a contract worker for a company that provided services to the mine (and contract workers could not join the union because they were not direct employees of the mine). One of the three was a prominent NUM shaft steward nicknamed Big Boy.

There was a distinctly staged quality to the arrests. If management had actually been concerned with identifying the perpetrators of the violence, why hadn't they had these arrests carried out *before* the Zulu workers were retrenched? Afterward, there was no social context for the continuance of memory of the Soweto Day murders. Those most knowledgeable had been shipped home to various locations in rural KwaZulu-Natal. A few stayed behind at Injalo squatter camp to look for work in the area, but a year after the murders, according to interviews, none of the Zulu former workers at Injalo realized that anyone had ever been arrested for the murders.

After a month, the charges were dropped—for want of further evidence. The NUM head office received its bail money back. And with this, the whole matter of identifying the murderers came to a close.

It was almost as if mine management and the NUM worked hand-in-glove, at the very end of the process, to sweep the Zulu matter under the rug. Clearly, management had an enormous investment in the NUM at Cinderella; in fact, company officials had been among its principal architects. Had a thorough investigation shown involvement by NUM shaft stewards in the Zulu killings, the result would presumably have unhinged the developing frame for industrial relationships at the mine.

In the very first meeting with NUM shaft stewards, the day after the murders, the industrial-relations manager at the mine asserted that some of the NUM shaft stewards themselves had been in the vicinity of the violence the previous evening. According to the minutes of the meeting on 17 June (at which Big Boy was present),

> Mr. Johnson stated that as a solution management proposed a full investigation into the assaults and deaths. Those found guilty of transgressions would face serious disciplinary action and criminal charges. He requested the assistance of the NUM. Secondly, he called for a joint condemnation of the violence and a brief to that effect signed by the NUM and management. Thirdly both parties should agree to sign a peace pledge. Further, a brief listing of unacceptable weapons would be drawn up and distributed. Mr. Johnson said that some of the NUM shaft stewards were in the vicinity of the violence and asked for assistance in identifying the perpetrators of violence. If they did not assist, they would be in breach of the recognition agreement, and management would have to look at possible suspensions.

But these strong words, on the morning after the violence, were never backed up by action. No one lost his job for participating in the beatings and killings — much less for being unwilling to cooperate in identifying the perpetrators of violence.

If the motives of management after Soweto Day were unclear, so also were those of the NUM. Why was the union so quick to provide bail, not only to one of their shaft stewards charged with murder, but also to a worker who was not even a member of the union? Didn't the head office need to investigate the matter before extending such support? Of course, in a situation like the Cinderella murders, unfounded accusations are always possible. Witnesses can be wrong or can invent stories to settle old accounts. But given what is known of how the NUM had been organized at Cinderella — the way that the shaft-steward committee had been grafted onto the amabutho — a question presents itself: were the three arrested, in fact, members of that secret gang?

As the compound manager, Mr. Robinson, emphasized, what happened on Soweto Day cannot be understood as the spontaneous outburst of crowd passion. It was, instead, a highly organized attack, spearheaded by a small group. The only group in the compound with that capacity (besides the Inkatha core) was the Xhosa regiment. The weapons—homemade clubs and spears—along with, according to some accounts, the use of *muti*, or traditional medicine, had all of the hallmarks of the amabutho. And as interviews with Madezi have shown, some men in the amabutho also served as officers in the NUM. Big Boy may have been one of those men who played dual roles.

If the regiment attacked the Zulus, what motivated them to do so? After one appreciates the politics of national liberation in South Africa—the rivalry between the ANC and Inkatha—one must turn to more local concerns to answer this question. Overwhelmingly, it was national politics that mine management used to understand the split between black workers at Cinderella. After all, within that schema, management saw itself as both blameless and essentially helpless to effect any resolution of the conflict that had erupted. How could management be expected to solve the country's problems? But national politics was not the only frame of reference for the amabutho. Union and compound politics were important as well, perhaps even more so. The regiment had allied itself with the NUM, but, to date, that alliance had produced no tangible returns. The strike in 1993, even though it had lasted a week, had yielded nothing for workers. As the wage negotiations for 1994 approached, the amabutho realized that the Inkatha core in the compound could divide the workforce in any future strike and hence weaken their power to transform the mine. One retrenched Zulu worker whom I interviewed in 1995—and who was not connected to Inkatha or to the squatter camp Injalo—claimed that he had heard Xhosa roommates, presumably the amabutho, plotting before Easter.

DONHAM: Who actually organized the attack on the Zulus?
S: Here I do not want to tell a lie. There were ten to fifteen people inside, people who were "blind" [township slang for "terrible," "feared"]. I can't tell you who they were. I wasn't watching this thing. I was doing my own "smuggling" [illegal activity].
D: So when did the ten to fifteen become visible?

s: About April last year it started when they were holding meetings. These ten to fifteen would have their own meetings inside. And at the very same time as NUM was having its own meetings.

D: The ten to fifteen were having meetings inside the hostel? Were they secret?

s: Yes, management didn't know about them. But the known meeting would be by the shop stewards of NUM. So the ten to fifteen would know about that meeting. They would take that to their group, and then they would influence others that NUM was wrong.

D: But the NUM guys would know about these people holding meetings? Would they go to these meetings?

s: Yes, they knew about these meetings. But sometimes they didn't go. NUM would take what was said in the meetings of the ten to fifteen and report to management. That is what was happening in the hostel.

D: So how were they having secret meetings?

s: They would just sit in a way that you wouldn't recognize that they were having a meeting. Other groups wouldn't know about their meetings. That way you would see them lying on their stomachs, and you wouldn't think, ah, there is a meeting.

D: How did you hear about these meetings?

s: Well, most of the time I was inside the hostel. I had friends who were attending these meetings. Others, I was staying with them in the room, and I heard them when they discussed things.

D: So they, the roommates were Xhosa?

s: Yes, Mpondo and Xhosa.

D: So these meetings planned to get rid of the Zulus?

s: The plans were made just before Easter. For things to go well on the mine, we must get rid of this union [UPUSA] and its people [the Zulus]. When things get better, we'll bring them back. That's what they were saying.

At another point in the interview, the man explained, "The thing that caused the problem was the unions. I can say that. Then UPUSA already existed and many people had joined UPUSA. The NUM gang saw that the UPUSA gang was strong. They could even take whites to court. After being taken to court, the whites would stop what they had been doing. Now the NUM gang said that they must take an opportunity to oust those people [UPUSA]. So that they would remain and be able to fix the problems on the mine."

So, frustration over wages and work issues, classic working-class concerns, appear to have been part of the motivation for the expulsion of the Zulus from the compound in April.[1] But this issue, real as it was, may not have been the only one. After all, the amabutho were workers of a special sort. As the example of moneylending shows, the informal pursuits of workers at Cinderella could offer higher rewards than mine salaries. The amabutho could make coercion pay by dominating the compound and its surrounds (the expanding squatter camps were a part of their space as well). Any other group who could exercise coercion could, ipso facto, become a competitor. By 1994, the only other such group was the Inkatha core.

As politicking at the national level heated up in early 1994 and Bloody Monday was brought into the compound via television news, it appears that certain members of the amabutho saw an opportunity to eliminate a potential rival—who also happened to represent an opposing political position at the national level. The rumor of a possible Inkatha attack on the compound during Easter weekend seems to have been manufactured. But, if so, its dissemination instantly unified the non-Zulu workforce and served to disguise what actually took place—namely, the amabutho's own aggression on Good Friday. Once again, the nature of the compound has to be taken into account: its social density, so effectively captured by Santu Mofokeng's photographs, made rumor a powerful weapon. Through rumor, the amabutho, led by ten to fifteen men, could mobilize many more. On Easter Sunday, over a thousand workers poured out through the gate to confront the returning Inkatha Zulu.

If the shaft stewards, as Madezi contended, used the amabutho in the organization of the union, the reverse must also have occurred. Because of its power to intimidate other workers in the compound, the regiment could dictate to the shaft stewards—as they apparently did during the 1993 strike. Indeed, the amalgamation of amabutho and the NUM at Cinderella explains local union politics in a way that is impossible to understand otherwise. The Cinderella murders therefore bear a final retelling, this time from the point of view of the amabutho.

On Good Friday, the regiment may have attacked any Zulu worker they could find, but their primary target was the Inkatha core of fighters. In this, they were motivated not by ethnicity (they had no problem with the Zulus who retained their jobs) or solely by national politics (though the latter must have added a layer of incentive). They were concerned about their own ability to control the compound and its environs—and to be seen as doing so. Performance and display were not byproducts in this context. They were themselves the point.

After the clash on Easter Sunday, the compound manager, Mr. Robinson, took the first step in "ethnicizing" the conflict, when he separated out Zulus from the compound on the basis of mine records. Afterward, some of those workers continued to feel sufficiently at ease in the compound, even after the attacks on Good Friday and the clash on Easter Sunday, that they returned to drink with their friends at the bar inside the compound.

The NUM shaft stewards at Cinderella took the next step in making the conflict ethnic. The majority of the Zulus taken from the compound were NUM members, but on the Monday after the Easter confrontation, the local NUM committee refused to represent their Zulu members.[2] Beholden to the amabutho, the shaft stewards—with Big Boy in attendance—explained, "The whole issue with the Zulus started when there were rumours that the Inkatha Freedom Party would attack employees in the hostel. Employees were threatened by the Zulus the previous week."[3] Management asked for the stewards' suggestions of how to proceed. After a recess in which the union representatives caucused, they responded, "He explained that the Zulus are not wanted in the workplace by other employees. The representative explained that the NUM members are here to work not to fight."[4] Management went immediately, on 4 April, to another meeting, with ten representatives chosen from the Zulus just separated out of the compound. Asked for their side of the story, the Zulus described being attacked by "Pondos in blankets." One Zulu reported that "On Friday night, Pondos were patrolling the hostel. As a result on Saturday morning, there were Zulus who left the hostel because they were scared of being attacked."[5]

Management quickly presented two proposals, on the first day after the Easter conflict: (1) that the Zulus could go home for a "cooling-off" period over the time of the approaching national elections; or (2) that the Zulus could accept a no-fault retrenchment package—leave pay plus R500, along with one week's payment for each year of service. Both were based on the assumption that it was the national political campaign that had divided the workforce. The first was premised on the hope that after political passions had dissipated, Zulus might be brought back to work, but this framing overlooked the stakes of the conflict as far as the amabutho were concerned: having chased away their rivals in the compound, they were not prepared to see them return.

In the ensuing days of negotiations in April, the Zulus themselves proposed mediation involving all of the political parties and labor unions involved at Cinderella, and management quickly agreed to pay the costs for IMSSA to carry out this process. But when management took this proposal to the NUM shaft stewards (whose participation clearly was required for any solution), the local committee postured and delayed: "NUM would like to play a neutral role in this issue. NUM is not prepared to meet together with the Inkatha Freedom Party and KwaZulu Government as we are not a political party"—never mind that NUM was the most political of unions, in full alliance with the ANC.[6] Pressed to join the mediation by management, the shaft stewards asked that a written description of the mediation process be sent to the NUM head office. "The union would like to deal with the Zulu formally."[7]

Over a hundred NUM members who happened to be Zulus had just been evicted from the compound. They were not working and were clearly in danger of losing their jobs. If labor issues had been the primary motivation for the shaft stewards, how could they have been so indifferent to the plight of their own (Zulu) members? So unconcerned, in fact, that they did not even consider the Zulus to be members? The NUM had long been, in alliance with the ANC, involved in the struggle for black liberation, but at that moment, a certain view of black nationalism trumped labor issues. By that point, all Zulus were seen as potential traitors to the nation.

After it was clear that management would receive no support from the shaft stewards for an investigative mediation—which had, after all, the potential to reveal the role of the amabutho—mine officials were pushed back to their original offer of a cooling-off period, or retrenchment. But because Mangosuthu Buthelezi, the leader of the IFP, had, at the very last minute, agreed to join the national election process, the proposed cooling-off period began to look like a more workable solution to management. The Zulus, many of whom were just beginning to understand the precariousness of their situations, were outraged. None wanted to accept the cooling-off period, even though they would be paid. "Why does management not get others to talk? They [other workers] are chasing other nations out. Zulus haven't attacked anyone. Who says the situation will change when we return. If we go home and others work, will that work out?"[8] Such fears proved to be well founded. They reflected the knowledge of workers who had lived in the compound, who knew how it was organized. After a certain amount of blustering, the Zulu workers reluctantly accepted the paid home stay, and they were shipped to KwaZulu on 15 April, with a guarantee of reemployment on 20 June—after the elections.

The supposed cooling-off began. When the elections took place peacefully, toward the end of April, and Buthelezi and the IFP joined the new coalition government—to the amazement of the world—mine managers turned optimistic, believing that the conditions that had produced the tensions at Cinderella had been significantly alleviated. But more was at stake than they realized. For the amabutho, the contest had turned into an exercise in dominance in the compound. Black mine workers had long celebrated their masculinity, as evidenced by their ability to survive the difficult and dangerous work underground (blacks who worked on the surface were often dismissed as "women"), so that contests for power among workers inevitably involved issues of masculine honor.

The solution that management had been forced to accept apparently offended that sense of honor. From the amabutho point of view, the Zulus had been sent home over the period of the elections on a paid vacation—while other workers were left to toil in their places. One story that I collected from several workers in the compound asserted that a Zulu returning on Soweto Day had proceeded to the bar, where he bragged drunkenly, "Yes, the Zulus are back. We were paid, while you guys worked for us." Whether any such provocation was ever made is difficult to say. At the very least, the story of the bigheaded Zulu appears to encapsulate the anxieties of the amabutho in their role as controllers of the compound. The Zulus—with the help of management now—had been placed in a position from which they could potentially condescend to the amabutho. Thus, far from cooling things off, the company's solution began to heat things up.

Aware of amabutho resentment, the NUM shaft stewards petitioned management to pay the rest of the workers the two month's pay that the Zulus had just received, but management considered this demand to be completely out of line. After the NUM had refused to become involved in solving the conflict, the company had gone to great effort to provide the conditions in which all workers could keep their jobs. From the perspective of mine management, the NUM was now using the conflict in the most irresponsible way. But the local NUM committee was not simply a labor organization. It was intertwined with the amabutho, and the amabutho reflected the social structure of the all-male compound, its world of gangs, and displays of force. In that context, the company's well-meant solution in fact destabilized the competition for determining male status.

Against the backdrop of the euphoria that developed in South Africa after the elections, mine management prepared for the return of the Zulus. During a meeting with the NUM shaft stewards on 24 May, management explained "that the Zulu employees will return to the mine on June 20, 1994, and management wants the Zulu employees to return to work when they arrive." The NUM representative "stated that he cannot comment at this stage about the Zulus' issue. He explained that his union's head office is busy with discussions regarding the Zulu issue—he will meet with his head office and give feedback to management at the next meeting."[9]

At the next meeting, on 7 June, Fabian Nkumane, the regional organizer from the NUM head office, was present, and when the Zulu issue came up, the minutes of the meeting recorded, "The NUM said that workers were unhappy that the Zulus were given two months' paid leave while other workers had to work. Some workers wanted to kill Zulus they said."[10] At the subsequent meeting between NUM and management, on 16 June—the very day of the murders—Nkumane would claim that the minutes of the 7 June meeting had misquoted him. At the very least, the regional organizer was attempting to impress on management just how strongly the workers felt—or at least some of them. In fact, the two-month pay issue created tensions between Nkumane and the workers at Cinderella, so much so that later he would tell the company that the union might not be able "to control the workers."[11]

Unbeknown to the NUM and Charles du Toit at management's head office, on 10 June local mine management met with representatives of the Zulus, who now presented themselves not as the old KwaZulu government but simply as the "Amakhosi," the Zulu chiefs. Management agreed that the date for returning the Zulus should be pushed forward to 15 June so as to accommodate the processing of all the workers. Lulled perhaps by the talk of reconciliation in the new South Africa and distracted by the yearly wage negotiations that were moving into high gear, local management did not notify the NUM shaft stewards of the change in date. When the first Zulu workers showed up at Cinderella on the 15th, no one on the NUM committee was expecting them.

Only on the following day, Soweto Day itself—the day of the murders—were the shaft stewards briefed on the return of the Zulus. At around 3:00 in the afternoon, management gathered with the NUM committee (including Big Boy). The regional organizer Nkumane asked once again that all workers be given an extra two months' salary. After industrial relations officers explained why it was impossible to respond to such a request, the general manager himself came into the meeting to introduce the idea of a peace pledge to be signed by all workers. The returning Zulus were already signing the document. The general manager asked for the assistance of the NUM in getting all of the workers to sign the pledge. Nkumane replied that the union committee was hardly opposed to the pledge—like everyone else in South Africa, they were committed to peace—but he objected to the unilateral way in which the pledge had been formulated. "It would have made sense if management had said let's come together, and this is our proposal on peace. The way that management is presenting this, I don't think it will be productive." After pressing the issue and being stymied, the general manager grandly proposed that at least those present at the meeting, beginning with himself, could sign. The NUM committee caucused and the minutes of the meeting recorded their refusal: "The representative expressed his gratitude for the caucus. He stated that unfortunately the peace pledge was presented at a wrong time. Even if we signed the paper, it will serve no purpose. We will take the paper to the workers and discuss it with them. We will give management feedback."[12]

Murder constituted the feedback, for after the television news that evening, the killing commenced. The clumsiness with which local management had handled the issue—that is, the unexpectedness with which the Zulus reappeared in the compound—may have added determination to the anger of the amabutho. In any case, the return of the Zulus had put the masculine honor of the amabutho to the test.

While ordinary workers would have been happy to receive an additional two months' salary, there is no evidence of widespread resentment against the Zulus for having been sent home with R500 a month, which was minimal pay. Had the Zulus been allowed to work, most would have earned much more than that. The Zulus themselves did not consider their paid home stay a benefit; they resisted it to the last minute. For the amabutho, the issue was not simply about pay—it involved their sense of position within the compound and its hierarchy.

Even taking these factors into account, some residue of incomprehensibility remains. The expulsion of the Zulus from the compound on Good Friday was one matter — the murders on Soweto Day were another. To some degree, the ratcheting of the conflict was a product of the process itself. Having chased the Zulus away, the amabutho was now vulnerable to counterattack if the Inkatha core were allowed to reside once again inside the compound. Fear and self-preservation can be powerful motives for murder, but something of the amabutho's worldview must also be appreciated. According to the traditional black understanding of the equation between blood and money on the mines, mine management once upon a time sacrificed coins to the snake who owned the earth so that death could be prevented and gold could be removed. But after many years of struggle against apartheid, the moral valences in the equation had been transformed: mine management was now understood to be like a witch, a vampire, a bloodsucker who trafficked in blood — for money.

Those black workers, like the Inkatha core, who seemed to ally with management at the moment of national liberation came, therefore, to be seen in a similar light — but perhaps as even more evil and witchlike than the company. It is impossible to know what went through the minds of those who beat, slashed, and stabbed Zulus who lay cringing on the ground that evening of Soweto Day 1994, I did not observe or interview the murderers, but the ferocity of the killings does suggest that some notion of moral purification, of wiping away the evil within the compound — and within the nation — may have been present.

The morning after the murders, everything had changed. Management was horrified. The extent of their misjudgment must have been clear. And the stakes for the NUM had changed as well. A new regional organizer, P. E. Mdeletshe, himself a Zulu, was immediately dispatched to the mine. (Madezi would not reappear at Cinderella until after the Zulus had been removed from mine property.) Mdeletshe reversed local union policy by reaching out to the Zulu workers (so much so that local shaft stewards apparently began to feel uneasy).

Given the pattern of events and given their sources of surveillance, management must have begun to suspect the role of certain NUM shaft stewards in the violence at Cinderella. But what could they do? In their view, the future of the mine depended on the NUM. In the aftermath of the murders, management met three times with the local NUM committee before meeting with the Zulus themselves. Four days after the murders, on Monday, 20 June, management finally expressed its regrets to the Zulus. It then conveyed two proposals from its meetings with the NUM: first, that the NUM shaft stewards meet with the Zulus; and second, that the two groups carry out a joint investigation into the violence, with the help of the clergymen. "The chairman [for management] asked that a committee be elected to discuss their problems with the NUM committee. He explained that an urgent meeting is scheduled for 4:00 and asked if the representatives were ready, they must bring forward their complaints to the meeting. The chairman explained that management would only play a neutral role in the mediation."[13]

Whereas the NUM had invoked its "neutrality" in April, it was management who took that stance after the murders. The head of UPUSA was distressed: "The representative asked why management would not be present in the mediation? He explained that the Zulu employees would not attend the meeting if management was not present because management was part of the problem. The representative asked for an independent mediator to assist with both parties' problems. The representative complained that management doesn't want to take action against other employees — there have been no arrests."[14] As the meeting continued, the Zulus eventually agreed to meet the NUM shaft stewards, but on condition that arrests be made first: "The Zulu representatives have agreed to meet with the NUM committee to mediate about their problems. The representative explained that some of the attackers can be identified. He asked that those people be arrested before the mediation starts. The Zulu employees are only prepared to mediate if those people are arrested. He stated that the Zulu employees are prepared to make statements to identify the people who attacked them."[15]

The Zulus then asserted that some of the attacks had taken place in the presence of management's own indunas in the compound, and "they asked that employees in section D be questioned about the attacks because the Zulu employees believe that it was those employees who started the attacks on the Zulus." Section D of Cinderella contained both the offices of the NUM shaft stewards and the room in which many of the amabutho were housed. In response, management agreed to call the South African Police to receive statements from the Zulus. These statements were to provide the basis for the arrests made after all of the Zulus had been retrenched.

Had management been in firm control of the situation, they would likely have instituted their own inquiry into what had happened, and they would have passed on the results to the South African Police, as they had done in the case of white violence the previous year, when van Zyl had shot a Mozambican in the cage. But with the NUM possibly implicated in the events of June 16th, the company was faced with an uneasy situation. Above all, it was worried about the survival of its enterprise. During the month of mediation that followed the murders, management repeatedly expressed concern that if the clergymen and police were not careful, they could provoke a strike. And, indeed, though there is no indication that management understood the role of the amabutho, the latter could easily have organized such a strike. In the end, no internal investigation took place, and in this vacuum, capitalist rationality met the Christian rhetoric of reconciliation at Cinderella—as it was soon to do in the wider South African transition. The needs of the first would find some fulfillment in the second. The efflorescence of discourse around reconciliation would serve to distract attention from the sacrifices and rank injustices that were being entailed in the restructuring and relegitimizing South African capitalism.

By Wednesday, 22 June, management had received agreement from both the NUM and the Zulus that they would meet under the aegis of a local committee of clergymen. Thus, the Zulus had been pressured into meeting without management present and without prior arrests of the perpetrators. The meetings were presided over by a man I shall call Rev. Mokoena, a member of an interracial committee of clergymen sponsored by the South African Council of Churches, who had been involved in attempts to quell the violence on the East Rand. Rev. Mokoena would later testify in Industrial Court on behalf of the retrenched Zulus. There, he came across as somewhat disorganized and sometimes misinformed about the conflict, as he himself would admit in court, but utterly idealistic about the possibility of the moral transformation of individuals and clear about where blame should lie in the case of the Soweto Day murders: the deaths were management's fault.[16]

At the conclusion of almost three days of testimony, in which the advocate for the company made Mokoena look increasingly clumsy as a mediator, the presiding judge politely asked the reverend, a year after the violence at Cinderella, "Are you still involved in peace work of a similar nature?" Mokoena responded,

> Actually since we ended up these matters, I've been involved in the Springs problem in KwaThema where . . . [people] killed each other,

more than a hundred students were killed. And I brought peace in that community. Today students are back in the classrooms, they are attending classes. There is peace in that community. People in the hostel of KwaThema, they were nearly actually thrown into a conflict with the township. I had a meeting of IFP people, together with other organizations. I've established a peace and reconciliation committee in that community. It is working effectively. I'm leaving this weekend for Durban. I've been called to come to help them. With the after-effects of the Second World War, the fall of the Berlin [Wall], people, the churches who find that they cannot reconcile their people now, they have called me. We are a team of ten people leaving on this Saturday to go to help those people. So I've been quite involved in this process since then.[17]

As with the Truth and Reconciliation Commission soon to unfold on the national stage, a distinctively Christian rhetoric began to supplement labor relations and laws about murder as the framework for response to the Cinderella violence.[18] In the case of the East Rand ministers, that rhetoric emphasized, as well, the centrality of the suffering of the poor and the oppressed, an emphasis that made it difficult for the ministers to consider management's concerns—for example, timetables and paying unproductive workers—on the same plane as preserving the lifework of black laborers.

In his personal notes during the mediation, Rev. Mokoena noted that another clergyman assisting him had "reiterated his divine role as a mediator."[19] In Industrial Court, Mokoena spoke of his own role "in preparing souls" for reconciliation.[20] (The ministers were concerned not only with the Cinderella murders, but also with the recent genocide in Rwanda, about which they conferred between meetings at Cinderella.) At Cinderella, Rev. Mokoena soon had NUM shaft stewards and Zulu representatives taking oaths for peace. Significantly, by that point, Big Boy, who had been among the most faithful of NUM shaft stewards in meetings, had disappeared from the deliberations.

> The Chairman proposed that leaders should make a solemn statement that they will work and build peace among their followers. Mr. Hudson Bunzi [NUM shaft steward] stood up and made a solemn promise. Mr. Zola Mayekiso [NUM shaft steward] supported him. Mr. Milton Ngema [Zulu and leader of Inkatha in the compound] made a statement that as a Catholic parishioner, he had not spilt anyone's blood. Therefore, he would work for peace. He was supported by Mr. Bongani

Nxumalo [Zulu, resident of Injalo squatter camp after the conflict and probably also an Inkatha member].[21]

The difficulty was that the ministers trusted so much in reconciliation that they expected the committee of ten—five NUM shaft stewards and five Inkatha Zulus—to identify the murderers. Under prodding by management, Rev. Mokoena had agreed that the South African Police should make no arrests until the ministers had accomplished their mission of peace. But the unlikelihood that the NUM shaft stewards would in fact identify amabutho murderers meant that Mokoena's (and management's) request to the police *not* to make arrests until the mediation had been accomplished, in effect, doomed the process. Without arrests of the perpetrators, the Zulus would be prepared to return to work only if they were moved out of Cinderella and given accommodation in the company's other, much smaller hostel at Far East, a situation in which they would be the overwhelming ethnic majority (approximately 350 out of 500). This is what the Zulus demanded. However, from the very beginning of the conflict in April, the company had made it clear that they were not prepared to set up a "Zulu" compound at Far East, which would, they claimed, only set the stage for more conflict (and, indeed, the amabutho would probably have seen any such move as provocative). Thus, even as the ministers prepared souls for reconciliation, they overlooked how their own measures, in fact, prevented a solution of the conflict. Their trust in the power of personal transformation worked against any such realization.

Not far into the mediation, the ministers, the Zulus, and the NUM (the company was absent) arrived at a convenient point of agreement: that the cause of the Cinderella murders was the divide-and-rule practices of mine management. This conclusion reflected the confluence of multiple interests. For the NUM committee, it deflected attention away from the fact that they had abandoned their Zulu members in April. For the Zulus, it emphasized their opposition to management in accepting the paid home stay in the first place. And for the ministers, the story fit into a larger (in some ways, justified) master narrative about apartheid: the black nationalist story. According to Rev. Mokoena's final report, "After mediating about this whole problem, we found that the option taken by management [in sending the Zulus on home stay with pay] created the whole problem. We believe that if this matter had been handled jointly with the NUM, it would not have created the kind of problem we are now facing. The matter should have been attended to purely as a labour matter, not being politicized and tribalised."[22] According to this narrative, it was management who had "tribalized" the issue. The ministers' interpretation of the conflict recast the situation, in which responsibility was distributed in the most complex of ways, as a matter of black and white.

Not long into the mediation, mine management lost all confidence in Rev. Mokoena. They were alarmed by some of his proposals, such as identifying the perpetrators of violence through a mass meeting of Zulus and Cinderella inhabitants. And even though the parties had begun to meet, there was no clear solution that would allow the Zulus to return safely to Cinderella compound. Not just management, but also the compound residents, according to an NUM mass meeting, rejected the idea of a Zulu-dominated hostel at Far East. By early July, management had decided that the only way to end the impasse was simply to retrench the Zulu workers, and on 13 July, it made a formal decision to do so.

For the ministers, management's decision to fire the Zulus was devastating. They were overcome by the sheer injustice of firing the victims of violence. The ministers contacted supporters abroad with the news, some of whom had just been to South Africa to observe the elections, in late April. The ministers issued a release to the South African press on the eve of 13 July.

> The East Rand Council of Churches is outraged and shocked by the decision taken by Cinderella mine to expel 350 Zulu speaking workers as from tomorrow. Our regional Organising Secretary Rev. Peter Mokoena was called by the local Peace Committee to mediate the problem. Through a mediation process, we managed to bring the two groups together, namely a Zulu-speaking group and a Xhosa-speaking group. A committee of ten people was established to implement the process of reintegrating the 350 workers who ran away during the conflict.

> We strongly condemn the inhuman decision of expelling poor people who have come to fend for their families. We view this decision as a senseless act spelling doom for the families of the expelled workers. It is our opinion that management is not happy to see the estranged groups coming together. However slow that process has been, it was taking the workers towards the future and the day when they will be one without thought of seeing one another as a Zulu or a Xhosa, as perceived by management. We are appealing to management to stop the system of divide and rule.

Our involvement in the process of peace and reconciliation does not mean that we are neutral. The church is always on the side of the poor and oppressed. We are biased towards justice. For us, justice is like an anchor of a ship during the storms at sea. We are shocked by the attitude of management of not being prepared to give us a grace period of 48 hours to finalise the process we have started.[23]

The ministers staged a sit-in in the offices of the mine and declared that they would not leave until management gave them an additional forty-eight hours to bring the workers together. "If management buses the workers out, they can bus the South African Council of Churches out," declared Rev. Mokoena.[24] When management assented, even giving the ministers more time than they had requested, Mokoena was effusive. The abbreviated minutes of the meeting recorded his response: "Don't have words to thank management. Very pleased. Thank management for the spirit of brotherhood. Praying for management. Send apologies if harm caused not intentional. Thank NUM, Mr. Mvelase, Prince Zulu and Mr. Mzizi for their role. May God forgive everyone for the mistakes that have been made. Not here to put the blame on management, not looking at the colour of skin."[25] But Rev. Mokoena *did* blame management. He had written so in his final report and in releases to the press, issued that very day, and he would reiterate that belief in court approximately a year after the event. From his perspective, management's system of divide and rule was responsible for the murders.

In some larger sense, of course, the migrant-labor system, apartheid, and the mines' construction of black ethnicity *were* responsible. They provided the indispensable background to the Cinderella murders; the killings could not have occurred, as they did, without that background. But Rev. Mokoena's moralism obscured the active participation of some black actors, the awful ironies of the situation. Because he could not appreciate these complexities, the reverend could not devise a solution that would effectively redress the situation. As another minister on his team suggested in one of the meetings, what was needed was an appreciation of how the mine as a capitalist enterprise was being restructured. The mine had once, not long before, run the compound as a dormitory for "boys," but in 1994 it was seeking to escape the role of patriarch and to create new systems of control that hailed black workers as modern individuals. As the company retreated from its old roles in the compound, it created a space in which ethnic gangs could flourish. At Cinderella, the amabutho stepped into that space. And when, during the last moments of the South African transition, Cinderella called the NUM to unionize its workforce, the regional organizer made the tactical decision to use the amabutho as enforcers. In a situation that increasingly looked like war, as national political parties struggled with negotiations while participating in violence, this decision may have seemed a wise one. But that decision had its consequences: the amabutho began to use the NUM for its own purposes.

These dynamics cannot be captured by a story in black and white. To be sure, Rev. Mokoena was not given the time or the resources to establish a more complex narrative, and it is possible that management may have chosen the reverend with just this in mind. But in any case, in failing in the mediation, he and the other ministers opened the way for the company and the NUM to sweep the matter from sight: that is, to let the amabutho get away with murder.

Compared with other tragedies in the South African transition, the Cinderella murders were insignificant (if, indeed, tragedies can be prioritized). A year later, even the Zulus themselves had forgotten a considerable amount of the detail. In the shadow of a nearby mine dump, under eucalyptus trees, its streets arrayed at right angles and its houses numbered and roofed with plastic sheet, Injalo was a sad approximation of proletarian dreams (fig. 19). But unlike in the compound, informal shops sold chilled soft drinks and white bread, and children played in its streets, and women lived in its houses (figs. 20–22).[26] Injalo's political alignment in 1975 is illustrated by figure 23, in which the squatter camp's Inkatha regiment readies to attend a rally in an adjacent township.

It took literally years to settle the case in Industrial Court, and in May 1996, the Zulus were given an addition to their retrenchment packages (depending on the extent of their unemployment after they were fired). In summing up for UPUSA, Advocate Kuny made an impassioned plea, arguing that, given the black unemployment rate in the country and the fact that many of the retrenched Zulus would probably never again find formal employment, the only way to compensate the workers was to reinstate them in their jobs. But Judge Shear was reluctant to take this alternative and to put himself in the position of ordering a settlement that could cause yet more violence. In his judgment, he asked, "How do I know that if the Zulus were to return to the hostel the same fate which awaited them on the night of 16 June will not befall them again?"[27]

19. Injalo squatter camp (photo by author)

20. A spaza, or informal shop, at Injalo (photo by author)

21. *A young girl at Injalo (photo by author)*

22. *A former mine worker's wife at Injalo (photo by author)*

23. *An* IFP *rally at Injalo (photo by author)*

THE AFTERMATH

"They Were Enjoying Our Freedom."

WERE THE SOWETO DAY MURDERS at Cinderella isolated events with no larger significance? Or were they in fact symptomatic of processes created by national liberation in South Africa? To begin to investigate this question, I would like to draw attention to three interconnected cases of violence that occurred on the West Rand two years later, in 1996. Unlike the Cinderella murders, the killings at East Driefontein, Leeudoorn, and Northam mines were so numerous that they could not be ignored by the public. President Mandela appointed a commission of inquiry, headed by Judge J. F. Myburgh, on 12 September 1996. Over the preceding two months, 42 black workers had been murdered and 203 injured in fighting that had cost an estimated 65 million rand. Like other commissions on violent events in South Africa, this one was directed by lawyers and, by the terms of its reference, could sit for only ten days. During that time, the commission produced a transcript of almost a thousand pages. Three policemen from the West Rand, four Gold Fields managers, one NUM official from the head office, an independent social anthropologist (Kent McNamara), an economist from the University of Cape Town, and one hostel resident (a local UWUSA shaft steward and chairman of the IFP at East Driefontein) gave testimony.

At all three mines, NUM members had turned on the Zulus in their midst—even Zulus who were members of the NUM—attacking and attempting to expel them from the compounds. According to management at Northam, a platinum mine (the other two were gold operations), an NUM shaft steward had aroused the compound against the Zulus by spreading a rumor that management had hired Zulus to kill members of the NUM. As at Cinderella, a rumor preceded an attack— which was in fact directed at the Zulus.

The clashes at each of these mines occurred after a rapid process of unionization by the NUM within a management group, Gold Fields, that had previously resisted it. As in the Cinderella case, the three conflicts began as yearly wage negotiations heated up and as local NUM branch committees attempted to put pressure on management. And in each case, the dispute appears to have begun as tensions developed between the recognized union, the NUM, and a minority union—in these cases, UWUSA, UPUSA's better-known, Inkatha-linked cousin. From reflecting union rivalries, each conflict, like the one at Cinderella, rapidly "ethnicized" and turned into a campaign against all Zulus.

In his presentation to the commission, the NUM official from the head office tried to widen the focus, deflecting attention from the immediate details of the incident to what he saw as the "underlying" causes—what some anthropologists have more recently called forms of "structural violence."[1] There had been many instances of violence on the mines since the 1970s. What triggered each case was in itself almost insignificant—a drunken argument over an insult, a fight over a woman. To focus solely on such details was, according to the union man, "to blame the victim." What was critical to understand were the deeper causes of the violence—the system of compounded, migrant labor inherited from apartheid and particularly the ways that Gold Fields continued to use apartheid practices of divide and rule in relation to its black employees. The economist who testified to the commission amplified on these points: "The simple but essential argument of this submission is that these compounds or, as I tend to call them, labor batteries are so abnormal that they are highly volatile places, liable to explode at any moment lit by a spark of anger, fuelled by any one of a dozen possible grievances."[2] That line was taken up by the ANC minister of labor when he discussed the report of the commission in parliament on 6 November 1996. After accepting the recommendations of the commission, the minister pointed out, "The Commission of enquiry confirms what we have long known. If you house thousands of men in single sex accommodation, divided on ethnic lines, then trouble will follow. As the NUM has said, 'If people are treated like animals, they will behave like animals.'"[3]

Thus, a great deal of the commission's attention was directed at Gold Field's policy of housing black workers along ethnic lines: Zulus in block FF, Sothos in BB, and so forth. This way of structuring the compound had been universal in the 1950s. By the mid-1990s, Gold Fields was probably the only mining group that continued this practice. But in what sense were compounds "abnormal"? They can be deemed so only when measured against an assumed standard of free wage labor—which is then naturalized by this terminology. And were compounds "powder kegs," just waiting go off? Surely not during the 1950s and 1960s. And, finally, were the immediate triggers of the violence so incidental that one does not need to pay attention to them? At Northam, as at Cinderella, certain local figures in the NUM had apparently spread incendiary rumors designed to cover their *own* aggression. Was this not a critical piece of information for understanding what happened?

Of the expert witnesses, only McNamara offered a deeper reading of the violence, one that effectively analyzed the role of ethnic housing in what transpired. Ironically, McNamara pointed out, what ethnic segregation allowed was a more effective resistance on the part of the Zulu minority. Unlike the case of Cinderella, where the Zulus were dispersed throughout the compound, those at East Driefontein, approximately 1,000 out of a total of almost 11,000 black workers, were housed together in their own block; when other workers attacked, the Zulus could therefore respond more effectively. The first two workers to die were, in fact, Xhosas, not Zulus. Those Xhosa deaths called for revenge, however, and over time, ethnic housing probably contributed to the longevity of the conflict and hence to the total number of deaths. The institutionalized knowledge of such an outcome—that any attack could be relatively easily repulsed and that any ensuing conflict would cost many lives, on all sides—may well have inhibited fighting under high apartheid.

Most submissions to the commission focused, then, on the continued presence of the past in the present. There were certainly burdensome legacies from apartheid, but narrating the violence in this way obscured what was actually new in the situation: namely, the vernacular black nationalism that had been created in the struggle for liberation, one that defined Zulus as unreliable and undeserving national subjects. In his decision, Judge Myburgh bristled,

> At all three mines NUM members turned on Zulu-speaking employees, including Zulu-speaking NUM members. NUM has furnished no explanation for the conduct of its members. Rather, it has adopted the stance that it need not give an explanation for what happened at each mine and that it would merely deal with what it called "the underlying causes of violence." An explanation should have been forthcoming. NUM prides

itself on its non-ethnic membership. NUM criticizes Gold Fields for what it regards as ethnic policies in regard to recruitment, housing and allocation of tasks. NUM should be sensitive to what was done to the Zulu-speaking employees, take responsibility for its members' behavior, and take positive steps to welcome the Zulu-speaking employees back onto the mines.[4]

What occurred at Cinderella in 1994 was thus not a singular event. It appears to have been a part of a wider process that unfolded at a number of sites — national liberation as it actually occurred.

How did Cinderella fare in the new South Africa? By 2005, the economic pressures on the mine had intensified. Only one out of the three shafts previously in operation continued to be worked. What had been a workforce of approximately 5,000 black workers in 1994 had been whittled down to less than 2,000: 558 from Mozambique, 95 from Lesotho, 55 from Swaziland, and 1,033 from South Africa. The mine no longer used ethnic categories to classify its workforce. While the percentage of foreign labor had declined compared to 1994, it was still significant.

More dramatic, the compound had been virtually abandoned. Only about 300 of the 1,741 black employees continued to live in the compound — the management of which had been subcontracted out by the mine. Far East Hostel, the smaller and more modern facility, had been rented out to a humanitarian organization as an AIDS hospice, but Cinderella compound remained — now in much greater disrepair. It had once been a lively, if dilapidated place. Now, it was clear that it would soon be abandoned (perhaps to be demolished and the land incorporated into the large new shopping mall that had just been built on adjacent property). Weeds had overgrown the tribal dancing arena, and the road that led to the compound gate was pitted with giant potholes.

The vast majority of the workers at Cinderella had elected to take a monthly "living-out allowance," R500, in addition to their salary, to live in the squatter camp that had mushroomed on mine property. A decade after my original fieldwork, the camp had expanded beyond all recognition. Along the way, it had reintegrated ethnic groups that had been pulled apart by the East Rand War. For example, one of the Zulus I had interviewed earlier in Injalo now lived in Ramaphosa squatter camp. Injalo, the old Zulu squatter camp, had moved and renamed itself Nxumalo, after the head of UPUSA. On the highway along Ramaphosa, a sign warned motorists that this was an area in which car-jackings regularly occurred.

But perhaps the most significant change at the mine was that it was now owned by a black South African, a man I shall call Mr. Molise. In a continuation of mine culture, Mr. Molise came to the mine in his Mercedes—not, however, in the large and staid version that Afrikaner managers had once preferred, but in a smaller and faster sports model. Automobiles were Molise's hobby. He had recently crashed his Lamborghini at a race track near Pretoria. Educated first in Lesotho and then in London, Mr. Molise had been active in the ANC abroad and in the anti-apartheid movement. He returned to South Africa after the ANC was unbanned, and when the new government was organized after the elections, he was appointed to a senior position in Pretoria. Gradually his business interests became more extensive, and in 1999 he left government to run his own ventures.

It was that year, 1999, that Cinderella went bankrupt. After years of warning, it finally happened: the mine's debt had grown so large, approximately 120 million rand, that the interest could not be paid, and the mine could obtain no further financing. By then, the government was a substantial stake holder in the mine (having given large loans to Cinderella in the 1980s). The state provided, as well, an annual subsidy to pump water from the bottom of the mine (and hence to preserve the other, surrounding mines on the East Rand). Molise, with majority participation from a foreign investor, put together a winning bid of 43 million rand to the bankruptcy court for Cinderella's assets. The shareholders were paid a fraction of the previous value of what they owned, and the mine reopened six months later. Through a series of transactions, Molise emerged a couple of years later as the majority owner of Cinderella, with enough tax credits gained from previous losses that the mine would never have to pay taxes again. A part of the bid to reopen the mine was a promise to rehire as many of the employees at the point of liquidation as possible.

Whether this transaction made "economic" sense in the usual ways that capitalists calculate is not clear. Without continued subsidy from the state and tax credits, Cinderella probably would not have been a viable enterprise in 1999. But then markets had never been "free" with respect to gold mining in South Africa—the state had always been involved. The one difference was the emergence of yet another fraction of the South African capitalist class—black men like Mr. Molise who used their contacts with the state and the ruling political party to build new business empires. In the middle of the twentieth century, significant numbers of Afrikaners, aided by the apartheid state, had joined the ranks of the English-speaking captains of industry. Now, black capitalists did so.

To be successful, Mr. Molise had not only to cultivate relations with the new state, but also to manage relations with the workforce, with the NUM as its representative. Racial and even some gender barriers had been removed (by 2004, some thirty women worked underground). But what one might term class struggle remained at Cinderella. When the workforce was dramatically reduced in October 2002, as Mr. Molise was taking over as majority owner, a four-day strike ensued in which the mine, according to its calculations, lost 9 million rand.[5] In the confrontation, three workers were killed by mine security and many more were injured before order could be restored. And in February of the following year, an incident of apparent arson took place underground and cost the mine another 15 million rand. (Whether the fire was the result of worker sabotage was never ascertained.)

The NUM, with a membership of roughly half of the black workforce at Cinderella, continued as the recognized union in 2005. The union had reluctantly agreed to negotiate Cinderella wages outside the Chamber of Mines and so to accept significantly lower rates of pay compared to wealthier mines. The only other option, it seemed, was no work at Cinderella at all.

What of the amabutho? Some insisted that it had disbanded soon after 1994. With Inkatha no longer a threat and with the transition to ANC rule complete, the rationale for its existence no longer obtained. But others were not so sure. The amabutho had set up Ramaphosa squatter camp on mine property in early 1994, and after 2002, (Sotho) Mr. Molise was coming into conflict with a Xhosa-speaking gang in the camp; the group had tapped into the mine's water supply and were charging camp residents for its use.

In June 2003, the confrontation widened to include the shaft stewards of the NUM (who remained overwhelmingly Xhosa). Significantly, a reference to the Soweto Day murders of 1994 became a bone of contention. The mine had agreed to rehire as many of the old workers as possible, and the head NUM shaft steward, Elijah, was in charge of vetting former workers when there were job vacancies. By 2003, the mine needed new drillers. According to management, it had exhausted the possibility of hiring any of the remaining former miners from the surrounding area. None had presented themselves with the required qualifications and health certificate. Management proceeded to recruit outside the borders of the nation, hiring twenty new drillers from Swaziland (Swazis had made something of an ethnic niche out of drilling). But when the Swazi recruits arrived at the mine, Elijah became upset and tried to delay their processing, asserting that there had not been enough consultation. A similar situation, he pointed out, had led to the Zulu killings of 1994. Frightened by Elijah's description of those events, the Swazis asked to be returned home.

Mr. Molise was furious. He, like the Swazis, interpreted Elijah's actions and comments as intimidation. How could he run a business when union leaders were threatening workers with attack? Mine management suspended five of the most influential NUM branch-committee members, pending an investigation into charges of intimidation and disorderly conduct. Months of struggle between Molise and the NUM ensued. Regional and head offices of the union demanded that the suspensions be lifted. Meanwhile, to stir up support, the fired stewards met with workers and former workers from the camps. Tensions rose. On 16 July, a handwritten note in English and Fanakalo, in the form that management used to communicate with the workers, was found at the shaft on which Elijah had worked.

MEMORANDUM

Who are you management to suspend our President? Elijah is the President of Cinderella like it or not. Molise you know everything. Your time will come. Month end of July if Elijah did not return to work, you will see. "White blood is needed at this time!" People work as slaves. It is July now. Where is our increase? This mine will be closed forever. Management: wena zihamba lapha futhi. wena "zinya double." Wena Molise sobuya ngawe. Wena zifa nja. Elijah, Qina, Qina. From The Workers Underground.[6]

Was this "memorandum" the work of some remnant of the amabutho? Had Molise's blood turned "white" by virtue of ownership? This time, management demanded an accounting. In early August, the outside attorney appointed to adjudicate the charges found three of the five branch members guilty of intimidation as charged and recommended dismissal—which the company promptly carried out. But a strike commenced the evening after the union men were dismissed. According to management, "Violence erupted during the night of the 4th of

August 2003 when a group of men forced their way into the compound and attacked employees with sjamboks, knobkerries and pangas resulting in the murder of at least one employee and the hospitalization of several others."[7]

Once again, a determined, if relatively small, group of workers had captured the gate, and even though the significance of the compound had been reduced considerably as the squatter camps had expanded, the group proceeded to dictate what workers were said to want: the reinstatement of the three dismissed stewards. The strike was declared illegal by the courts on 6 August, but workers did not return underground until the evening of the next day, after the NUM head office and the company had agreed to refer the case of the three dismissed stewards for a rehearing by an independent arbitrator. After eight days of testimony in September and October, presided over by lawyers for both sides, the arbitrator upheld the dismissal of the most influential NUM member, the branch chairman, Elijah. The firings of the other two stewards were found to be "unfair," but the arbitrator did not reinstate them, recommending compensation instead.

The struggle between the new black-directed management at Cinderella and the NUM did not end there. October brought wage negotiations, and in that context, the head office at NUM demanded, again, that all three stewards be reinstated. In response, Mr. Molise went so far as to assert that the NUM leadership at Cinderella was unrepresentative of the workforce, particularly in its distribution across ethnic groups. When the dust of the negotiations settled, Elijah remained without work, but the other two stewards had been reinstated—on the condition that new elections of shaft stewards would be held, supervised by an independent outside authority, not by the NUM itself. At the end of April 2004, those elections were held by the Electoral Institute of Southern Africa. According to the results, the head office's candidate, the (Xhosa) steward Madume, had been defeated as the new branch chairman. Once again, the NUM head office refused to accept the result, and after they conducted their own elections, Madume became the new chairperson of the branch.

Mr. Molise interpreted this wall of support by the NUM head office (presided over by a Xhosa at that point) as ethnic patronage and, indeed, the union was increasingly beset by charges of ethnic discrimination in the decade after 2000.[8] An independent mediator agreed with Molise that Elijah's comments and actions had constituted an unacceptable threat. Let me, however, offer a different interpretation, set against the background of discourses on the nation and the system of inequality that had crystallized in the new South Africa.

Jeremy Seekings and Nicoli Nattrass have presented an examination of what they call South Africa's new distributional regime—the way that policies of the state interact with the economy to produce a characteristic pattern of social stratification.[9] They argue that before apartheid ended, in 1994, the primary basis of inequality had already shifted from race to class. The result was a pyramid with a small top composed of the upper classes (the 12 percent of households that received 45 percent of income), a broader middle strata of the core working class and others (the 48 percent who received 45 percent of income), and finally, a base of the marginally employed and the unemployed (the 41 percent of households with only 10 percent of income).[10]

Black empowerment helped to begin to integrate the top of the pyramid, where men like Molise took their place. In the middle, one finds those workers who had managed to hang onto their jobs. Labor unions are sometime thought to represent people at the "bottom" of a social system, but in the new South Africa, unions like the NUM actually represented workers in the middle. There were many, many others who were worse off—namely the majority in Ramaphosa's shack settlement. Thousands of Cinderella workers had lost their jobs after 1994, and few had gone back to the countryside (where economic opportunities were even fewer).

In part because the new ANC government continued policies from the apartheid past that favored capital-intensive growth, there was little if any job creation in the decade after liberation. Thus, the economic interests of the three layers of society diverged. The elite, particularly the black elite, benefited from the business-friendly policies of the new government and from black empowerment. The labor unions, still in alliance with the ANC, chafed at such policies, but when they demanded wage increases for their workers in the middle, they succeeded, some claimed, only at the expense of more jobs for those at the very bottom of the system. Life in Ramaphosa camp hardly improved after 1994. It only attracted more and more of the unemployed, including those beyond the borders of South Africa.

As this pattern of stratification solidified after liberation, particularly after Thabo Mbeki became president, what I call "nationalism from above" did much to obscure the economic stakes for differently positioned black South Africans.[11] Mbeki, for example, talked of two nations, one black and one white, as if black South Africans still shared the same essential interests.[12] But there was, as well, a "nationalism from below"—one less thought out, but no less passionately held, principally by those at the bottom of society—that could rouse strong feelings of betrayal directed not only at the ANC government but at others as well.

According to Gillian Hart, the interaction of these two nationalisms constitutes a central nexus in the new South Africa.

> To grasp the hegemonic power of official articulations of nationalism as well as their limits, we have to look carefully to how they work in and through ongoing invocations of the struggle for national liberation and the suffering for freedom that our people have endured. This is not just a cynical manipulation from above; it carries powerful moral weight and connects with specific histories, memories, and meanings of racial oppression, racialised dispossession, and struggles against apartheid. Precisely because official articulations of nationalism tap into popular understandings of freedom, justice, and liberation from apartheid racial oppression, they bolster the ANC state's hegemonic project. Yet the deep grounding of popular understandings of nationalism and liberation is a razor blade that cuts both ways. [It is] potentially vulnerable to the current counter-claims of betrayal.[13]

The potentially explosive mix of narratives of national redemption in a context of largely unchanged and even diminishing economic realities for a significant portion of the population provides the background for the continuation of violent patterns in post-apartheid South Africa. Unlike other so-called post-conflict societies, South Africa continues to exhibit, as Gary Kynock has argued, an unusual amalgam of crime with other spheres of life.[14] Within the more circumscribed arena of labor relations, strikes persist, unusually as violent affairs. Karl von Holdt gives part of the explanation for this continuation: "Workers articulate a somewhat inchoate but nonetheless strong sense of grievance about their location in post-apartheid society which legitimates recourse to familiar tactics of struggle, including repertoires of collective violence."[15]

With this background in place, let me return to Elijah at Cinderella in 2003. When he recounted to the increasingly apprehensive (non–South African) Swazis how Zulus had been murdered a decade before, this may have been motivated by a knowledge of just how South

Africans in the squatter camp felt, or at least, how the gang that mobilized coercion in the camp felt. In 1994, the local NUM had made a devil's pact with the amabutho: it unionized with amabutho help, but in doing so it conferred power on the amabutho in return. How the squatter camp was organized in 2003 is unclear, but we do know the camp had been founded by the amabutho. If some version of the regiment remained, the union at Cinderella could hardly expect to control it, and Elijah may well have been trying to prevent violence rather than threaten it. On this reading, support for Elijah from the NUM head office reflects not ethnic patronage but an appreciation of the compromises made by shaft stewards in the process of unionization. Neither Mr. Molise, nor the arbitrator had this knowledge, but Elijah and his union lawyer could hardly explain these connections in an official proceeding.

Violence eventually *did* occur in Ramaphosa — not against the ANC government but against black foreigners in the camp (such as the Swazis that management had attempted to bring to Cinderella). Like many other sites around Johannesburg in May 2008, Ramaphosa erupted into a pogrom against *makwerekwere* or foreigners. Two foreign black workers at Cinderella were killed in this violence. A young man who had participated in the attacks at Ramaphosa explained to reporters that the *makwerekwere* were taking jobs from black South Africans: "They were," he said, "enjoying our freedom."[16]

In 2005, I bumped into the deposed shaft steward, Elijah, who continued to live in Cinderella housing (his wife worked for the mine and so qualified for the housing). Tall and powerfully built, a man in his late thirties, thoughtful but guarded, Elijah seemed to embody the progress of national liberation. When I mentioned the amabutho of more than a decade before, he was well informed — so much so that he unconsciously alternated in English between "they" and "we" when referring to the regiment. I did not ask him whether he had been a member. Without a mine job, Elijah was running as an ANC member for a place on the local city council (a position he later won). When I asked how he felt about the past decade, about how things had changed and stayed the same, he replied that if you were outside the ANC, then you would be very disillusioned by now, but if you were inside, as he was, then you would know that the party had plans for a real transformation in the lives of black people by the time of the World Cup scheduled for South Africa in 2010.

The World Cup was recently played in South Africa, to international acclaim, but whether residents of places like Ramaphosa now see their lives as transformed is unclear. A few months after the pogroms of 2008, the ranks of the unemployed in the squatter camp were expanded yet again when underground flooding forced Cinderella to cease all underground work. The mine retrenched 1,400 workers. After more than a hundred years of operation, mining at Cinderella came to a close.

CONCLUSION

I HAVE COMPLETED MY ACCOUNT of "ethnic violence," a label that can now be understood as deceptive. At Cinderella, Xhosas did attack Zulus, but there were more than 800 Xhosa workers at Cinderella in 1994, and, at most, perhaps 150 belonged to the amabutho. Moreover, some members of that group did not participate in the killings, and there were Xhosa outside the regiment who assisted their Zulu friends in escaping. The amabutho was Xhosa-speaking, but it did not attack because of ethnic hatred; rather, it targeted the Inkatha core of Zulus, who had wreaked havoc on black communities of the East Rand. But because the distinction between Inkatha and Zulus blurred in the eyes of the amabutho, in the end all Zulus became objects of attack.

But the story has yet more layers. While the framing that the liberation struggle offers is essential, local interests also played their part, and how black nationalism interacted with those quotidian considerations is key to what happened. Leaders of the amabutho, "blind" men like Big Boy and Whitey, may have hated Inkatha, but dominating the compound also enabled them to acquire critical resources: receipts from the open-air shebeen, some control over moneylending, and so forth. When the compound was replaced by the squatter camp, similar but different opportunities presented themselves.

The way that black nationalism and economic interests intertwined in the present case provides wider insights into post-apartheid South Africa. Critical in this regard is the very notion of national liberation. Unlike, for example, the idea of social revolution which looks forward, national liberation refers backward. It denotes "freedom from"—from the past, from white domination. The content of the future is left unspecified. This blankness was probably necessary for the kind of transition that took place in South Africa in 1994. To simplify somewhat, Mandela and the ANC struck a deal to protect capitalist property at the price of giving citizenship to blacks, creating in the process a new state that mandated the rise of a small fraction of black citizens—particularly leaders of the national struggle—to the ranks of the truly wealthy and powerful. But the economic situation of many, perhaps as much as 40 percent of black South Africans, was *not* improved; to date, it may even have deteriorated, as this group has become a more or less permanently unemployed underclass.[1]

As the chasm between the promise and reality of "liberation" became ever more evident—but as a few black actors, like the new owner of Cinderella, became spectacularly successful—the pressures increased within a vernacular black nationalism to expel and expunge those who did not qualify as authentic national subjects. At the heart of any nationalism is the notion of deep fraternal bonds among national subjects.[2] As Elie Kedourie argued long ago, however, this sentiment cannot, by itself, furnish a stable foundation for the adjudication of power. Nationalism's dynamic, in situations of conflict, can turn explosively inward.

> Nationalist leaders inculcate in their followers the belief, and themselves perhaps believe, that political action will institute a reign of love in society and state. But the love which they speak of, though tender, is also merciless. Only through a tender mercilessness and a loving chastisement will men be brought to know and realize their own deepest urge, which is to love and be at one with the fellow members of their nation. It is therefore no surprise that the nationalists' avenging sword often claims more victims among their own brethren than among the alien fore. Of this many examples can be quoted, but one may now suffice: the Mau Mau killed two thousand fellow Africans as against thirty-two European civilians.[3]

Zulus at Cinderella in 1994, and again at East Driefontein, Leeudoorn, and Northam in 1996, lost their jobs, and some their lives, because they were seen by others as less than South African. By the time of the national elections of 1999, the ANC had adroitly undermined the IFP as a political force that had to be reckoned with. That process seemed complete toward the end of 2007, when Jacob Zuma, a Zulu, became president of the ANC.[4] As Zulus became more securely bound within South Africa, however, the nationalist dynamic continued to play out with respect to others on the edge of the nation, and pogroms against Mozambicans and Zimbabweans emerged in May 2008 in numerous locations around Johannesburg—including Cinderella.

It is easy to tell a story about any of these conflicts that simplifies their awful complexity—their exquisite shades of gray. Political actors at Cinderella, from mine management to union leadership to national political parties, all made decisions that did not match their ideals. Afterward, it was common practice to cover up those discrepancies with "set" stories. In nationalist narratives, the invocation of apartheid will not soon fade in South Africa since it furnishes such a convenient evil, and for virtually everyone else across our interconnected world, ethnic stories make sense before the fact. In this context, telling deep stories—that capture the dialectic between intention and consequence in particular contexts—will not automatically improve the world, but attempting to do so seems the necessary, if not sufficient, condition for hope.

POSTSCRIPT

Doing Fieldwork at the End of Apartheid

I HAVE THUS FAR EMBEDDED THEORY AND METHOD in this study, rather than separating them out for overt comment and formulation, but I will take this opportunity to be more explicit about the background and the stakes of my analysis. Perhaps most critical to note is the tradition of anthropological work in southern Africa associated with the name of Max Gluckman and the work of the Rhodes-Livingstone Institute. While anthropologists studying other areas of Africa were satisfied with functionalist accounts of self-contained social worlds, Rhodes-Livingstone anthropologists, as early as the 1940s and 1950s, fashioned analyses that emphasized cultural heterogeneity and connection to a wider political economy. Even seemingly traditional structures such as rural black households were understood as interlinked with local capitalist enterprises and the modern colonial state.[1] In many ways, this analytical vision prefigured later developments in French and North American anthropology after 1968—work more explicitly in dialogue with Marx and advanced by scholars such as Claude Meillassoux, Eric Wolf, and Sidney Mintz.[2]

For Rhodes-Livingstone scholars, the problem was that the closer a researcher got to the heart of the beast—to South Africa itself and the gold mines that dominated the entire southern region of the continent—the more difficult it became to do research. Even the rural areas of South Africa were challenging; after beginning fieldwork, Gluckman himself was expelled from Zululand, in 1939.[3] Afterward, when he assumed the directorship of the Rhodes-Livingstone Institute, its work was located not in South Africa, but farther to the north, in colonial Northern Rhodesia. There, Gluckman encouraged the formation of a cadre of students, among them A. L. Epstein and Clyde Mitchell, who would take up issues that were central to South African society—like urban settlement, ethnic relations, and trade unions—but that could not be investigated in South Africa, because of political restrictions.[4] Even in Northern Rhodesia, Epstein could not obtain permission to enter mine premises in the town he studied.[5]

This structure of colonial power affected historians as well, for archives were also controlled. In the 1960s, when Charles van Onselen began research on the history of black-labor recruitment, the institution of the compound, and the social worlds that migrant workers had created in southern Africa, it was difficult to gain access to South African archives. Like anthropologists, he turned to sites farther north—in his case, to Southern Rhodesia—that were less tightly controlled but manifested many of the same patterns found in South Africa.[6]

As the National Party consolidated power in South Africa, in 1948, ethnographic work became even more difficult, even though it must be said that a limited but distinguished tradition of local work continued. The situation began to change fundamentally only after Nelson Mandela was released from prison. When I arrived in South Africa in 1993, for example, I found an exhilarating sense of the epochal opening-up under way for scholars. Even so, it took six months of personal diplomacy to arrange access to a gold mine. I returned to Johannesburg, in 1994, to begin work just after the famous elections that had brought Mandela to power. I had obtained permission from the management of a mine I am calling Cinderella and from the union recognized to represent black workers, the NUM. I would eventually obtain permission as well from a labyrinth of organizations of mostly white workers, including the Mine Surface Officials' Association of South Africa, the Underground Officials' Association of South Africa, the South African Technical Officials Association, and the Council of Mining Unions.

The NUM was interested in my study precisely because it held out the possibility of understanding the contexts that had produced violence among black workers—of which there had been many recent instances. In a letter of permission for my research, dated 27 May 1993, the then acting general secretary of NUM, wrote,

> The mines are one of the nodes of oppression and racism in the South African economy and it will be extremely difficult to re-structure them, even once the official policy of Apartheid has been abandoned. The NUM has participated in numerous commissions of inquiry to investigate the causes of violent incidents on the mines. These inquiries are usually directed by lawyers and have a narrow focus. They are always conducted

under rigid time constraints. The union itself undertakes opinion surveys of its members on a regular basis, but these are always issue-related. We believe that a dispassionate and in-depth study of the complex social relations on a South African mine, unlinked to any particular incident, could provide valuable insights into the continuing process of change in South Africa's hallmark industry.

At that point, of course, neither I nor the union could know that a particular incident of violence would divide the black workforce at Cinderella in 1994, just after the democratic transition, and just before I was to begin my research.

That the NUM supported my proposed study is not surprising. They assumed, correctly, that I was sympathetic to their cause. But if the union's support was extended relatively easily, there was virtually no reason for a South African gold mine to allow an independent researcher to snoop around its business — a business that was steeped in a past rapidly being repudiated. Without company permission, support from the NUM was meaningless.

In the beginning, I assumed that if I were to have any chance at all of gaining access to a gold mine, it would be with the most liberal of companies, Anglo American. As early as 1975, after a series of violent clashes among its black workers, the Industrial Relations Division at Anglo had approached T. Dunbar Moodie, a South African sociologist, to carry out an ethnographic study of the compounds and workplaces at one of its mines in the Orange Free State. Moodie hired four black university graduates to do participant observation — to live in the compound and to work underground. Thus began a long-term research program that would eventually include several other sets of black participant observers, archival research, and interviews with retired miners in the countryside.[7]

When I approached Anglo American in 1993, I was not told no. Rather, it was suggested that what I needed to do was to convince Anglo mine managers that my proposed study would somehow benefit them, teach them how to do their jobs better. Even had I wanted to pursue this strategy, I had no idea how to show mine managers how to improve their business. As I began to cast about for alternatives, I attached myself to a group of local activist-scholars at the Sociology of Work Unit at the University of the Witwatersrand. There, I eventually met the director of human resources at the mining house that managed Cinderella.

Until the early 1990s, that management group had taken a far more conservative approach to labor relations than had Anglo American, but by 1993, it managed only a handful of marginal mines, in which the old ways of doing things were clearly not working. With the transition to black majority rule on the horizon, the mining house began to scramble to adapt its business to the coming new order. The new director, who had been an undergraduate sociology major at the University of the Witwatersrand and something of a student activist, was called to work at the head office toward the end of 1991, to help "modernize" labor relations.

In another life, Charles du Toit, as I call him, might have become an academic. Rather than cover up the mines' problems, he pointed them out. And he was not intimidated by critics. He realized that engaging with different points of view gave legitimacy to the process he was attempting to institute, namely, to bring the mines out of the past into the present. Given the military command structure of gold companies, I needed only his support (which he made contingent on permission from the NUM). Du Toit sent me to Cinderella because it was in the early stages of the transition that he was attempting to engineer. The general manager at the mine, the man who held overall responsibility on the spot, did as he was told, and I began fieldwork.

As such things go, my entry into a gold mine and its compounds in 1994 was conditioned by a set of unique circumstances. A couple of years earlier, I would not have been given permission, and a couple of years later, I was, in fact, denied authorization, after du Toit had left the head office. Liberal companies like Anglo American had no reason in 1994 to sponsor an independent researcher. They had led the way in changing industrial relations in the gold industry. They felt they were where they should be. And richer and more conservative companies, such as Gold Fields, had dug in their heels and were insisting that they had no problems in labor relations. They did not want anyone around telling them otherwise.

I finally arrived at the mine itself in early August 1994, several months after the murders. No other scholar had been offered the kind of access that I had stumbled into. In August, I followed white managers around, a day at a time, even going underground, two miles deep, as they did, in some of the tensest moments of my fieldwork (fig. 24). And I began to drink at the bar in the compound and to interview black workers with the assistance of an interpreter, an educated black clerk who had grown up on the mine and who spoke most of the languages

24. *Underground level 67, with the author in the background*

of the compound. (Most of these interviews were taped and later transcribed.) My request to live in the compound had been turned down. In September, I accompanied human-resources personnel from the mine to Industrial Court in Pretoria, where I first became aware of the violence that would become the subject of this book.

The mine's former Zulu employees—fired in July—were in court by September with a case against mine management. As part of its defense strategy, management flooded the court with documents. Additionally, three top officials of management at the mine, including the compound manager, testified for ten days in court, and nine Zulu workers, including the head of the IFP in the compound, were examined and cross-examined. Finally, a Christian minister, whom I have called Rev. Mokoena, and who had been involved in attempts to mediate the conflict at Cinderella, testified, as did Kent McNamara, a social anthropologist who had spent his career studying mine violence.

I supplemented review of written materials—thousands of pages of court transcripts with associated documents—with my own interviews with local NUM shaft stewards and other workers, regional organizers from the NUM head office, Zulu workers still resident around the mine in squatter camps, and management officials at various levels. Eventually, the incident of June 16th became an awful and irritating puzzle I had to try to understand, and I came to realize how my materials could be used to say something about the new South Africa and about how to read ethnic violence more generally.

The fieldwork itself provided my topic. I did not go to South Africa to study collective violence (I had intended to study the changes to the organization of production after the end of apartheid). Violence overtook me as a topic in a way not unlike the more consequential ways it overtook ordinary black workers at Cinderella. My methodology focused on gathering as many narratives of what had transpired as possible and fitting them together into what would become, in the end, my own narrative in this book. Perhaps the most difficult part of my work was reconstructing the contexts—political, economic, and ideological—in which actors had done what they did (later recalled in certain ways). Besides the inherent difficulty of reconstructing murder (never easy, for obvious reasons), complications arose from the continuing political stakes in the new South Africa of recounting just how national liberation had occurred in this case.

Elsewhere I have argued, following philosophers of history, that "telling a story" is itself what might be called a theoretical construction.[8] It imparts knowledge. Narrative "converts congeries of events into storied concatenations—a task whose object is not so much to isolate social laws as to develop an understanding of contingent connections."[9] But if this is so for analysts like anthropologists, it also true, as Bakhtin argued, for others.[10] The way ordinary people act in the world depends, in part, on *their* narrative constructions of the conditions around *them*. In other words, so-called objective reality rarely imposes itself upon human actors in a unilateral way. Therefore, analytical narratives are required to understand complex forms of collective human action. By offering stories of stories, such narratives take on depth, revealing unexpected insights.[11]

To this day, significant parts of the story of 1994 in South Africa remain untold. When the ANC was legalized, in 1990, it agreed to forego the armed struggle. By 1994, however, some ANC-aligned labor unions appear to have been secretly armed with modern weapons. This was the case at Cinderella. The amabutho, with its traditional weapons, was only a part of a wider network. In any conflict, had machetes and knobkerries failed, others with AK-47s would have been called into battle. If and when more information surfaces about those days in 1994, when the country was perhaps on the very brink of civil war, the story I have told here may need revision — perhaps in important ways. Analyses of collective violence almost inevitably arrive in this place of uncertainty. What I hope to have conveyed in this book is how to problematize the data of violence — how to read its stories without succumbing to their apparent certainties.

NOTES

PREFACE

1. Donham, *Marxist Modern*.
2. See ibid., 8–12; and Donham, "Thinking Temporally or Modernizing Anthropology."
3. See Seekings and Nattrass, *Class, Race, and Inequality in South Africa*, 340–75.

INTRODUCTION

1. In order to protect the identities of individuals I discuss, I have chosen not to use the real name of the mine. "Cinderella" was originally the name of another gold mine in South Africa, long defunct by the 1990s. The name evokes so much of mining that I have chosen to use it here. The real Cinderella, like the mine I describe in this book, was located on the East Rand. The Rand—an abbreviated version of Witwatersrand, Afrikaans for "white watershed"—was the high arc along which gold was discovered in 1886. Johannesburg evolved as the principal mining center on the Rand, eventually serving as the point from which the East and West Rand were defined.

In 1994, the owners of Cinderella consisted predominately of foreign investors, particularly large French and British banks, sometimes as representatives of retirement funds for European workers. No one controlled enough shares to determine outright the management of the mine. One of the large mining houses in South Africa owned a minority stake in Cinderella and held the management contract.

2. I use the North American term *black*, rather than *African*. In South Africa, *black* is commonly used to refer to all nonwhites, whether Indian or African or "colored" (racially mixed), for example. Since there were only a handful of Indian and colored workers at Cinderella and none in the compound, my use of *black* should not introduce confusion.

3. "Apartheid," Afrikaans for "separateness," is a shorthand expression for a (changing) bundle of racially discriminatory policies after 1948. See Seekings and Nattrass, *Class, Race, and Inequality in South Africa*, 19–20, for

a table of the different components of apartheid. On the wider process of decolonization on the African continent, see Cooper, *Decolonization and African Society*. South Africa, of course, was different from the rest of the continent in having a centuries-old and exceptionally significant degree of European settlement.

4. Quoted in Sparks, *Tomorrow Is Another Country*, 178.

5. South Africa–based academics have been in closer touch than foreign scholars with the complexities of the 1994 transition. See Bonner and Nieftagodien, "The Truth and Reconciliation Commission and the Pursuit of 'Social Truth'"; Belinda Bozzoli's account of events in the township of Alexandra, in *Theatres of Struggle and the End of Apartheid*; and Karl Von Holdt's account of the unionization of black metalworkers in *Transition from Below*. See also Marais, *South Africa, Limits to Change*; Bond, *Elite Transition* and *Against Global Apartheid*; and Alexander, *An Ordinary Country*.

6. Crush, Jeeves, and Yudelman, *South Africa's Labor Empire*; James, *Our Precious Metal*.

"Villagers," the first locally produced television program in South Africa, in 1976, was about (white) life on a gold mine. The South African Broadcasting synopsis of the first episode runs as follows.

> The Village Reef Gold Mine is being run by an elderly General Manager, Harry Styles. He, however, dies of a heart attack when he hears of yet another accident underground. Everybody expects that the Assistant General Manager, Buller Wilmot, will become the new General Manager. Unfortunately, life on the Village Reef is not quite as simple as that. The job is given to Hilton McRae, because he has higher qualifications than Buller. The Village Reef people however, believe that Hilton got the job because his wife is the daughter of the Chairman of Vaal Investments.

On the pervasiveness of mines in black music, see Coplan, *In the Time of Cannibals*; for an example of a black novel set in the mines, see Abrahams, *Mine Boy*. Wilbur Smith's *Gold Mine* is a work of white popular fiction, whose back cover reads,

> The Sonder Ditch was more than a gold mine to Rod Ironsides. It was life and death itself. His love of the gold, the mine and those who toiled deep in the belly of the earth had begun to rival even his passion for the beautiful Theresa. But there are those who wish to destroy Rod's world. Far beyond the law, and more powerful than the government, a fanatical group of financiers are plotting to flood the Transvaal mines for their own evil ends—regardless of the cost in human lives. When disaster threatens Sonder Ditch, Rod is plunged headlong into a sea of violence, greed and chicanery in a desperate race to save the previous metal of the mines upon which rests his destiny and the future of the nation.

7. Fanon, *The Wretched of the Earth*.

8. The other area of the country particularly affected by this kind of systemic violence was Zululand. On the complexity of the killing that devel-

oped in one rural area, see chap. 3 of Sarah M. Mathis's dissertation, "After Apartheid" (75–120).

9. Chipkin, *Do South Africans Exist?*, 123.

10. Bonner and Ndima, "The Roots of Violence and Martial Zuluness on the East Rand."

11. Ellis, "The Historical Significance of South Africa's Third Force."

12. Turton, introduction to *War and Ethnicity*, 3.

13. See Chipkin, *Do South Africans Exist?*

14. Fanon, *Wretched of the Earth*, 1.

15. See, for example, Kynoch, *We Are Fighting the World*.

16. At least five other major projects have been based on interviewing and participant observation in southern African mines. See Burawoy, *The Colour of Class on the Copper Mines* and "The Hidden Abode of Underdevelopment"; Gordon, *Mines, Masters, and Migrants*; McNamara, "Black Worker Conflicts on South African Gold Mines"; Leger, "Talking Rocks." Finally, the most comprehensive work is perhaps *Going for Gold*, by T. Dunbar Moodie, with Vivienne Ndatshe.

17. For an extended description of the methodological issues involved here, on which the next few paragraphs are based, see Donham, "Staring at Suffering."

18. The interdisciplinary literature on "ethnicity" is sprawling, yet many analysts have not attended to what I would call the complexity of ethnic attribution. Ethnic "groups" are rarely groups in a concrete, sociological sense. Rather, individuals in specific contexts claim or impute connection to ethnic categories. Some of these contentions will fall flat, while others will have far-reaching social effects. In this book I provide a narrative of how ethnic attribution came to have wide social recognition in the case at Cinderella, even though it obscured what was actually happening. As David Carr and other philosophers of history have argued, narrative is itself a kind of "theory," albeit one different from social-science generalization. See Carr, *Time, Narrative, and History*.

19. Cohen, *Colonialism and Its Forms of Knowledge*.

20. Compare to Stanley Tambiah's discussion in *Leveling Crowds*:

Two concepts that may be employed to describe the trajectory of such riots are *focalization* and *transvaluation*. These are linked processes by which a series of local incidents and small-scale disputes, occasioned by religious, commercial, interfamilial, or other issues, and involving people in direct contact with one another, cumulatively build up into larger and larger clashes between growing numbers of antagonists only indirectly involved in the original disputes. This progressive involvement of the ethnic public coincides with their coming under the sway of the rhetoric of propagandists and the horror tales of rumormongers, who appeal to larger, deeper, certainly more emotive and enduring—and therefore less local-context-bound—loyalties and cleavages, such as race, religion, language, national, or place of origin. To sum up: focalization progressively denudes local incidents and disputes of their contextual particulars, and transvaluation distorts, abstracts, and aggregates those incidents into larger collective issues of national or ethnic interest. (81)

Unfortunately, in a book that contains so many cases, how focalization and transvaluation worked in each is sometimes unclear.

21. John and Jean Comaroff take a different tack in *Ethnicity, Inc.*: "In its *lived* manifestations, cultural identity appears ever more as two antithetical things at once: on the one hand, as a precipitate of inalienable natural essence, of genetics and biology, and, on the other, as a function of voluntary self-fashioning, often through serial acts of consumption. *Both* innate and constructed. *Both* blood and choice . . . this doubling is endemic to cultural identity in the neoliberal age" (40).

22. See Carr, *Time, Narrative and History*.

23. Scarry, *The Body in Pain*; Taussig, "Culture of Terror, Space of Death."

24. Not speaking is often assumed to present it own burdens. See Caruth, *Trauma*. See also LaCapra, *Writing History, Writing Trauma*; and Jackson, *The Politics of Storytelling*.

25. Malkki, *Purity and Exile*.

26. Horowitz, *The Deadly Ethnic Riot*, 28–33. Horowitz is confident of the data: "For many incidents, there are complete accounts covering all the questions to be pursued, in multiple sources that lend themselves to factual cross-checking" (29).

27. For a comparative study that makes this point, see Eller, *From Culture to Ethnicity to Conflict*.

28. For example, Peter Novick, in *The Holocaust in American Life*, has questioned whether a too-easy popularity of Holocaust museums in the United States has contributed to an uncritical American support of Israeli policies — policies that may have spawned yet more violence.

CHAPTER 1. PICTURING A SOUTH AFRICAN GOLD MINE

1. Goldblatt and Gordimer, *On the Mines*. See also Luli Callinicos's popular history, *Gold and Workers 1886–1924*.

2. By the 1990s, the term that representatives of the South African gold industry used for black worker domiciles was *hostel*, not *compound*. I use both designations, but because the principal structure that housed black workers at Cinderella was so obviously not a modernized "hostel," I primarily use the term *compound* in this book, as did both black and white workers at the mine.

3. Mofokeng, *Santu Mofokeng*.

4. Moodie, *Going for Gold*, 119–58. See also Harries, "Symbols and Sexuality." Moodie has expanded his argument somewhat in "Black Migrant Mine Labourers and the Vicissitudes of Male Desire." On the particular role of white compound managers in encouraging male-male relations, see Beinart, "Worker Consciousness, Ethnic Particularism and Nationalism," 294.

5. Niehaus, "Renegotiating Masculinity in the South African Lowveld," 85.

6. Ibid., 84.

7. According to Robert Gordon, "Of all the senior officials at the mine, his [the compound manager's] was the only position *not* based on technical qualifications. Traditionally, they gain their 'experience' as ex-policemen, Department of Bantu Administration officials, or more uncommonly as youths who have grown up in the black areas and are fluent in one or two of the Bantu languages" ("The Celebration of Ethnicity," 222).

8. The design of mine compounds, as it crystallized in early-twentieth-century South Africa, reflected perhaps most fundamentally white anxieties about controlling large concentrations of black men close to urban areas. As Dunbar Moodie has argued in chapter 3 of *Going for Gold*, however, this organization of space proved, on the whole, useful for capitalists.

9. Moodie, *Going for Gold*, 86.

10. For a reprise of the race-class debates in South African studies, see Hart, "Changing Concepts of Articulation."

11. Patrick Harries describes clashes among black workers on Witwatersrand gold mines before the turn of the twentieth century (see *Work, Culture, and Identity*, 121–24). While some of these fights were not "tribal," instead pitting the workers of one mine against those of another, many were cast at the time as ethnic confrontations. Harries argues that these fights were, indeed, one of the principal means by which ethnic boundaries were constructed on the mines: "Group fighting was preeminently about erecting the social boundaries of inclusion and exclusion through which workers carved out and created a place for themselves in a turbulent and unpredictable world. Faction fighting gave a physical content to their notions of community and a coherence to their sense of justice, hierarchy and self-respect" (ibid., 124). Faction fights may well have had such effects, and I present a similar argument with regard to the present case, but effects, of course, cannot be used to determine the causes of fights.

12. Mayer and Mayer, "Socialization by Peers."

13. Gordon, "The Celebration of Ethnicity."

14. Moodie, *Going for Gold*, 231.

15. De Tocqueville, *The Old Régime and the French Revolution*. Kent McNamara emphasizes the relevance of de Tocqueville's insights in "Culture, Consciousness and Change," 150.

16. See Seekings and Nattrass, *Class, Race, and Inequality in South Africa*, chap. 5, "The Rise of Unemployment under Apartheid," 165–87.

17. See McNamara, "Inter-Group Violence among Black Employees on South African Gold Mines" and "Estimated Incidence of Inter-Group Violence on Gold Mines since 1987."

18. Liebenberg, "Militance and Violence on the Mines," 37–38.

19. *Sunday Times*, 9 March 1975, as quoted by McNamara, "Black Worker Conflicts on South African Gold Mines," 4.

20. See, for example, Pandey, *The Construction of Communalism in Colonial North India.*

CHAPTER 2. WHITE STORIES

1. The title of this chapter is inspired by J. M. Coetzee's *White Writing.*

2. Record of Appeal of the Judgment by Mr. L. F. Shear (hereafter referred to as "Record of Appeal"), vol. 30, 3286–301.

3. Record of Appeal, vol. 10, 1006–8.

4. Record of Appeal, vol. 11, 1179–80.

5. After a previous clash that year, on Easter Sunday, all of the Zulu workers had been sent home for a "cooling off" period during the time of the elections. The Zulus just happened to begin returning to work as the first Soweto Day was being celebrated.

6. In a study of thirty-eight gold-mine compounds in 1975, J. K. McNamara and P. de Bruyn noted, "Most [compound managers] had been in close contact with Black people, particularly in their youth on farms in the Orange Free State, Natal and Transkei. Two hostel managers from the Transkei had been trader and recruiter respectively. Eight hostel managers spoke Nguni (Xhosa/ Zulu), two spoke Sotho, and one Shangaan. Most were proficient in 'Fanakalo'" ("Hostel Organisation and Management in the Gold Mining Industry," 13).

7. Record of Appeal, vol. 10, 1026–27.

8. According to A. Momberg and J. K. McNamara, the origin of the system of tribal representation on the Witwatersrand mines in the early 1890s reflected a complex intersection of white and black interests—not just a white strategy of divide and rule. See "The Tribal Representative System on Gold Mines." In the late nineteenth century, some rural headmen or indunas, involved in recruitment for the mines, requested to come to the mine and to be employed "to look after their workers" (3).

9. J. A. Gemmill, "Native Labour on the Gold Mines."

10. Hamilton, *Terrific Majesty.*

11. Sean Moroney noted the role of Zulus as policemen in the early twentieth century: "On the Reef, workers from Natal and Zululand remained a small proportion of the labour force during the period under review [1901–1912] and earned a reputation for strength and cruelty against workers from other tribes. They suited the role of collaborator perfectly in the eyes of management and the state, and apparently monopolized the position in the compound and state black police force" ("Industrial Conflict in a Labour Represssive Economy," 43).

12. The stereotype of the Shangaan as an especially submissive worker dates back to the end of the nineteenth century. Patrick Harries, for example, quotes a Chamber of Mines report, published in 1898, to the effect that "the greatest advantage of employing the East Coast native [as the area that would become Mozambique was called then] is that you have no diffi-

culty with him underground as compared with natives from other sources" (*Work, Culture, and Identity*, 192).

13. In fact, there were as many Sotho as Xhosa, but many of the Sotho were from Lesotho and thus "foreign" by 1994.

14. Record of the Commission of Enquiry into the Violence on Three Goldfields Mines, 470–71.

15. Guy and Thabane, "Technology, Ethnicity and Ideology" and "Basotho Miners, Ethnicity and Workers' Strategies."

16. Joshua Amupadhi and Mungo Soggot, "Mine's Race Policy Aided Murders," *Weekly Mail and Guardian*, 18 October 1996.

17. Here I am focusing on discourse and the kinds of claims that get mobilized in situations in which black workers compete for jobs.

18. Badenhorst and Mather, "Tribal Recreation and Recreating Tribalism."

19. Tracey, *African Dances of the Witwatersrand Gold Mines*, from the acknowledgments.

20. According to *Mining News*, March 1995, mine dances continued at conservative Gold Fields mines even after the 1994 elections. As such, mine dancing indexes much about the culture of labor relations.

21. Tracey, *African Dances of the Witwatersrand Gold Mines*, 1.

22. Chamber of Mines Publication P.R.D. Series No. 164, Swan Press, Johannesburg.

23. Industrial Relations Department, Manpower Resources Division, Anglo American Corporation of South Africa, "The Perceptions and Behaviour Patterns of Black Mineworkers on a Group Gold Mine," 27–29.

24. In a study of a Namibian mine in the 1970s, Gordon reported that white supervisors felt that they could spur production by encouraging ethnic competition among black workers and that they attempted to stimulate ethnic consciousness by insulting blacks in ethnic terms (*Mines, Masters and Migrants*, 70).

25. At one shaft—out of the three at Cinderella—the section manager, the highest official located at the shaft, had three mine captains beneath him. (The offices of the manager of mining and of the general manager were located away from the shafts, in a Cape Dutch-styled building called the "time office" by black and white workers.) One mine captain was in charge of development, of blasting out new areas; the other two were in charge of day-to-day production. Of the latter two, one supervised four shift bosses, and those four supervised nine miners in sum. The other mine captain supervised five shift bosses, under whom worked eleven miners.

26. See van Onselen, "The Main Reef Road into the Working Class," in *Studies in the Social and Economic History of the Witwatersrand*, vol. 2.

27. Gouldner, *Patterns of Industrial Bureaucracy*.

28. Leger, *Towards Safer Underground Gold Mining*, 50–51.

29. "The Perceptions and Behavior Patterns of Black Mineworkers on a Group Gold Mine," 16.

30. Webster and Leger, *Reconceptualising Skill Formation in South Africa*, 61–62.

31. Nesbitt, *Gold Fever*, 87.

32. In the inverted world of the mine, a kind of hell in which the devil ruled in place of God, "Satan" could also refer to black miners themselves. See Coplan, *In the Time of Cannibals*, 146.

33. McNamara, on the basis of work in the 1970s, reports some more benevolent black nicknames for white compound managers: Malungisa, "The one who puts things right"; Thandabantu, "The one who likes people"; and Mxolisi, "Peacemaker." Along with these, however, are also Bopuntwalo, "Pack and go!" and Mabulal' ehleka, "The one who kills you while laughing." See McNamara, "Brothers and Work Mates" 309.

34. Chamber of Mines of South Africa, *Statistical Tables 1994*, 16.

35. South African mine managements consciously adjusted the ethnic mix of black workers on their mines. For example, Mr. Eksteen from Gold Fields mines, testified to the Myburgh Commission in 1996 that his group of mines never let a black ethnic group grow to more than 25 percent of the total. If the percentage went higher, "problems" resulted, according to Eksteen.

36. "In most cases the chief induna was selected from the largest ethnic group in the hostel" (A. Momberg and J. K. McNamara, "The Tribal Representative System on Gold Mines," 7). Each mine had its own formula for the minimal number of workers that would be assigned their own induna. In Momberg and McNamara's sample of six mines in the mid-1970s, the minimum ranged from 300 to 1,000 (13).

37. Vail, *The Creation of Tribalism in Southern Africa*, 15.

38. See, for example, Oomen, *Chiefs in South Africa*.

39. "The general public in South Africa shows a remarkable facility for assimilating all manner of conflict within the African population into the 'tribal' paradigm, and they appear to assume that if virtually any outbreak of violence is labeled a 'tribal' or 'faction' fight, there is no need to seek for further explanation in contemporary circumstances" (Skalník, "Tribe as Colonial Category," 68).

CHAPTER 3. WAYS OF DYING

1. I take the title for this chapter from the novel *Ways of Dying*, by the South African writer Zakes Mda. Francis Wilson's description of drilling, as seen in the epigraph, remained broadly apposite for the 1990s. Consider the process in the 1890s:

> As the subterranean works were extended, "hammer boys," or the drillers who made up about 60 percent of the underground labour force, rapidly became an elite. To enter the mines they either walked in their bare feet down an incline shaft or descended to the clatter and confusion of the working level in

elevators or cages, an experience that was perhaps the most quotidian source of terror. Each driller was armed with a four-pound hammer, about five hand-sharpened steel drills of varying lengths, a supply of twelve-ounce candles, matches, an old cloth swab, and a can of water. After the white miner indicated to the men under his charge where they were to drill in the stope [the work-face that contained the seam of gold ore], the men fixed candles to the rock face or the nearby timbering and, because of the heat, removed much of their clothing. In the flickering light, the shadowy figures applied their hammers to the short starter drills, which they turned with their free hand after each blow to loosen the interior of the hole. Every few minutes the miner lubricated the drills by squirting a mouthful of water into the hole. The cloth swab was wrapped round the drill to protect him from the ensuing slush and this was re-moved, from time to time, with a wooden peg. The miner completed the hole, generally, a meter deep, with a 1.7 meter-long "jumper" drill. Mechanical drills were employed in shaft driving and tunneling, but only rarely in the stopes, as their weight and bulk required an enlarged and uneconomical working face. (Harries, *Work, Culture, and Identity*, 115)

2. Chamber of Mines of South Africa, *Statistical Tables 1994*, 8.

3. Quoted in Eddie Koch, "And the Latest Gold Price Floods of Blood," *Weekly Mail and Guardian*, 19 May 1995.

4. A twenty-five-year-old worker from Lesotho with about a year of ex-perience on the mine (quoted in Molapo, "Job Stress, Health and Percep-tions of Migrant Mineworkers," 89).

5. A forty-one-year-old Lesotho miner with sixteen years of experience, who may have exaggerated the number of deaths he had witnessed (quoted in ibid., 91).

6. South Africa produced 583.9 metric tons of gold in 1994, while suffer-ing 357 deaths (Chamber of Mines of South Africa, *Statistical Tables 1994*, 47, 8, respectively).

7. Niehaus, "Coins for Blood and Blood for Coins."

8. Ibid., 39–40.

9. Packard and Coetzee, "White Plague, Black Labour Revisited."

10. Teba is the central recruiting agency for black workers on the mines. Originally, black workers called it KwaTeba, "the place of Mr. Taberer," an early and influential leader of the organization. Later, it was formally named the Employment Bureau of Africa, TEBA. Now it is simply referred to as Teba.

11. Sundkler, *Bantu Prophets in South Africa*.

12. In his study of black workers in a copper mine in Namibia during the 1970s, Robert J. Gordon emphasized the central role of drinking among black workers in cementing bonds of "brotherhood" (*Mines, Masters and Migrants*, 116–20). Charles van Onselen presents a wider political economy of alcohol, in "Randlords and Rotgut 1886–1903," in *Studies in the Social and Economic History of the Witwatersrand*, vol. 1.

13. Fiona Ross, *Bearing Witness*.

14. It is possible of course that some of the Zulus were afraid or were suspicious of my motives or were inhibited by any number of other considerations. I cannot absolutely rule out these possibilities, but from what I could discern, my informants really did not know who had attacked them. At the point at which I interviewed them, Zulu workers had little to lose by identifying the culprits; in fact, just after the Soweto Day murders, the Zulus had demanded that a process be set up to identify the perpetrators.

15. Record of Appeal, vol. 28, 3138, Exhibit B, "Minutes of Meeting between Management and Zulu Representative Held on Monday 20 June 1994 at Cinderella Main Office."

16. The toyi-toyi, which involves defiant singing and dancing, was a pervasive part of anti-apartheid demonstrations from the 1980s onward.

17. Record of Appeal, vol. 12, 1276.

18. All statements given to mediators in July are contained in the Record of Appeal, vol. 28, 3162–64. I have changed these statements from the third person into the first — which undoubtedly was how the workers themselves had related their stories to Mvelaze.

19. Record of Appeal, vol. 28, 3162–3.

20. Record of Appeal, vol. 13, 1398. The English has been corrected from the court interpreter's version.

21. Record of Appeal, vol. 28, 3163.

22. Record of Appeal, vol. 28, 3164.

23. Record of Appeal, vol. 28, 3162.

24. Record of Appeal, vol. 28, 3164.

25. Record of Appeal, vol. 23, 2460.

26. Record of Appeal, vol. 23, 2426.

27. "Cockroach" was the Hutu term for Tutsis during the Rwandan genocide, which had had just taken place in 1994.

28. Bozzoli, *Theatres of Struggle and the End of Apartheid*.

CHAPTER 4. GOOD FRIDAY AT CINDERELLA

1. In a survey done on an Orange Free State mine in 1979, two-thirds of black mine workers claimed to be Christian. See Moodie, "Mine Migration and the Struggle for Redemption."

2. Sacrifice was a central motif in the form of Christianity most common in the compound, that is, independent African churches that mixed European Christian with African beliefs. While Christmas was relatively unmarked in the practices of independent churches, Good Friday and Easter were the ritual high points of the year. See West, *Bishops and Prophets in a Black City*.

3. Watjen, *Workers and Warriors*, 14–20.

4. The "third force" was real enough in certain instances, but in the context of widespread black beliefs in witchcraft, it occupied a larger space in

popular explanations of events in the 1990s than it might otherwise had. See Ashforth, *Witchcraft, Violence, and Democracy in South Africa*, 273–78.

5. Like mine compounds, but provided and controlled by city administrations, municipal hostels housed black migrant workers who were employed in a variety of enterprises in the city.

6. Ellis, "The Historical Significance of South Africa's Third Force."

7. See Mazzarella, "Culture, Globalization, Mediation," for a review of recent anthropological work on mediation. He formulates a useful notion of "close distance": "Mediation produces and reproduces certain configurations of close-distance, mediated self-understandings that depend on the routing of the personal through the impersonal, the near through the far, and the self through the other. Close distance is therefore a figure for the dialectic of engagement and alienation inherent in all cultural politics" (361).

8. This polarization was made yet more complex by the fact that isiZulu functioned as the lingua franca of the black townships around Johannesburg.

9. The event was also referred to as the "Johannesburg massacre" and, in time, the "Shell House massacre," Shell House being the ANC headquarters, in front of which the most politically charged deaths took place.

10. Windrich, "The Johannesburg Massacre."

11. Thembinkosi offered this as an example during an interview.

12. Record of Appeal, vol. 19, 2023–24.

13. Report on the Inquiry Conducted by the Committee of Inquiry into the Violence at Tokoza, R. J. Goldstone, Pretoria, 17 November 1992, 56–57: "The committee is satisfied that at least some of the rumour is deliberately initiated as part of the power struggle and as a cover or to raise the level of suspicion and hence of polarization."

14. It is noteworthy that a year later, when I interviewed Mr. Oosthusizen, or "Oosie," at the local Gold Fields security office for Cinderella regarding the Easter events, he reversed the polarity of the rumors in his memory. According to him, security was aware of rumors that the Zulus would attack other political parties from around 20 March (rather than what was recorded at the time: namely, that the Pondos would attack the Zulus). From 20 March onward, according to Oosie, Gold Fields had undercover agents in the hostel, looking for information. This is an example of how memory can be affected by subsequent events.

15. Such moments always offer the possibility of emphasizing how whiteness is required to prevent black violence. For example, an Afrikaans newspaper reported a conflict between Sotho and Xhosa workers on a Free State mine in 1974, in which a Sotho-speaking white man, Mr. T. C. Muller, was brought to the mine to address the Sotho workers: "'Children of Moshesh, grandchildren of Mokhachane who were carried on the back in a rhebuck pickaback skin, I greet you!' The words went through the Sothos like a shock wave, and dead silence descended on the compound. Standing very

straight and in a powerful voice the lean Mr. Muller addressed the 2,000 Sothos around him. After he had spoken, a deafening cry of peace burst out. The Sothos dispersed and many left their weapons behind" (quoted in McNamara, "Black Worker Conflicts on South African Gold Mines," 206).

16. Crush, "Scripting the Compound."

17. Self-Defense Units (SDUS) were ANC-aligned vigilante groups in the townships. On the other side, Inkatha-aligned vigilante groups were called Self-Protection Units (SPUS). In both cases, the notions of protection and defense were sometimes used to cover acts of aggression.

18. Gordon, *Mines, Masters and Migrants*, 170–71.

19. I have emphasized the efflorescence of the notion of black ethnic essence in twentieth-century South Africa. This should not obscure, and it does not contradict, the situational quality of ethnic attribution. See for example, Niehaus, "Ethnicity and the Boundaries of Belonging."

20. Lashing, one of the lowliest, most "unskilled" jobs, involved loading cars underground with ore to be transported to the surface.

21. Record of Appeal, vol. 27, 3065–66.

22. Mann, *The Dark Side of Democracy*.

CHAPTER 5. FREEING WORKERS AND ERASING HISTORY

1. Susan Buck-Morss, "Hegel and Haiti."

2. There is a long and distinguished tradition of reflection on South Africa's peculiar pattern of industrialization. See, for example, Trapido, "South Africa in a Comparative Study of Industrialization."

3. On paternalism, see van Onselen, "The Social and Economic Underpinning of Paternalism and Violence" and "Race and Class in the South African Countryside." With respect to the mines in particular see James, "The Erosion of Paternalism on South African Gold Mines."

4. Many white miners in midcentury South Africa had grown up in rural areas (see Breckenridge, "The Allure of Violence," 679–81). Thus, there was a direct sociological link between the culture of the mines and the paternalism that van Onselen describes for white farmers and their black sharecroppers.

5. James, "The Erosion of Paternalism on South African Gold Mines," 1–2.

6. Nadine Gordimer, *The Lying Days*, p. 33.

7. Quoted in Breckenridge, "The Allure of Violence," 686.

8. Ibid., 686–87. See also Kuckertz, *Creating Order*.

9. From the other side of the relationship, black men at times saw their white supervisors as less than real men—unable to do hard work and unable to fight.

10. Breckenridge, "The Allure of Violence."

11. Ibid., 689.

12. I have already pointed out that boss boys were often the source of white miners' practical knowledge of mining.

13. See, among others, McNamara, "Inter-Group Violence Among Black Employees on South African Gold Mines"; Crush, Jeeves, and Yudelman, *South Africa's Labor Empire*; James, "The Erosion of Paternalism on South African Gold Mines" and *Our Precious Metal*; Moodie, *Going for Gold.*

14. See the classic statements of this thesis: Johnstone, *Class, Race and Gold*; Wolpe, "Capitalism and Cheap Labour-Power in South Africa."

15. See Patrick Harries, *Work, Culture, and Identity* for an account of how black wages were actually decreased toward the end of the nineteenth century, as deep-level mining commenced.

16. Crush, Jeeves, and Yudelman, *South Africa's Labor Empire*, 1.

17. Yudelman, *The Emergence of Modern South Africa.*

18. Cited in Frances Wilson, *Labour in the South African Gold Mines, 1911–1969*, 32.

19. Jeeves, *Migrant Labor in South Africa's Mining Economy.*

20. Van Onselen, "The Modernization of the Zuid Afrikaansche Republiek."

21. Thompson, *A History of South Africa*, 137.

22. For a narrative that implicitly reviews the historigraphical controversy that began with Hobson's economic explanation of the Boer War, see ibid., 132–41.

23. Simkins, "Agricultural Production in the African Reserves of South Africa, 1918-1969."

24. Crush, Jeeves, and Yudelman, *South Africa's Labor Empire*, 3; Leger and van Niekerk, "Organisation on the Mines," 69.

25. Chamber of Mines of South Africa, *Statistical Tables 1994*, 37.

26. See James, *Our Precious Metal*, 108, table 6.2, which is based on Philip Albert Hirschsohn, "Management Ideology and Environmental Turbulence."

27. Crush, Jeeves, and Yudelman, *South Africa's Labor Empire*, 162.

28. Ibid., 166.

29. Ibid. According to Philip Albert Hirschsohn, even the most liberal mining house, Anglo American, pursued a divide-and-rule policy after the 1987 strike, by attempting to replace militant Transkeian workers with Zulus and Mozambicans, who were thought less likely to join the union ("Management Ideology and Environmental Turbulence," 42).

30. McNamara, "Gate Politics," 64, and "Inter-Group Violence among Black Employees on South Africa Gold Mines," 30.

31. James, *Our Precious Metal*, 93.

32. Ibid., 96–97.

33. Bundy, *The Rise and Fall of the South African Peasantry.*

34. Quoted in Crush, Jeeves, and Yudelman, *South Africa's Labor Empire*, 189.

35. James, *Our Precious Metal*, 91. For an account commissioned by the union, see Allen, *The History of Black Mineworkers in South Africa.*

36. James, *Our Precious Metal*, 106–7.

37. Chamber of Mines of South Africa, *Statistical Tables 1994*, 15.

38. Moodie, "Mine Migration and the Struggle for Redemption," 17.

39. Adam, Slabbert, and Moodley, *Comrades in Business*.

CHAPTER 6. UNIONIZATION FROM ABOVE

1. In a survey of six gold mines, A. Momberg and J. K. McNamara reported that four still had holding "cells," though one of these was scheduled to be phased out ("Report on the Tribal Representative System on Gold Mines," 13).

2. In an account commissioned by the union, V. L. Allen makes the organizational problems at the head office clear. Writing of the mid-1980s, he says, "There were instances where individual members, who were not officials, collected subscriptions without the authorization of the union and did not pass them on to it" (*The History of Black Mineworkers in South Africa*, 115).

3. There were, in addition, approximately 2,500 workers at home who would eventually shuttle back to work on the mines as others left. With such a large labor reservoir at home, home stays became longer than black workers wanted, and this became an issue for many workers in the early 1990s. The mine may have kept a fuller complement of black labor than it needed because it was expensive to retrench workers—they had to be provided a severance package equivalent to several months pay. Mine management may also have wanted to keep relatively skilled workers, who would come into demand as the new shaft came into production.

4. The full-time shop stewards were paid by the company (at the top of the category 1–8 pay scale) to do union business full-time. They were brought online in the middle of 1994, approximately a year after recognition of the NUM at Cinderella.

5. This was a fund into which all workers, union and nonunion alike, were required to pay. The fund was then used, at the joint discretion of management and the NUM, to support all workers' welfare. For example, if union officials from the head office were involved in dispute resolution at a mine, their expenses could be covered by the fund.

6. Selections from Investigation Diary, Gold Field Security, 4 April 1993, from 14:00 onward.

7. Independent Mediation Service of South Africa, Arbitration Award, Elna Revelas, 1 July 1993, 2.

8. *Business Day*, 7 April 1994.

9. See McNamara, "Social Life, Ethnicity and Conflict in a Gold Mine Hostel."

10. The classic study is Mayer, *Townsmen or Tribesmen*.

11. Kynoch, "Crime, Conflict and Politics in Transition-Era South Africa."

12. Van Onselen, "The Regiment of the Hills—Umkosi Wezintaba," in *Studies in the Social and Economic History of the Witwatersrand 1886–1914*.

13. Gangs that trace their lineage to Nongoloza still exist in South African prisons (Steinberg, *The Number*).

14. Breckenridge, "Migrancy, Crime and Faction Fighting"; Beinart, "Worker Consciousness, Ethnic Particularism and Nationalism."

15. Bonner, "Family, Crime and Political Consciousness on the East Rand, 1939–1955"; Kynoch, "Marashea on the Mines."

16. A glimpse of this underworld is afforded by the records of a Gold Fields security raid on a moneylender in Cinderella in February 1994, in this case, a Shangaan team leader from Mozambique. Security found a plastic bag of approximately eighty TEBA Cash Savings Books in the moneylender's room. It turned out that these had been taken as security against loans to Cinderella workers that totaled approximately R15,000. The rate of interest charged was high. For example, one Tao Chithanga borrowed R100 from the moneylender sometime in February, agreeing to hand over his TEBA Cash Savings Book as security and to repay R150 by 8 March. The R50 was interest. Clearly, as long as his moneylending business continued undetected, the Mozambican team leader was earning far more from his undercover activities than from his salary. Being a worker at Cinderella was a kind of cover. It would be interesting to know, of course, just who tipped off security about this Shangaan moneylender. Was it the Russians, who ran their own operation?

17. Allen, *The History of Black Mineworkers in South Africa*, 3:532.

18. Ibid., 3:535.

19. Ibid., 3:613.

20. The role of nationality, as it intertwined with ethnicity, becomes clear in Madezi's calculations. There were approximately as many Sotho speakers as there were Xhosa speakers at Cinderella, but many of the Sotho were Lesotho nationals, not South Africans. As a new nation was being created in South Africa, in the early 1990s, South African workers therefore began to occupy a (potentially) superior structural position vis-à-vis "foreign" workers. Under apartheid, this "national" effect had not been in operation, since all black workers had been subordinated to white power in the same way. The change that the creation of a new nation entailed was charged by the fact that foreign workers, Mozambicans in particular, tended to dominate the highest-paying jobs at Cinderella.

21. The history of the violence on East Rand has not yet been described well. The best account, a critique of the narrative developed by the Truth and Reconciliation Commission, is Philip Bonner's and Noor Nieftagodien's "The Truth and Reconciliation Commission and the Pursuit of 'Social Truth.'" See also Bonner and Ndima, "The Roots of Violence."

22. Moodie, "Becoming a Social Movement Union," 168.

23. Allen, *The History of Black Mineworkers in South Africa*, 3:173–76.

24. Report of the Commission of Inquiry, Vaal Reefs South Mine and National Union of Mine Workers, Kathy Satchwell, Chair, 1995, 18.

25. Ibid., 17.

26. Ibid., 42.

27. Ibid., 44.

CHAPTER 7. MOTIVES FOR MURDER

1. This was also the interpretation made by Patrick, the head of the full-time shaft stewards: that the people who had chased Zulus out of the compound wanted to prevent splits in the black workforce to maximize their power in the compound and in negotiations with management.

2. In his judgment, L. F. Shear noted, "The parties, especially the recognized union, had no right to turn its back on the dispute, solely under the disguise that the dispute was political, when it affected the relationship between management and a not inconsiderable group of employees, some of whom were NUM members. The impression that NUM had its own agenda, possibly a conflict of interest which it desired to protect, is almost inescapable" See Judgment by L. F. Shear, 33–34.

3. Record of Appeal, "Minutes of Meeting between Management and NUM Held on Monday 4 April 1994 at Main Office," vol. 27, 3065–66.

4. Ibid., 3066.

5. Record of Appeal, "Minutes of the Meeting between Management and Zulu Representatives Held on Monday April 4 1994 in the Training Centre at 10:30," vol. 27, 3069.

6. Record of Appeal, "Minutes of Meeting between Management and NUM held on Wednesday, 6 April 1994 at Hostel," vol. 28, 3080.

7. Record of Appeal, "Minutes of Meeting between Management and NUM held on Friday, 8 April 1994 at Main Office, 10:00," vol. 28, 3086.

8. Record of Appeal, "Delegation of 6 Zulus, GM, HRM, RE, IRM, CTO & CS Meeting 9:20 on 12 April 1994," vol. 28, 3095. This meeting was the result of a protest march by Zulus to the general manager's office.

9. Record of Appeal, "Minutes of the Meeting between Management and NUM Branch Committee held on Tuesday 24 May 1994 at the Main Office Conference Room," vol. 30, 3309.

10. Record of Appeal, "Minutes of the Meeting between Management and NUM Branch Committee held on 7 June 1994 at the Main Office Conference Room at 14:30," vol. 30, 3313.

11. Record of Appeal, "Minutes of a Meeting between Management and NUM Branch Committee Held on Friday 17 June 1994 at 12:00," vol. 28, 3132.

12. Record of Appeal, "Minutes of the Meeting between Management and NUM Branch Committee Held on Thursday, 16 June 1994 in the Conference Room at 14H50," vol. 28, 3125.

13. Record of Appeal, "Minutes of Meeting between Management and Zulu Representatives Held on Monday 20 June 1994 at Main Office," vol. 28, 3138.

14. Ibid.

15. Record of Appeal, "Minutes of Meeting between Management and

Zulu Representatives Held on Monday 20 June 1994 at Main Office," vol. 28, 3140.

16. Record of Appeal, vol. 18, 1897.

17. Record of Appeal, vol. 19, 2005.

18. See Richard A. Wilson, *The Politics of Truth and Reconciliation in South Africa*; and Posel and Simpson, *Commissioning the Past*; Ross, *Bearing Witness*.

19. Record of Appeal, "Meeting of 13 July 1994," vol. 30, 3360.

20. Record of Appeal, vol. 18, 1912.

21. Record of Appeal, "Meeting of 13 July 1994," vol. 30, 3366–68.

22. Record of Appeal, "Report on Our Intervention Ministry," vol. 28, 3194.

23. Record of Appeal, "Press Statement by the East Rand Branch of the South African Council of Churches," vol. 30, 3354.

24. Record of Appeal, "Minutes of the Meeting between South African Council of Churches, NUM, IFP, KwaZulu Natal Government and Peace Committee held on 13 July 1994 at 10:30 in Technical Manager's Office," vol. 28, 3169.

25. Ibid., vol. 28, 3180.

26. Figures 19–23 are my own photographs. Because Santu Mofokeng had come close to being attacked after attempting to photograph an Inkatha march, and was therefore not comfortable visiting Injalo, I had to resort to my own devices (and the continuing privilege of whiteness).

27. Judgment by L. F. Shear, 51.

CHAPTER 8. THE AFTERMATH

1. See Scheper-Hughes and Bourgois, *Violence in War and Peace*, 31. This position has become common within recent anthropology. See Donham, "Staring at Suffering," for the limitations of this approach.

2. Record of the Commission of Enquiry into the Violence on Three Gold Field Mines, 844.

3. National Assembly Question Paper, Interpellations for Wednesday, 6 November 1996, response by the Minister of Labour to Mr. G. G. Olipant.

4. Judge J. F. Myburgh, "Report of the Commission of Enquiry into the Recent Violence and Occurrences at the East Driefontein, Leeudoorn and Northam Mines, 5 October 1996, 49.

5. Founding Affidavit in the Labour Court of South Africa held at Johannesburg, 6 August 2003, 10.

6. Founding Affidavit in the Labour Court of South Africa, 6 August 2003, appendix AW12, 64. The Fanakalo passage was translated in the Record of the Arbitration by Tokiso Dispute Settlement as: "You will come here again. You will shit double. You, Molise, we are coming back to you. You are going to die, you dog. Elijah, Power, Power" (60–61).

7. Founding Affidavit in the Labour Court of South Africa, 6 August 2003, 18.

8. Bulungu and Bezuidenhout, "Union Solidarity under Stress."

9. Seekings and Nattrass, *Class, Race, and Inequality in South Africa.*

10. Ibid., 254.

11. Chipkin, *Do South Africans Exist?*, chap. 4.

12. Seekings and Nattrass, *Class, Race, and Inequality in South Africa*, 342–45.

13. Hart, "Changing Concepts of Articulation," 94.

14. Kynoch, "Crime, Conflict and Politics in Transition-Era South Africa."

15. Von Holdt, "Institutionalisation, Strike Violence and Local Moral Orders," 128.

16. Thembelihle Tshabalala and Monako Dibetle, "Inside the Mob," *Mail and Guardian*, 23 May 2008.

CONCLUSION

1. See Seekings and Nattrass, *Class, Race, and Inequality in South Africa.*

2. Anderson, *Imagined Communities.*

3. Kedourie, *Nationalism in Asia and Africa*, 135.

4. Gillian Hart argues that Zuma was able to wrest control of the ANC from Mbeki by seizing the mantle of the liberation struggle.

> Positioning himself as the hero of national liberation is the key to Zuma's capacity—at least for the time being—to articulate multiple, often contradictory meanings into a complex unity that appeals powerfully to "common sense" across a broad spectrum. They include his asserting himself as a man of the left (much to the chagrin of many on the left who point to his support of GEAR [Mbeki's neoliberal economic policy], as well as his links to certain fractions of capital); as a traditionalist who dons leopard skins on key occasions (and as one who brought peace to KwaZulu-Natal, helping to end the violent civil war of the early 1990s); and as an anti-elitist (his regular reference to himself as "not educated"—but, by implication, extremely smart—is a direct attack on the technocratic elite surrounding Mbeki, often portrayed by Zuma supporters as arrogant and self-serving, and as not having served in the trenches of the revolutionary struggle). ("Changing Concepts of Articulation," 97–98)

POSTSCRIPT. DOING FIELDWORK AT THE END OF APARTHEID

1. See, in particular, Gluckman's "Analysis of a Social Situation in Modern Zululand." In many ways, the strategy of this book represents an extended elaboration of Gluckman's so-called extended-case-study method.

2. For an attempt to clarify the essential theoretical core of this position, see Donham, *History, Power, Ideology.*

3. MacMillan, "Return to the Malungwana Drift."

4. Epstein, *Politics in an Urban African Community*; J. C. Mitchell, *The Kalela Dance*. For an account of the formation of the Rhodes-Livingstone Institute and of the so-called Manchester school of social anthropology, see Schumaker, *Africanizing Anthropology*.

5. "Initially I was able to secure the full co-operation of the Mine Management at the Roan Antelope for the study. Shortly afterwards, as a result of a series of unfortunate misunderstandings, this support was withdrawn, and for the greater part of my stay in the town I was denied personal access to the mine compound. Inevitably this has meant that at many points my data are not as full as I would have wished" (Epstein, *Politics in an Urban African Community*, xvii–xviii). The word *compound* here refers to the family housing provided by the mine for black workers, not to the single-sex structures on South African mines.

6. Van Onselen, *Chibaro*. Afterward, when van Onselen turned to the early social history of Johannesburg, he was denied permission to use the archives of the Chamber of Mines and Barlow Rand (see his preface to *Studies in the Social and Economic History of the Witwatersrand 1886–1914*, 1:xi–xii).

7. Moodie, *Going for Gold*.

8. Donham, *Marxist Modern*, 8–12.

9. Ibid., 8.

10. Bakhtin, *The Dialogic Imagination*.

11. For what counts as a "deep" story, see Donham, "Thinking Temporally or Modernizing Anthropology," 145.

BIBLIOGRAPHY

UNPUBLISHED SOURCES
IN THE AUTHOR'S POSSESSION

Agency for Industrial Mission. "Another Blanket: Report on an Investigation into the Migrant Situation," June 1976.

Anglo American Corporation of South Africa, Industrial Relations Department, Manpower Resources Division. "The Perceptions and Behavior Patterns of Black Mineworkers on a Group Gold Mine," November 1976.

Arbitration Award, Independent Mediation Service of South Africa, Elna Revelas, 1 July 1993.

Arbitration Award, Tokiso Dispute Settlement, Patrick Deale, 11 November 2003.

[Cinderella] Mine, annual reports, 1985–1994.

De Vries, P., N. L. Robertson, and J. K. McNamara. "Mine Hostel Arrangements for Black Workers." Human Resources Laboratory, Chamber of Mines of South Africa Research Organisation, Report 37/78, August 1978.

Founding Affidavit, Labour Court of South Africa, held at Johannesburg, 6 August 2003.

Gemmill, J. A. "Native Labour on the Gold Mines." Paper presented at the Seventh Commonwealth Mining and Metallurgical Congress, 1961.

Judgment by L. F. Shear in Industrial Court of South Africa, held at Pretoria, 20 September 1995, with addendum dated 10 May 1996.

Leatt, James, Paulus Zulu, Manoko Nchwe, Mark Ntshangase, and Richard Laughlin. "Reaping the Whirlwind? Report on a Joint Study by the National Union of Mineworkers and Anglo American Gold Division on the Causes of Mine Violence," 1986.

McNamara, J. K. "An Approach to the Investigation of Disturbances in Gold Mine Hostels." Human Resources Laboratory, Chamber of Mines of South Africa Research Organisation, Report 79/76, December 1976.

———. "The Underlying Causes and Resolution of Labour Conflict at Matla Colliery." Report for Trans-Natal and the NUM, November 1988.

McNamara, J. K., and P. De Bruyn. "Hostel Organisation and Management in the Gold Mining Industry." Human Resources Laboratory, Chamber of Mines of South Africa Research Organisation, Report 73/75, September 1975.

Momberg, A., and J. K. McNamara. "The Tribal Representative System of Gold Mines." Human Resources Laboratory, Chamber of Mines of South Africa Research Organisation, Report 10/77, June 1977.

Record of Appeal of the Judgment by Mr. L. F. Shear in the Industrial Court of South Africa, held at Pretoria, dated 20 September 1995 and delivered on 22 September 1995. Labour Appeal Court, Transvaal Provincial Division, 31 vols.

Record of the Arbitration, 26, 27 August 2003; 25, 26 September 2003; 29, 30 September 2003; 1 October 2003, Patrick Deale, Tokiso Arbritration.

Record of the Commission of Enquiry Between Vaal Reefs Exploration and Mining Co. and the National Union of Mineworkers into the Violence at No. 9 Shaft Village and subsequent Deaths and/or Injuries on 1 and 9 April 1995, D. Moseneke, Chairman, 1995.

Record of the Commission of Enquiry into the Violence on Three Gold Fields Mines, Justice J. F. Myburgh, Chairman, 1996.

Report of the Commission of Enquiry into the Recent Violence and Occurrences at the East Driefontein, Leeudoorn, and Northam Mines, J. F. Mybrugh, 5 October 1996.

Report of the Commission of Enquiry into the Violence on 28 and 29 January 1995 at No. 8 Hostel, Vaal Reefs South Mine, and National Union of Mine Workers, Kathy Satchwell, Chair, 1995.

Report of the Commission of Enquiry into Violence at 9 Village Vaal Reefs East Mine, 1 and 9 April 1995, E. Moseneke, Chair, 1995.

Report on the Enquiry Conducted by the Commission of Enquiry into the Violence at the Durban Roodepoort Deep Gold Mine During December 1992, Independent Mediation Service of South Africa, 1993.

Report on the Enquiry Conducted by the Committee of Enquiry into the Violence at Tokoza, R. J. Goldstone, Pretoria, 17 November 1992.

PUBLISHED SOURCES

Abrahams, Peter. *Mine Boy*. New York: Knopf, 1955.

Adam, Heribert, Frederik Van Zyl Slabbert, and Kogila Moodley. *Comrades in Business: Post-Liberation Politics in South Africa*. Cape Town: Tafelberg, 1997.

Aijmer, G. and J. Abbink, eds. *Meanings of Violence: A Cross-Cultural Perspective*. Oxford: Berg, 2000.

Alexander, Jocelyn, JoAnn McGregor and Terence Ranger. *Violence and Memory: One Hundred Years in the Dark Forests of Matabeleland*. Oxford: James Currey, 2000.

Alexander, Neville. *An Ordinary Country: Issues in the Transition from Apartheid to Democracy in South Africa*. Pietermaritzburg: University of KwaZulu-Natal Press, 2002.

Allen, V. L. *The History of Black Mineworkers in South Africa.* Vol. 3. Keighley, U.K.: Moor Press, 2003.

Alverson, Hoyt. *Mind in the Heart of Darkness: Value and Self-Identity among the Tswana of Southern Africa.* New Haven: Yale University Press, 1978.

Anderson, Benedict. *Imagined Communities: Reflections on the Origin and Spread of Nationalism.* Rev. edn. London: Verso, 1991.

Appadurai, Arjun. *Fear of Small Numbers: An Essay on the Geography of Anger.* Durham: Duke University Press, 2006.

Ashforth, Adam. *Witchcraft, Violence, and Democracy in South Africa.* Chicago: University of Chicago Press, 2005.

Badenhorst, Cecile, and Charles Mather. "Tribal Recreation and Recreating Tribalism: Culture, Leisure and Social Control on South Africa's Gold Mines, 1940–1950." *Journal of Southern African Studies* 23 (1997): 473–89.

Bakhtin, Mikhail. "Forms of Time and of the Chronotope in the Novel," *The Dialogic Imagination,* ed. Michael Holquist, 84–254. Austin: University of Texas Press, 1981.

Beinart, William. "Conflict in Qumbu: Rural Consciousness, Ethnicity and Violence in the Colonial Transkei." *Hidden Struggles in Rural South Africa,* William Beinart and Colin Bundy, 106–37. Berkeley: University of California Press, 1987.

———. "Political and Collective Violence in Southern African Historiography." *Journal of Southern African Studies* 18 (1992): 455–86.

———. *The Political Economy of Pondoland, 1860 to 1930.* Cambridge: Cambridge University Press, 1982.

———. "Worker Consciousness, Ethnic Particularism and Nationalism: The Experiences of a South African Migrant 1930–1960." *The Politics of Race, Class and Nationalism in Twentieth Century South Africa,* ed. Shula Marks and Stanley Trapido, 286–309. London: Longman, 1987.

Besteman, Catherine, ed. *Violence: A Reader.* New York: New York University Press, 2001.

Bond, Patrick. *Against Global Apartheid: South Africa Meets the World Bank, IMF and International Finance.* Cape Town: University of Cape Town Press, 2001.

———. *Elite Transition: From Apartheid to Neoliberalism in South Africa.* London: Pluto, 2000.

Bonner, Philip. "Family, Crime and Political Consciousness on the East Rand, 1939–1955." *Journal of Southern African Studies* 14 (1988): 393–420.

———. "The 1920 Black Mineworkers' Strike: A Preliminary Account." *Labour, Townships and Protest: Studies in the Social History of the Witwatersrand,* ed. Belinda Bozzoli, 273–97. Johannesburg: Ravan, 1979.

Bonner, Philip, and Noor Nieftagodien. "The Truth and Reconciliation Commission and the Pursuit of 'Social Truth': The Case of Kathorus." *Commissioning the Past: Understanding South Africa's Truth and Reconciliation Commission,* ed. Deborah Posel and Graeme Simpson, 173–203. Johannesburg: Witwatersrand University Press, 2002.

Bonner, Philip, and Vusi Ndima. "The Roots of Violence and Martial Zuluness on the East Rand." *Zulu Identities: Being Zulu, Past and Present*, ed. Benedict Carton, John Laband and Jabulani Sithole, 363–82. New York: Columbia University Press, 2009.

Bozzoli, Belinda. *Theatres of Struggle and the End of Apartheid*. Johannesburg: Witwatersrand University Press, 2004.

Brass, Paul R. *Theft of an Idol: Text and Context in the Representation of Collective Violence*. Princeton: Princeton University Press, 1997.

Breckenridge, Keith. "An Age of Consent: Law, Discipline and Violence on the South African Gold Mines, 1910–1933." PhD dissertation, Northwestern University, 1995.

————. "The Allure of Violence: Men, Race and Masculinity on the South African Goldmines, 1900–1950." *Journal of Southern African Studies* 24 (1998): 669–93.

————. "Migrancy, Crime and Faction Fighting: The Role of the Isitshozi in the Development of Ethnic Organisations in the Compounds." *Journal of Southern African Studies* 16 (1990): 55–78.

Brown, David. "The Basements of Babylon: Language and Literacy on the South African Gold Mines," *Social Dynamics* 14 (1988): 46–56.

Buck-Morss, Susan. "Hegel and Haiti." *Critical Inquiry* 26 (2000): 821–65.

Buhlungu, Sakhela, ed. *Trade Unions and Democracy*. Pretoria: Human Sciences Research Council, 2006.

Buhlungu, Sakhela, and Andries Bezuidenhout. "Union Solidarity under Stress: The Case of the National Union of Mineworkers in South Africa," Sociology of Work Unit, University of the Witwatersrand, n.d.

Bundy, Colin. *The Rise and Fall of the South African Peasantry*. London: Heineman, 1979.

Burawoy, Michael. *The Colour of Class on the Copper Mines: From African Advancement to Zambianization*. Zambian Papers No. 7. Lusaka: Institute of African Studies, 1972.

————. "The Hidden Abode of Underdevelopment." *The Politics of Production*, 209–52. London: Verso, 1985.

Callinicos, Luli. *Gold and Workers 1886–1924*. Johannesburg: Ravan, 1981.

Campbell, Catherine. "Learning to Kill? Masculinity, the Family and Violence in Natal." *Journal of Southern African Studies* 18 (1992): 614–28.

————. *"Letting them Die": Why HIV/AIDS Prevention Programmes Fail*. Bloomington: Indiana University Press, 2003.

Carr, David. *Time, Narrative, and History*. Bloomington: Indiana University Press, 1986.

Carton, Benedict, John Laband, and Jabulani Sithole, eds. *Zulu Identities: Being Zulu, Past and Present*. New York: Columbia University Press, 2009.

Caruth, Cathy. *Trauma: Explorations in Memory*. Baltimore: Johns Hopkins University Press, 1995.

Chamber of Mines of South Africa. *Statistical Tables 1994*. Johannesburg: Chamber of Mines of South Africa, 1994.

Chipkin, Ivor. *Do South Africans Exist? Nationalism, Democracy and the Identity of "the People."* Johannesburg: Witwatersrand University Press, 2007.

————. "Nationalism as Such: Violence During South Africa's Political Transition." *Public Culture* 16 (2004): 315–35.

Coetzee, J. M. *White Writing: On the Culture of Letters in South Africa.* New Haven: Yale University Press, 2000.

Cohen, Bernard S. *Colonialism and Its Forms of Knowledge.* Princeton: Princeton University Press, 1996.

Comaroff, John L., and Jean Comaroff. *Ethnicity, Inc.* Chicago: University of Chicago Press, 2009.

————. "The Madman and the Migrant: Work and Labor in the Historical Consciousness of a South African People." *American Ethnologist* 14 (1987): 191–209.

Cooper, Frederick. *Colonialism in Question: Theory, Knowledge, History.* Berkeley: University of California Press, 2005.

————. *Decolonization and African Society: The Labor Question in French and British Africa.* Cambridge: Cambridge University Press, 1996.

Coplan, David B. *In the Time of Cannibals: The Word Music of South Africa's Basotho Migrants.* Chicago: University of Chicago Press, 1994.

Crush, Jonathan. "Power and Surveillance on the South African Gold Mines." *Journal of Southern African Studies* 18 (1992): 825–44.

————. "Scripting the Compound: Power and Space in the South African Mining Industry." *Environment and Planning D: Society and Space* 12 (1994): 301–24.

Crush, Jonathan, Alan Jeeves, and David Yudelman. *South Africa's Labor Empire: A History of Black Migrancy to the Gold Mines.* Boulder, Colo.: Westview, 1991.

Das, Veena. *Life and Words: Violence and the Descent into the Ordinary.* Berkeley: University of California Press, 2007.

————, ed. *Mirrors of Violence: Communities, Riots and Survivors in South Asia.* Delhi: Oxford University Press, 1990.

Das, Veena, Arthur Kleinman, Mamphela Ramphele, and Pamela Reynolds, eds. *Violence and Subjectivity.* Berkeley: University of California Press, 2000.

Davies, Rob. "The 1922 Strike and the Political Economy of South Africa." *Labour, Townships, and Protest: Studies in the Social History of the Witwatersrand,* ed. Belinda Bozzoli, 298–324. Johannesburg: Raven, 1979.

de Tocqueville, Alexis. *The Old Régime and the French Revolution.* Translated by Stuart Gilbert. New York: Doubleday, [1865] 1955.

de Vries, Hent, and Samuel Weber, eds. *Violence, Identity, and Self-Determination.* Stanford: Stanford University Press, 1997.

Donham, Donald L. *History, Power, Ideology: Central Issues in Marxism and Anthropology.* 2nd edn. Berkeley: University of California Press, 1990.

————. *Marxist Modern: An Ethnographic History of the Ethiopian Revolution.* Berkeley: University of California Press, 1990.

————. "Staring at Suffering." *States of Violence: Politics, Youth, and Memory in Contemporary Africa,* ed. Edna G. Bay and Donald L. Donham, 16–33. Charlottesville: University of Virginia Press, 2006.

————. "Thinking Temporally or Modernizing Anthropology." *American Anthropologist* 103 (2001): 134–49.

Elder, Glen S. *Hostels. Sexuality, and the Apartheid Legacy: Malevolent Geographies*. Athens: Ohio University Press, 2003.

Eller, Jack D. *From Culture to Ethnicity to Conflict: An Anthropological Perspective on International Ethnic Conflict*. Ann Arbor: University of Michigan Press, 1999.

Ellis, Stephen. "The Historical Significance of South Africa's Third Force." *Journal of Southern African Studies* 24 (1998): 261–300.

Epstein, A. L. *Ethos and Identity: Three Studies in Ethnicity*. London: Tavistock, 1978.

————. *Politics in an Urban African Community*. Manchester: Manchester University Press, 1958.

Fanon, Frantz. *The Wretched of the Earth*. Translated by Richard Philcox. New York: Grove, [1961] 2004.

Fardon, Richard. "'African Ethnogenesis': Limits to the Comparability of Ethnic Phenomena." *Comparative Anthropology*, ed. Ladislav Holy, 168–88. Oxford: Basil Blackwell, 1987.

————. "'Crossed Destinies': The Entangled Histories of West African Ethnic and National Identities." *Ethnicity in Africa: Roots, Meanings and Implications*, ed. Louise de la Gorgendière, Kenneth King, and Sarah Vaughan, 117–46. Edinburgh: Centre of African Studies, University of Edinburgh, 1996.

Feinstein, Charles H. *An Economic History of South Africa: Conquest, Discrimination and Development*. Cambridge: Cambridge University Press, 2005.

Feldman, Allen. *Formations of Violence: The Narrative of the Body and Political Terror in Northern Ireland*. Chicago: University of Chicago Press, 1991.

Friedman, Jonathan, ed. *Globalization, the State, and Violence*. Walnut Creek, Calif.: Altamira Press, 2003.

Girard, René, *Violence and the Sacred*. Translated by Patrick Gregory. Baltimore: Johns Hopkins University Press, [1972] 1977.

Gluckman, Max. "Analysis of a Social Situation in Modern Zululand." *Bantu Studies* 14 (1940): 1–30, 147–74.

Godoy, Ricardo. "Mining: Anthropological Perspectives." *Annual Review of Anthropology* 14 (1985): 199–217.

Goldblatt, David, and Nadine Gordimer. *On the Mines*. Cape Town: C. Struik, 1973.

Gordimer, Nadine. *The Lying Days*. London: Gollancz, 1954.

Gordon, Robert J. "The Celebration of Ethnicity: A 'Tribal Fight' in a Namibian Mine Compound." *Ethnicity in Modern Africa*, ed. Brian M. du Toit, 213–31. Boulder, Colo.: Westview, 1978.

————. *Mines, Masters, and Migrants: Life in a Namibian Mine Compound*. Johannesburg: Ravan, 1977.

Gouldner, Alvin W. *Patterns of Industrial Bureaucracy*. London: Routledge and Kegan Paul, 1955.

Guy, Jeff, and Motlatsi Thabane. "Basotho Miners, Ethnicity and Workers' Strategies." *Workers in Third-World Industrialization*, ed. Inga Brandell, 74–103. London: Macmillan, 1991.

———. "Technology, Ethnicity and Ideology: Basotho Miners and Shaft-Sinking on the South African Gold Mines." *Journal of Southern African Studies* 14 (1988): 257–78.

Hamerton-Kelly, Robert G., ed. *Violent Origins: Walter Burkert, René Girard, and Jonathan Z. Smith on Ritual Killing and Cultural Formation*. Stanford: Stanford University Press, 1987.

Hamilton, Carolyn. *Terrific Majesty: The Powers of Shaka Zulu and the Limits of Historical Invention*. Cambridge: Harvard University Press, 1998.

Hansen, Thomas Blom. *Wages of Violence: Naming and Identity in Postcolonial Bombay*. Princeton: Princeton University Press, 2001.

Harries, Patrick. "Symbols and Sexuality: Culture and Identity on the Early Witwatersrand Gold Mines." *Gender and History* 2 (1999): 318–36.

———. *Work, Culture, and Identity: Migrant Laborers in Mozambique and South Africa, c. 1860–1910*. Portsmouth, N.H.: Heinemann, 1994.

Hart, Gillian. "Changing Concepts of Articulation: Political Stakes in South Africa Today." *Review of African Political Economy* 111 (2007): 85–101.

———. *Disabling Globalization: Places of Power in Post-Apartheid South Africa*. Berkeley: University of California Press, 2002.

Harvey, Penelope, and Peter Gow, eds. *Sex and Violence: Issues in Representation and Experience*. London: Routledge, 1994.

Hinton, Alexander Laban. *Annihilating Difference: The Anthropology of Genocide*. Berkeley: University of California Press, 2002.

Hirschsohn, Philip Albert. "Management Ideology and Environmental Turbulence: Understanding Labour Policies in the South African Gold Mining Industries." M.S. dissertation, University of Oxford, 1988.

Horowitz, Donald L. *The Deadly Ethnic Riot*. Berkeley: University of California Press, 2001.

Hunter, Monica. *Reaction to Conquest: Effects of Contact with Europeans on the Pondos of South Africa*. 2nd edn. London: Oxford University Press for the International African Institute, 1961.

Jackson, Michael. *The Politics of Storytelling: Violence, Transgression, and Intersubjectivity*. Copenhagen: Museum Tusculanum Press, 2002.

James, Wilmot G. "The Erosion of Paternalism on South African Gold Mines." *Industrial Relations Journal of South Africa* 12 (1992): 1–16.

———. *Our Precious Metal: African Labour in South Africa's Gold Industry, 1970–1990*. London: James Currey, 1992.

Jay, Martin. *Refractions of Violence*. London: Routledge, 2003.

Jeeves, Alan. *Migrant Labor in South Africa's Mining Economy*. Kingston: McGill-Queen's University Press, 1985.

Jochelson, Karen, Monyaola Mothibeli, and Jean-Patrick Leger, "Human Immunodeficiency Virus and Migrant Labor in South Africa." *International Journal of Health Services* 21 (1991): 157–73.

Johnstone, Frederick A. *Class, Race and Gold: A Study of Class Relations and*

Racial Discrimination in South Africa. London: Routledge and Kegan Paul, 1976.

Kedourie, Elie, ed. *Nationalism in Asia and Africa*. London: Routledge, 1974.

Kuckertz, Heinz. *Creating Order: The Image of the Homestead in Mpondo Social Life*. Johannesburg: University of the Witwatersrand Press, 1990.

Kynoch, Gary. "Crime, Conflict and Politics in Transition-Era South Africa." *African Affairs* 104 (2005): 493–514.

———. "Marashea on the Mines: Economic, Social and Criminal Networks on the South African Gold Fields, 1947–1999." *Journal of Southern African Studies* 26 (2000): 79–103.

———. *We Are Fighting the World: A History of the Marashea Gangs in South Africa, 1947–1999*. Athens: Ohio University Press, 2005.

LaCapra, Dominick. *Writing History, Writing Trauma*. Baltimore: Johns Hopkins University Press, 2001.

Legassick, Martin. "Capital Accumulation and Violence." *Economy and Society* 3 (1974): 253–91.

Leger, Jean P. "Talking Rocks: An Investigation of the Pit Sense of Rockfall Accidents amongst Underground Gold Miners." PhD dissertation, University of the Witwatersrand, 1992.

———. *Towards Safer Underground Gold Mining: An Investigation Commissioned by the National Union of Mineworkers*. Labour Studies Research Report 1. Johannesburg: University of the Witwatersrand, Sociology of Work Program, 1985.

Leger, Jean, and Phillip van Niekerk. "Organisation on the Mines: The NUM Phenomenon." *South African Review* 3: 68–78. Johannesburg: Ravan, 1986.

Liebenberg, Johan. "Militance and Violence on the Mines." *Industrial Relations Journal of South Africa* 17 (1987): 37–43.

MacMillan, H. "Return to the Malungwana Drift: Max Gluckman, the Zulu Nation and the Common Society." *African Affairs* 94 (1995): 39–65.

Malkki, Liisa. *Purity and Exile: Violence, Memory, and National Cosmology among Hutu Refugees in Tanzania*. Chicago: University of Chicago Press, 1995.

Mamdani, Mahmood. *Citizen and Subject: Contemporary Africa and the Legacy of Late Colonialism*. Princeton: Princeton University Press, 1996.

Manganyi, N. Chabani, and André du Toit, eds. *Political Violence and the Struggle in South Africa*. London: Macmillan, 1990.

Mann, Michael. *The Dark Side of Democracy: Explaining Ethnic Cleansing*. Cambridge: Cambridge University Press, 2005.

Marais, Hein. *South Africa, Limits to Change: The Political Economy of Transformation*. London: Zed, 1998.

Marks, Shula, and Richard Rathbone, eds. *Industrialisation and Social Change in South Africa: African Class Formation, Culture and Consciousness 1870–1930*. London: Longman, 1982.

Mathis, Sarah M. "After Apartheid: Chiefly Authority and the Politics of

Land, Community and Development." PhD dissertation, Emory University, 2008.

Mayer, Philip, ed. *Black Villagers in an Industrial Society: Anthropological Perspectives on Labour Migration in South Africa.* Cape Town: Oxford University Press, 1980.

———. *Townsmen or Tribesmen: Conservatism and the Process of Urbanization in a South African City.* Cape Town: Oxford University Press, 1961.

Mayer, Philip, and Iona Mayer. "Socialization by Peers: The Youth Organization of the Red Xhosas." *Socialisation,* ed. Philip Mayer, 159–89. London: Tavistock, 1970.

Mazzarella, William. "Culture, Globalization, Mediation." *Annual Review of Anthropology* 33 (2004): 345–67.

Mbembe, Achille. *On the Postcolony.* Berkeley: University of California Press, 2001.

McNamara, J. K. "Black Worker Conflicts on South African Gold Mines: 1973–1982." PhD dissertation, University of the Witwatersrand, 1985.

———. "Brothers and Work Mates: Home Friend Networks in the Social Life of Black Migrant Workers in a Gold Mine Hostel," *Black Villagers in an Industrial Society,* ed. Philip Mayer, 305–53. Cape Town: Oxford University Press, 1980.

———. "Culture, Consciousness and Change: The Origins of Worker Revolt on South African Gold Mines." *Culture and the Commonplace,* ed. Patrick McAllister, 137–55. Johannesburg: University of the Witwatersrand Press, 1997.

———. "Estimated Incidence of Inter-Group Violence on Gold Mines since 1987." Unpublished manuscript, 1997.

———. "Gate Politics: Competing Interests in Mine Hostels." *Crossing Boundaries: Mine Migrancy in a Democratic South Africa,* ed. Jonathan Crush and Wilmot James, 62–67. Cape Town: Institute for Democracy in South Africa, 1995.

———. "Inter-Group Violence among Black Employees on South African Gold Mines: 1974 to 1986." *South African Sociological Review* 1 (1988): 23–38.

———. "Social Life, Ethnicity, and Conflict in a Gold Mine Hostel." M.A. dissertation, University of the Witwatersrand, 1978.

Mda, Zakes. *Ways of Dying.* New York: Picador, 1995.

Minnaar, Anthony, ed. *Communities in Isolation: Perspectives on Hostels in South Africa.* Pretoria: Human Sciences Research Council, 1993.

———, ed. *Conflict and Violence in Natal / KwaZulu: Historical Perspectives.* Pretoria: Human Sciences Research Council, 1991.

Mitchell, J. C. *The Kalela Dance.* Rhodes-Livingstone Paper no. 27. Manchester: Manchester University Press, 1956.

Mofokeng, Santu. *Santu Mofokeng.* Johannesburg: David Krut / French Institute of South Africa, 2001.

Molapo, Matsheliso Palesa. "Job Stress, Health and Perceptions of Migrant

Mineworkers." *Crossing Boundaries: Mine Migrancy in a Democratic South Africa*, ed. Jonathan Crush and Wilmot James, 88–100. Cape Town: Institute for Democracy in South Africa, 1995.

Moodie, T. Dunbar. "Becoming a Social Movement Union: Cyril Ramaphosa and the National Union of Mineworkers." *Transformation* 72/73 (2010): 152–80.

———."Black Migrant Mine Labourers and the Vicissitudes of Male Desire." *Changing Men in Southern Africa*, ed. Robert Morrell, 297–315. Pietermaritzburg: University of Natal Press, 2001.

———. *Going for Gold: Men, Mines and Migration.* With Vivienne Ndatshe. Berkeley: University of California Press, 1994.

———. "Mine Migration and the Struggle for Redemption." Unpublished paper, Hobart and William Smith Colleges, n.d.

———. "The Moral Economy of the Black Miners' Strike of 1946." *Journal of Southern African Studies.* 13 (1986): 1–35.

Moroney, Sean. "Industrial Conflict in a Labour Repressive Economy: Black Labour on the Transvaal Gold mines 1901–1912" B.A. Honors dissertation, University of the Witwatersrand, 1976.

Murray, Colin. *Families Divided: The Impact of Migrant Labour in Lesotho.* Cambridge: Cambridge University Press, 1981.

Nash, June. *We Eat the Mines and the Mines Eat Us: Dependency and Exploitation in Bolivian Tin Mines.* New York: Columbia University Press, 1979.

Nesbitt, L. M. *Gold Fever.* London: Jonathan Cape, 1936.

Niehaus, Isak. "Coins for Blood and Blood for Coins: From Sacrifice to Ritual Murder in the South African Lowveld, 1930–2000." *Etnofoor* 13 (2000): 31–54.

———. "Ethnicity and the Boundaries of Belonging: Reconfiguring Shangaan Identity in the South African Lowveld." *African Affairs* 101 (2002): 557–83.

———. "Renegotiating Masculinity in the South African Lowveld: Narratives of Male-Male Sex in Labour Compounds and in Prisons." *African Studies* 61 (2002): 77–97.

Niehaus, Isak, with Eliazaar Mohlala and Kally Shokane. *Witchcraft, Power and Politics: Exploring the Occult in the South African Lowveld.* London: Pluto, 2001.

Novick, Peter. *The Holocaust in American Life.* Boston: Houghton Mifflin, 1999.

Oomen, Barbara. *Chiefs in South Africa: Law, Power, and Culture in the Post-Apartheid Era.* Oxford: James Currey, 2005.

Packard, Randall, and David Coetzee. "White Plague, Black Labour Revisited: TB and the Mining Industry." *Crossing Boundaries: Mine Migrancy in a Democratic South Africa*, ed. Jonathan Crush and Wilmot James, 101–15. Cape Town: Institute for Democracy in South Africa, 1995.

Pandey, Gyanendra. *The Construction of Communalism in Colonial North India.* Delhi: Oxford University Press, 1990.

————. *Routine Violence: Nations, Fragments, Histories*. Stanford: Stanford University Press, 2006.

Peluso, Nancy Lee, and Michael Watts, eds. *Violent Environments*. Ithaca: Cornell University Press, 2001.

Phimister, Ian, and Charles van Onselen. "The Political Economy of Tribal Animosity: A Case Study of the 1929 Bulawayo Location 'Faction Fight.'" *Journal of Southern African Studies* 6 (1979): 1–43.

Posel, Deborah, and Graeme Simpson, eds. *Commissioning the Past: Understanding South Africa's Truth and Reconciliation Commission*. Johannesburg: University of the Witwatersrand Press, 2002.

Robins, Steven L., ed. *Limits to Liberation after Apartheid: Citizenship, Governance and Culture*. Oxford: James Currey, 2005.

Ross, Fiona C. *Bearing Witness: Women and the Truth and Reconciliation Commission in South Africa*. London: Pluto, 2002.

Scarry, Elaine. *The Body in Pain: The Making and Unmaking of the World*. New York: Oxford University Press, 1985.

Scheper-Hughes, Nancy, and Philippe Bourgois. *Violence in War and Peace*. Oxford: Blackwell, 2004.

Schmidt, Bettina E., and Ingo W. Schroder, eds. *Anthropology of Violence and Conflict*. London: Routledge, 2001.

Schumaker, Lyn. *Africanizing Anthropology: Fieldwork, Networks, and the Making of Cultural Knowledge in Central Africa*. Durham: Duke University Press, 2001.

Seekings, Jeremy, and Nicoli Nattrass. *Class, Race, and Inequality in South Africa*. New Haven: Yale University Press, 2005.

Sharp, John S., and Andrew D. Spiegel. "Vulnerability to Impoverishment in South African Rural Areas: The Erosion of Kinship and Neighbourhood as Social Resources." *Africa* 55 (1985): 133–52.

Simkins, Charles. "Agricultural Production in the African Reserves of South Africa, 1918–1969." *Journal of Southern African Studies* 7 (1981): 256–83.

Sitas, Ari. "The New Tribalism: Hostels and Violence." *Journal of Southern African Studies* 22 (1996): 235–48.

Skalník, Peter. "Tribe as Colonial Category." *South African Keywords: The Uses and Abuses of Political Concepts*, ed. Emile Boonzaier and John Sharp, 60–78. Cape Town: David Philip, 1988.

Smith, Wilbur. *Gold Mine*. London: William Heinemann, 1970.

Sparks, Allister. *Tomorrow Is Another Country*. Johannesburg: Jonathan Ball, 1995.

Standing, Guy, John Sender, and John Weeks. *Restructuring the Labour Markets: The South African Challenge*. Geneva: International Labor Organization, 1996.

Steinberg, Jonny. *The Number: One Man's Search for Identity in the Cape Underworld and Prison Gangs*. Johannesburg: Jonathan Ball, 2004.

Steinberg, Jonny, and Gay Seidman. "Gold Mining's Labour Markets: Legacies of the Past, Challenges of the Present." Labour Studies Research Report 6, Sociology of Work Unit, University of the Witwatersrand, 1995.

Stewart, Pamela J., and Andrew Strathern. *Violence: Theory and Ethnography*. London: Continuum, 2002.

Sundkler, Bengt G. M. *Bantu Prophets in South Africa*. 2nd edn. London: Oxford University Press, 1961.

Tambiah, Stanley J. *Leveling Crowds: Ethnonationalist Conflicts and Collective Violence in South Asia*. Berkeley: University of California Press, 1996.

Taussig, Michael. "Culture of Terror, Space of Death: Roger Casement's Putumayo Report and the Explanation of Torture." *Comparative Studies in Society and History* 26 (1984): 467–97.

———. *The Devil and Commodity Fetishism in South America*. Chapel Hill: University of North Carolina Press, 1980.

Taylor, Christopher C. *Sacrifice as Terror: The Rwandan Genocide of 1994*. Oxford: Berg, 2001.

Thompson, Leonard. *A History of South Africa*. New Haven: Yale University Press, 1990.

Tracey, Hugh. *African Dances of the Witwatersrand Gold Mines*. Johannesburg: African Society, 1952.

Trapido, Stanley. "South Africa in a Comparative Study of Industrialization." *Development Studies* 7 (1971): 309–20.

Turton, David, ed. *War and Ethnicity: Global Connections and Local Violence*. San Marion: Center for Interdisciplinary Research on Social Stress, Boydell Press, 1997.

Vail, Leroy, ed. *The Creation of Tribalism in Southern Africa*. Berkeley: University of California Press, 1989.

van Onselen, Charles. *Chibaro: African Mine Labour in Southern Rhodesia 1900–1933*. London: Pluto, 1976.

———. "The Modernization of the Zuid Afrikaansche Republiek: F. E. T. Krause, J. C. Smuts, and the Struggle for the Johannesburg Public Prosecutor's Office, 1989–1899." *Law and History Review* 21 (2003): 483–526.

———. "Race and Class in the South African Countryside: Cultural Osmosis and Social Relations in the Sharecropping Economy of the South Western Transvaal, 1900–1950." *American Historical Review* 95 (1990): 99–123.

———. "The Social and Economic Underpinning of Paternalism and Violence on the Maize Farms of the South-Western Transvaal, 1900–1950." *Journal of Historical Sociology* 5 (1992): 127–60.

———. *Studies in the Social and Economic History of the Witwatersrand 1886–1914*. 2 vols. London: Longman, 1982.

Von Holdt, Karl. 2003. "Institutionalisation, Strike Violence and Local Moral Orders." *Transformation* 72/73 (2010): 127–51.

———. *Transition from Below: Forging Trade Unionism and Workplace Change in South Africa*. Pietermaritzburg: University of KwaZulu-Natal Press, 2003.

Warren, Kay B., ed. *The Violence Within: Cultural and Political Opposition in Divided Nations*. Boulder, Colo.: Westview Press, 1993.

Watjen, Thembisa. *Workers and Warriors: Masculinity and the Struggle for Nation in South Africa.* Urbana: University of Illinois Press, 2004.

Webster, David. "Abafazi Bathonga Bafihlakala: Ethnicity and Gender in a KwaZulu Border Community." *Tradition and Transition in Southern Africa,* ed. A. D. Spiegel and P. A. McAllister, 243–71. Johannesburg: Witwatersrand University Press, 1991.

Webster, E. C., and Jean P. Leger. "Reconceptualising Skill Formation in South Africa." *Perspectives in Education* 13.2 (1992): 53–68.

Webster, Edward, and Karl Von Holdt, eds. *Beyond the Apartheid Workplace: Studies in Transition.* Pietermaritzburg: University of KwaZulu-Natal Press, 2005.

Werbner, Richard. "The Manchester School in South-Central Africa." *Annual Review of Anthropology* 13 (1984): 157–85.

Werbner, Richard, and Terence Ranger, eds. *Postcolonial Identities in Africa.* London: Zed, 1996.

West, Martin. *Bishops and Prophets in a Black City: African Independent Churches in Soweto Johannesburg.* Cape Town: David Philip, 1975.

Whitehead, Neil L., ed. *Violence.* Santa Fe, N.M.: School for American Research Press, 2004.

Wilmsen, Edwin N., and Patrick McAllister, eds. *The Politics of Difference: Ethnic Premises in a World of Power.* Chicago: University of Chicago Press, 1996.

Wilson, Francis. *Labour in the South African Gold Mines, 1911–1969.* Cambridge: Cambridge University Press, 1972.

Wilson, Richard A. *The Politics of Truth and Reconciliation in South Africa: Legitimizing the Post-Apartheid State.* Cambridge: Cambridge University Press, 2001.

Windrich, Elaine. "The Johannesburg Massacre: Media Images of the South African Transition." *Africa Today* 43 (1996): 77–96.

Wolpe, Harold. "Capitalism and Cheap Labour-Power in South Africa: From Segregation to Apartheid." *Economy and Society* 1 (1972): 425–56.

———. "The 'White Working Class' in South Africa." *Economy and Society* 5 (1976): 197–240.

Yudelman, David. *The Emergence of Modern South Africa: State, Capital and the Incorporation of Organized Labor on the South African Gold Fields, 1902–1939.* Westport, Conn.: Greenwood, 1983.

Breckenridge, Keith, 112–13, 114
Bunzi, Hudson, 103, 128, 165
Buthelezi, Mangosuthu, 3, 89–93, 108, 158–59

Capitalism: creative destruction and, 115, 173; free versus bound labor, 110–11, 123–24; gold mines and, 115–18; mining financial power as, 116, 119; paternalism of, 18; on public/private space, 17–18
Chamber of Mines: on black labor recruiting, 116, 118–19; statistics, 70, 72; studies by, 18; on tribal dancing, 58; unionization and, 110–12; wage negotiation and, 179
Christian rhetoric, 165
Cinderella (pseud.) gold mine, 16, 25–44, 193; abandoned compound, 14; access to, 191–93; alcohol and drug use in, 16, 18, 19, 20, 75, 141–48; bankruptcy of, 178; black management of, 178–82, 187; class struggle in, 179; closing of, 185; compound life, 14–19; compound schematic, 19; funeral policy, 73–74; gate to compound, 101, 101–2, 135; hostel, 12, 13, 14–17, 15, 100, 166, 167, 177; housing, 61, 62–63; human resources director, 191–92; injuries and death, 69–70, 71–74; living-out allowance, 177; management on Zulus, 107–8; migrant workers, 16, 89, 168; racism, 136–37; regional organizers (NUM), 138, 143, 149, 160–61, 162, 169; retrenchments, 127, 151–52, 157–58; shafts, 2, 14; social activities, 14–17; subsistence agriculture in, 20; traditions of violence, 22–23; union compromise, 106; wages, 67, 137, 156, 179; white management and NUM, 6, 120, 126, 132, 138–39, 142–43, 146–48, 152–53, 157–64, 175,

181, 188; Zulus banished from, 4, 5–6, 151–52, 155–56, 155–58, 158. See also Strikes
Cinderella (pseud.) gold mine murders, 1–2, 4; accounts of, 5–6, 46–48, 51–53, 75–86, 90–103, 154–55; aftermath of, 174, 177–82; alleged Zulu threats, 94, 102; amabutho and, 154, 156–66, 169, 173; analysis of, 100–108; court testimonies, 49–51, 54–55, 78, 79, 92, 95, 164–65, 193; documentation by induna, 96–98; as ethnic violence, 4, 5, 88, 107, 157, 167; identification of murderers, 151–53, 163, 166; incidents leading to, 88–90; lack of investigation, 86–87, 151, 153; logbook entries, 45–48, 96, 98; management responsibility for, 166, 168; mine security response, 1, 45–48, 50, 53, 75, 77, 80, 96, 98, 102, 106, 151–52; national liberation and, 162, 174, 177, 194; NUM on, 6, 110; paid home visit for Zulus, 106; plot against Zulus, 95–96; sacrifice and, 88; shaft stewards and, 56, 110, 157–58, 162–63; tensions prior to, 93, 96; unions as cause, 155; as unrecorded, 69; video surveillance of, 99
Class, ethnicity as, 20, 179
Cold War, end of, 3
Collective narratives. See under Narratives
Collective violence. See Violence
Colonial power and anthropological studies, 190
Color bar, 45, 60, 64, 113, 121
Company cars, 61
Cosmologies, black, 70–71

Dagga use. See Alcohol and drug use
Death, attitudes toward, 70
Decolonization: end of apartheid

and, 1; racial restrictions and, 118; as violent, 4

De Klerk, F. W., 90, 91, 108

Drug use. *See* Alcohol and drug use

Du Toit, Charles: on black labor, 131–32; character of, 192; fired from position, 173; as human resources director, 131, 191–92; on strike, 148; on unionization, 132–33

East Driefontein mine killings, 174, 187

Easter, 88, 94–95, 98, 102

East Rand Council of Churches, 167

East Rand War, 3, 23, 177

Elijah, 179–81, 183–84

Ellis, Stephen, 90

Epstein, A. L., 189–90

Ethnicity: class and, 20, 179; as descriptor, 7, 48, 67–68, 102–4, 106–7, 139–40; job skills and, 56–57; nation and, 109; purification and, 90–91, 162; stereotypes of, 59–60; violence and, 4, 5, 7, 88, 107, 157, 167, 175, 186

Ethnographic studies, 189–90, 194

Faction fights, 20–21, 22, 75, 201 n. 11

Fanon, Frantz, 2, 4

Far East Hostel, 12–14, *13, 15,* 100, 166, 167, 177

Gangs: history of mines and, 5; mine social structure and, 160, 168–69; strikes and, 141–42, 149, 156; tensions among, 147; violence and, 140, 160. *See also* specific gangs, e.g. Amabutho

Gemmill, J. A., 55

Gluckman, Max, 189

Gold Fields: company, 120, 125, 175–76, 177, 192; security, 46, 98, 99, 101, 103, 211 n. 16

Gold mines: access to, 191–92; capi-

talism and, 115–18; clerk-mine worker relationship, 103–4; compound architecture, 100–101; conflicts in 1970s, 119–20; divide and rule practices, 55, 167, 168, 175, 209 n. 29; drilling description, 204 n. 1; ethnicity in, 20; gold standard, 115–16, 118; hierarchy in, 64–65; indunas and, 55, 67, 120, 204 n. 36; injuries and deaths, 17, 22, 69–72; migrant labor, 16, 89, 100, 113, 168; mine marriages, 17; paternalism of, 111–12, 115, 118, 120–22; police intervention, 21; segregated hostels, 12; statistics, 123; stop orders, 122, 130, 132–33; stories, 72; as symbol of South Africa, 1; violence in West Rand, 174–75; wages, 19, 21, 67; worker expectations, 18–19

Goldstone Commission, 95

Gordimer, Nadine, 36, 112

Gordon, Robert J., 103–4

Gouldner, Alvin, 65

Grootvlei gold mine, 149–50

Guy, Jeff, 57

Hart, Gillian, 183

Hatred, role of, 4, 8, 186

Healers and traditional medicine, 74–75, 144–45

Hobson, J. A., 116

Home, concept of, 18

Horowitz, Donald, 9

Identity, ethnic: classification of, 7, 48, 67–68, 102–4, 106–7, 139–40; projected past and, 8–9

IFP. *See* Inkatha Freedom Party (IFP)

Independent Mediation Service of South Africa (IMSSA), 92, 151, 158

Indunas, 55, 67, 120, 204 n. 36. *See also* Sam

Industrial Court testimonies, 49–51, 54–55, 78, 79, 92, 95, 164–65

Injalo squatter camp, 76, 92, 98, 142, 152, 169, 170–73, 177–78

Inkatha Freedom Party (IFP): amabutho and, 162, 186; ANC on, 89–90, 154, 187; attack on, 156–57; betrayal and, 90; Bloody Monday and, 91, 94, 156; Cinderella workers as members, 93; court testimony, 193; domination of hostels by, 90–91; election of, 159; on migrant labor, 89; national liberation and, 91; squatter camp, 98; on Zulu ethnicity, 3; Zulus in, 5, 91

Internal Stability Unit, 98, 99, 100, 102

Isitshozi, 140

Katorus, violence in, 3

Kedourie, Elie, 187

Kloof gold mine, 121–22

KwaZulu Natal, 108, 152

Labor unions. See Unions, black labor

Leeudoorn mine killings, 174, 187

Leger, Jean, 66

Liberation. See National liberation

Liebenberg, Johan, 22

Madezi, 137, 139, 143–49, 154, 156

Madiba, 129–30

Mandela, Nelson, 90, 91; on black citizenship, 186–87; coalition government of, 108; on oppression, 1; release from prison, 3, 89, 190; Xhosa background, 91; on West Rand murders inquiry, 174

Marijuana use. See Alcohol and drug use

Masculine honor, 22, 159, 161

Mbeki, Thabo, 182–83, 214 n. 4

McNamara, Kent, 95, 174, 176, 193; on faction fights, 21

Migrant labor: apartheid and, 168, 175; in gold mines, 16, 89, 100, 113, 168; housing, 100, 176; pogroms

against, 5, 184, 187; required return home, 16, 89; social groups and, 139–40, 190

Mine dancing. See Tribal dancing

Mine marriages. See Same-sex relationships

Mine Surface Officials' Association of South Africa, 190

Mineworkers' Union, 60

Mitchell, Clyde, 189–90

Mofokeng, Santu, 11, 14, 61, 125, 142, 156; photo gallery, 25–44

Mokoena, Rev. Peter: on Cinderella management, 166, 168; court testimony, 164, 193; final report, 166–67; as mediator, 164–69

Molapo, Matsheliso, 70

Molise, Mr. (new black owner of Cinderella), 178–82

Moodie, T. Dunbar: compound schematic, 18, 19; compound studies, 191; on faction fights, 21; on mine marriages, 17; on mine worker expectations, 19; on NUM strategy, 123; Ramaphosa interview, 149

Mozambicans, 5, 13, 59, 67, 133–34, 143, 146, 187

Mpondo, 140–42, 145, 152

Myburgh Commission, 56, 57, 174

Myburgh, J. F., 174, 176–77

Narratives: collective, 7–8, 10; comparing, 10, 194

Nationalism and nation: from above/below, 182–83; Afrikaner, 60; after decolonization, 4–5; apartheid and, 188; black, 5, 6, 108, 123, 158, 166, 176, 186–87; discourse on, 182; ethnicity and, 5, 20, 98, 109, 158, 187, 211 n. 20; IFP and, 90; mines as symbols of, 1; national subjects and, 187; politics of, 107; sacrifice for, 5, 53, 88; violence and, 91; Zulus and, 98, 158. See also National liberation

Sam (induna), 49, 51–52, 53, 55, 67, 68, 85

Sebokeng, violence in, 3

Seekings, Jeremy, 172

Setona, Lira, 149

Sex, control of, 140–41

Shaft stewards, 44; amabutho and, 153, 156, 157, 166, 179, 194; Cinderella conflict and, 56, 110, 157–58, 161–63; compromise with, 106, 158–59, 181, 184; fired workers, 180–81; pay scale, 210 n. 4; on peace pledge, 161, 165; on piccanins, 114; as union members, 6, 132, 148–49; as Xhosa, 56, 149; Zulu return to mine and, 160–61; on Zulu workers, 107. See also specific individuals

Shangaans: change and, 109; as foreigners, 108; roles in mines, 55, 56, 57, 59–60, 67; smuggling and, 141; stereotype of, 59–60, 203 n. 12; unions and, 143; women and sacrifice, 71

Social stratification, 182

Sothos: ethnic conflicts, 21, 120, 150; mine song, 70; Russians gang, 140–41, 150; as shaft sinkers, 56, 57; women and sacrifice, 71

South African Communist Party (SACP), 123, 143

South African Police, 21, 46–47, 77, 98, 135, 151–52, 163–64, 166

South African Technical Officials Association, 190

South African War (1899–1902), 117

Soviet Union, disintegration of, 3, 123

Soweto Day murders. See Cinderella (pseud.) gold mine murders

Soweto Uprising (1976), 4

Squatter camps: abandoned mines and, 12; amabutho and, 156; ANC control of, 91; compound re-

placed by, 181, 186; ethnic identity of, 142; Injalo, 76, 92, 98, 142, 152, 169, 170–73, 177–78; near Cinderella, 5, 144, 177; Ramaphosa, 142, 179, 183–85; Russians control of, 141; violence in, 3, 90, 144–45

Stewards. See Shaft stewards

Stick fighting, 21, 140

Stokisi, 125–26

Stop orders, 122, 130, 132–33

Strikes: control of, 121–22; enforcement during, 6; gangs and, 141–42, 149, 156; legality of, 128, 181; mine operation and, 106, 126; mine security response, 22, 138, 179; organizing, 134–35, 145–49, 152, 164; results of, 154; use of strikebreakers, 61; violence during, 21–22, 112, 138–39, 145–46, 179–81, 183

Subsistence agriculture, 20, 117

Swazis, 56–57, 150, 180, 183, 184

Testimonies. See Industrial Court testimonies

Thembinkosi, 92, 96, 98–99

Tocqueville, Alexis de, 21

Tokoza, violence in, 3

Tracey, Hugh, 57, 58

Traditional medicine. See Healers and traditional medicine

Tribal dancing, 16, 57–59

Underground Officials' Association of South Africa, 190

Unemployment, black, 21, 119, 148, 169

Unions, black labor, 67, 90, 111, 155, 182, 194. See also National Union of Mineworkers (NUM)

United People's Union of South Africa (UPUSA), 106–7, 127–30, 132, 139, 143, 155, 163, 169, 175

United Workers Union of South Africa (UWUSA), 90, 128, 129, 132, 175

University of Witwatersrand, Sociology of Work Unit, 191
UPUSA. *See* United People's Union of South Africa (UPUSA)
UWUSA. *See* United Workers Union of South Africa (UWUSA)

Van Onselen, Charles, 140, 190, 208 n. 4
Van Zyl, Johannes, 133, 135, 136, 164, 187
"Villagers" (television series), 198 n. 6
Violence: black, and whiteness, 207 n. 15; as catharsis, 2, 162; collective narratives of, 7–8, 10, 194; critical methodology for, 7–10; decolonization and, 4; effect of, 75; ethnic, 4, 5, 7, 88, 107, 157, 167, 175, 186; faction fights, 20–21, 22, 75, 201 n. 11; focalization and transvaluation in, 199 n. 20; gangs and, 140, 149–50, 169, 173; around Johannesburg, 2–3; new nationhood and, 91; NUM and, 149–50, 174–75; purification and, 90–91, 162; strikes and, 21–22, 112, 138–39, 145–46, 179–81, 183; structural, 175; uncertainty and, 8, 23, 195. *See also* Cinderella (pseud.) gold mine
Von Holdt, Karl, 183

Wages: at Cinderella mine, 67, 137, 156, 179; increase in, 21, 119, 120, 146; mine success and, 117; NUM strategy and, 123, 137; recruitment and, 117–18; worker expectations, 19, 21
Wealth: acquiring, 71–72; black citizenship and, 187; black labor and, 118, 123–24; mining and, 1, 179; redistribution of, 4

Weapons, 3, 140, 141, 194–95
White labor, 61–67
Whitey, 144, 145, 146, 186
Wilson, Francis, 69
World Cup (2010), 184–85

Xhosas: amabutho and, 142, 145, 154; change and, 109; continuation and innovation of, 141; ethnic conflicts, 2–4, 21, 98, 120, 146, 150, 186; identification as murderers, 152; as Mandela's background, 91; self-identification as, 104; as shaft stewards, 56, 149; stereotypes of, 59; stick fighting and, 21; strikes and, 146–47; unions and, 6, 143–44, 149. *See also* Cinderella (pseud.) gold mine murders

Zamakile, 126–27, 129–31
Zimbabweans, 5, 187
Zulus: alleged threats by, 94–95, 102; Amakhosi, 160; banished from Cinderella mine, 4, 5–6, 151–52, 155–58, 193; Bloody Monday and, 93–94; change and, 108–9; ethnic conflicts, 2–4, 23, 98, 107, 146, 186; evacuation of from compound, 88, 100, 102, 107, 166; nation and, 5, 98, 107, 158; NUM violence against, 174–75; paid home visit, 106, 158–59; peace pledge by, 161, 165; political parties and, 5, 91; proletarianization for, 55; racial legacy, 55–56; retrenchment packages, 157, 169; return to mine, 151, 160–61; systematic intimidation of, 98. *See also* Cinderella (pseud.) gold mine murders
Zuma, Jacob, 5, 187

DONALD L. DONHAM is a professor of anthropology at
the University of California, Davis. He is the author of
*Marxist Modern: An Ethnographic History of the Ethiopian
Revolution* (1999), and coeditor, with Edna G. Bay, of *States
of Violence: Politics, Youth, and Memory in Contemporary
Africa* (2006).

Library of Congress Cataloging-in-Publication Data

Donham, Donald L. (Donald Lewis)
Violence in a time of liberation : murder and ethnicity at
a South African gold mine, 1994 / Donald L. Donham ;
with photographs by Santu Mofokeng.
p. cm.
Includes bibliographical references and index.
ISBN 978-0-8223-4841-2 (cloth : alk. paper)
ISBN 978-0-8223-4853-5 (pbk. : alk. paper)
1. Ethnic conflict — South Africa.
2. Violence — South Africa.
3. Post-apartheid era — South Africa.
I. Mofokeng, Santu, 1956– II. Title.
HN801.Z9S636 2011
305.896′806822109049 — dc22   2011006407